MW01098111

Queerly Remembered

Studies in Rhetoric/Communication
Thomas W. Benson, Series Editor

Queerly Remembered

Rhetorics for Representing
the GLBTQ Past

Thomas R. Dunn

THE UNIVERSITY OF SOUTH CAROLINA PRESS

© 2016 University of South Carolina

Published by the University of South Carolina Press
Columbia, South Carolina 29208

www.sc.edu/uscpress

Manufactured in the United States of America

25 24 23 22 21 20 19 18 17 16
10 9 8 7 6 5 4 3 2 1

Library of Congress Cataloging-in-Publication Data
can be found at http://catalog.loc.gov/.

ISBN: 978-1-61117-670-4 (hardcover)
ISBN: 978-1-61117-671-1 (ebook)

CONTENTS

ILLUSTRATIONS

SERIES EDITOR'S PREFACE

On June 24, 2016, President Barack Obama designated a new "Stonewall National Monument," the first National Park landmark to honor the LGBT community's role in national life. The monument, which includes the Stonewall Inn and immediate surrounding area in New York City, commemorates a community uprising that took place at the site after a police raid on June 28, 1969. The designation of the national monument came less than two weeks after a gunman at a gay nightclub in Orlando, Florida, killed forty-nine people and a century after the founding of the National Park Service.

In *Queerly Remembered: Rhetorics for Remembering the GLBTQ Past,* Thomas R. Dunn explores in a series of case studies a "turn toward memory" as a political and rhetorical action by members of a community sometimes erased by history. Dunn's studies of monuments, memorials, statues, gravestones, textbooks, and publications recovers, celebrates, and interrogates memory and forgetting as rhetorical actions in a conflicted, fluid, and changing community seeking to contribute to "queer persuasion."

Queerly Remembered is a lucid and penetrating study, sure to be of interest for memory studies, gay and lesbian studies, queer theory, and rhetorical studies.

Thomas W. Benson

ACKNOWLEDGMENTS

At its heart, queer monumentality is about publicly acknowledging the meaningful moments and people from our collective pasts that have made our presents and futures more livable and empowering. In these few paragraphs, I would like to recognize the many people and institutions that contributed in ways large and small to the completion of this book, lest they be forgotten.

This project would have been impossible without the unflagging intellectual and financial support from three outstanding institutions of higher learning. Support from the Department of Communication and Rhetorical Studies and a Graduate School Summer Fellowship, both from Syracuse University, facilitated a summer of reflection that spawned the initial considerations of this book. These concerns were further crystalized through a research fellowship provided by the School of Arts and Sciences during the first year of my Ph.D. program at the University of Pittsburgh. The School of Arts and Science also provided a summer research grant for travel and study in Toronto, Ontario, in 2008. My research in Scotland, England, and Ireland in the summer of 2009 was made possible by a grant from the Frank and Vilma Slater/Scottish Nationality Room Committee at Pitt. In addition, a generous grant from Pitt's Women's Studies Program Student Research Fund enabled archival investigations and fieldwork in San Francisco, California, Washington, D.C., and Princeton, New Jersey. The Department of Communication Studies at Colorado State University has also been hugely supportive of this project, offering encouragement, time to write, and financial support.

Likewise, several people, organizations, and institutions have generously supported this book and its earlier instantiations by granting this scholar their support, insights, and/or permission to reproduce materials. In doing so, they have helped make the final product infinitely better. For their generosity, I would like to thank Patricia Cronin, Jessea Greenman, Del Newbigging,

Dennis O'Connor, Congressional Cemetery, the San Francisco GLBT Historical Society, the Daniel E. Koshland San Francisco History Center at the San Francisco Public Library, the Manuscript Division of Princeton University Library, and the late David B. Boyce. Thanks also to Michigan State University Press for granting permission to reproduce and extend chapter 3, which was previously published in *Rhetoric & Public Affairs*, and to Taylor & Francis for granting permission to reproduce chapter 2, previously published in the *Quarterly Journal of Speech*. In addition, my heartfelt thanks to the staff at the University of South Carolina Press, who expertly saw this book from slapdash ideas on a page to final product.

I have also been particularly lucky to spend several years working on this book in the company of outstanding scholars whose input enhanced this manuscript. For their proofreading, hole-poking, and merrymaking, I must thank Brita Anderson, Josh Beaty, David Landes, Katie Kavanagh O'Neil, Joe Packer, John Rief, Brent Saindon, and Joe Sery. Thanks to Kendall Phillips for introducing me to the study of public memory and nudging me to stick with academia and to Chuck Morris for exemplifying for me and many others the queer paths backward that so enrich this project. Very special thanks also go to John Lyne, Kirk Savage, and Ronald Zboray. Each has offered me endless support, advice, and expertise. Collectively they pushed me to do my best work and worked together fabulously—no small achievement in itself. Other colleagues, mentors, and friends who helped me immeasurably in this journey include Kari Anderson, Eric Aoki, Hamilton Bean, John Crowley, Carl Burgchardt, Bernadette Calafell, Greg Dickinson, Sonja Foss, Katie Gibson, Stephen Hartnett, Linda Hobgood, James Janack, Lisa Keränen, John Lynch, Brent Malin, Nick Marx, Mari Lee Mifsud, Gordon Mitchell, Shanara Reid-Brinkley, Belinda and Bjørn Stillion Southard, Barbara Warnick, Elizabeth Williams, and Mary Zboray, as well as anyone I may have forgotten.

To my mentor and friend Lester Olson go my most heartfelt thanks. Over countless classes, e-mails, lunches, and discussions, you have been my biggest supporter, most encouraging voice, and most exacting interlocutor. Thank you for pushing me to ask tough questions, to interrogate my own assumptions, and to stay true to myself. Thank you also for encouraging me to pursue my insights vigorously, to avoid simplistic answers, to seek out complexity, and always to keep in mind how the tasks at hand might be done in life-affirming ways. It has been both a pleasure and an honor to work with you.

For me the hardest part of writing this book was letting go of the cherished moments that might have been spent with an unbelievably supportive family. As this book demonstrates, not all GLBTQ people have been fortunate to have families on whom they can rely. My family has always been there for me, and I am so thankful for them every day. To Matt, Dan, Grace,

Jillian, and Carly—thank you for the phone calls, the laughs, the encouragement, the visits, and all the moments you had my back. To my parents, Gary and Barbara, I aspire every day to make you proud. The completion of this book was possible only because of the countless books you read to me and with me decades ago. Thank you for the family dinner table, asking me how my day was, making me do my homework, and allowing me to learn from my mistakes. Thank you for believing in me always, loving me no matter what, and for all of the persistent words of support you have given me my entire life. Finally, to my husband Craig: thank you for sharing nearly every adventure and misadventure of this project. Thank you for indulging my nerdy interests, putting up with my trips abroad, sticking by me in good and bad times, having faith in me always, moving across the country with me, keeping me well fed and constantly laughing, and always being your amazing self, proudly and without fear. You still make me happier than I thought I could be. I love you and I am grateful for you every day. You are my everything.

Finally, this project is dedicated to the countless GLBTQ people in the past and present who—despite overwhelming odds to the contrary—found ways to live, to speak, to be heard, and to persevere so that others might learn to speak in a queer voice.

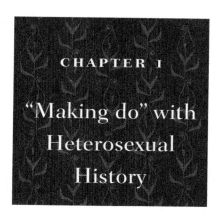

CHAPTER I

"Making do" with Heterosexual History

IN 1914 DR. WILLIAM J. ROBINSON, a physician, sexologist, and chief of the Department of Genito-Urinary Diseases at Bronx Hospital who examined individuals suspected of being homosexual "inverts," published an account of his views on homosexuality.[1] Castigating his sexological colleagues who argued that same-sex desire was a normal part of human existence, Robinson reasserted that homosexuality was "a sad, deplorable, pathological phenomenon. Every sexual deviation or disorder which has for its result an inability to perpetuate the race is *ipso facto* pathological, *ipso facto* an abnormality, and this is pre-eminently true of true homosexuality." He concluded that, despite his opposition to overly harsh legal penalties for those engaging in same-sex acts and/or gender nonconformity, homosexual persons "did not have a great or even capable thinker among them," were all "distinctly inferior to the normal man," and that the "world could get along very well without these step-children of nature."[2]

Ten years later Robinson had been persuaded otherwise. While still unprepared to regard homosexuality as favorably as possible, after a decade of research listening to "lovable, sympathetic types" of early gay men and lesbians "of high intelligence," Robinson's position on homosexuality evolved. In an article published in 1925 he stated: "My attitude towards homosexuals of both sexes has undergone some change, has become broader, more tolerant, perhaps even sympathetic." While still convinced that there was something "'not quite right' with the male or female homo," Robinson was nevertheless prompted to alter his professional recommendations. In regard to the study, care, and treatment of homosexual "inverts," Robinson adopted the position of his new friend and homosexual advocate, Dr. Magnus Hirschfeld. Like Hirschfeld, Robinson began to argue that "inverts" were not pathological or a menace to society but rather should be considered "merely a 'variation,' an intersex or a third sex."[3] For at least one contemporary researcher of the medicalization of homosexuality, Robinson's conversion (if only a conversion

from antagonism to neutrality) signaled a "notable instance" of queer persuasion in early-twentieth-century scientific and popular discourse.[4]

What contributed to the persuasion of this one famous skeptic and his
prominent early sexological views of homosexuality? Robinson largely attributed his shift to conversations with numerous homosexual individuals
over ten years of research and counseling. Robinson first had opportunities
for such conversations early in his career as a physician; however, his "homophile" contacts expanded exponentially later in his career when he began to
receive letters from homosexual readers in his role as editor of the *Journal
of Urology and Sexology,* many of which Robinson chose to publish.[5] In the
early 1920s Robinson's interactions with the homophile community deepened further when Hirschfeld invited him to Germany for an extended visit
to the Berlin Institute for Sexual Science.[6] While some of the individuals
with whom Robinson interacted were important leaders of the homophile
movement—Hirschfeld the most notable example—most of them were everyday people awash in mixed feelings of pride, guilt, shame, acceptance,
and regret about their "condition."

Those who met with Robinson throughout his career came with different motives and desires. Robinson believed that the vast majority of his homosexual visitors approached him because they were unhappy and sought a
"cure." In fact, early in his career Robinson declared that all the homosexual
individuals he had ever met "considered their condition a great punishment,
tho some of them were resigned to it."[7] By contrast, it has been suggested
that, as Robinson's prestige grew in scientific and popular circles, he became
a targeted audience for homosexual activists.[8] These later visitors almost
all seemed compelled at some level to defend their homosexual feelings as
reasonable. In doing so, they relied upon a particular kind of appeal to justify their being in the world. The appeal was so repetitive that Robinson
made note of it in his publications: "the thing that struck me peculiarly in
almost all homosexuals is their pathetic eagerness *to claim . . . as homosexuals* people whose homosexuality is extremely doubtful. . . . Thus they speak
of Shakespeare, Byron, and Whitman as belonging to their class, as if their
homosexuality . . . were a well-established historical fact."[9]

While the text demonstrates that Robinson doubted the veracity of these
statements and was far from convinced that these homosexual reclamation
projects of accomplished historical individuals were either credible or merited attention, we can see simultaneously within this account a tactical form
of argumentation in process. As a scene juxtaposing a scientist with his
subject—an empowered, supposedly heterosexual man against his disempowered, homosexual patient—we might be tempted to view the exchanges
between Robinson and the individuals interviewed as invasive confession-
als in which homosexual persons were subjected to the disciplinary force

of modern science and medicine.[10] Doubtless much of this dynamic was in play and, in such settings, little agency might be expected of those who were considered by society at the time to be mentally ill patients, prisoners, or criminals. However, on the contrary, these conversations exemplified important moments in the formation of early gay and lesbian subjects—the budding utterances of a gay and lesbian rhetoric of resistance. In short, these conversations reveal a calculated, persuasive appeal by a nascent gay and lesbian community to defend itself from disciplinary apparatuses and heteronormative culture—"the institutions, structures of understanding, and practical orientations that make heterosexuality seem not only coherent . . . but also privileged."[11] At the very heart of these persuasive appeals that sought to influence Robinson's view of his patients as pathological was a deep and abiding rhetorical maneuver—the calculated deployment of homosexual historical representations aimed at a powerful heterosexual audience. As such, the anonymous patients' interactions with Dr. Robinson illustrate in microcosm the central question of this book: How have gay, lesbian, bisexual, transgender, and queer (GLBTQ)[12] advocates of the past and present represented and contested history in endeavors to influence or persuade the judgments by dominant, apparently heterosexual citizens?

The Robinson anecdote is only one example of how GLBTQ people, institutions, and communities have and continue to use their collective pasts to shape sustainable selves and spaces within a deeply heteronormative world. This task is not simple. GLBTQ communities are and have always been richly diverse, not only with regard to gender, sex, and sexuality but also with deeply intersectional experiences of race, ethnicity, class, ability, nationality, and age (among others) that have shifted in importance and articulation through time. Such diversity has frequently instigated contentious debates among GLBTQ persons about how and why communal pasts should be represented. These debates are valuable for understanding not only the fissures they produce but the participation, forethought, and critical self-reflection such debates demand. At the same time, deploying GLBTQ pasts in rhetorical ways—with the intent to shape the perceptions of audiences at the level of the public—has regularly been complicated by a pervasive drive to forget GLBTQ people within heterosexual cultures. While forgetting can provide important opportunities for communities to form, to be renewed, and to "begin again,"[13] the erasure of entire sets of people from history also functions to sustain dominant culture, its privileges, and its attendant power structures. Heterosexual individuals, at the center of dominant culture, have regularly exerted and reexerted a constellation of forgetting practices (both consciously and unconsciously) against GLBTQ pasts—including heteronormativity, misrepresentation, the subjugation of knowledge, destruction of records, disqualification of evidence, and "mnemonicide," among many others—to resecure that center.[14] At times GLBTQ people themselves, for very different reasons, have contributed to this will to forget.[15] Nonetheless, as Charles E. Morris III has suggested, GLBTQ communities in recent years have made a prominent queer *"turn toward* memory," one that I argue has actually been a reliable, though less evident, resource for these communities' survival for nearly 150 years.[16] In doing so GLBTQ people have imbedded themselves within a popular and interdisciplinary project interested in *public memory.* While the particulars of this term are contested, in this book *public memory* refers to the use of the past in diverse but always shared ways by a particular community to respond to a present need.[17] Through appeals to public memory, GLBTQ people and communities activate their pasts in powerful ways to shape the present and drive social change.

As an epigram, the early-twentieth-century gay men and lesbians who drew upon the past in their attempts to persuade Robinson ask us likewise today to reflect upon how contemporary GLBTQ persons in Western culture utilize their pasts to appeal to audiences or publics: In what ways do modern GLBTQ persons in the West remember the past?[18] Do GLBTQ persons today remember the past in the same way, or what patterns typify diverse representations of GLBTQ history? Whom do we remember for doing certain deeds in the past? How do we determine what sorts of symbolic and material deeds are worthy of remembering or forgetting? How do we go about doing remembering as individuals and as groups? Whom do we remember as a community and, given the underlying roles of institutions and organizations such as publication outlets and archives, what symbolic and material costs does such memory require? As we will see, these questions are deeply historical, rhetorical, and queer. They also form the foundational themes of this project.

Indeed GLBTQ histories, or more specifically GLBTQ public memories, are key rhetorical devices addressed to audiences or publics, devices that have grown more pervasive, more complex, and more controversial as they have been used to influence not only GLBTQ audiences but heterosexual audiences as well. In remembering these pasts GLBTQ communities have not only preserved often overlooked, ignored, disqualified, or willfully misrepresented ways of being in time, but they have also sought to shape the present and the future of queer life in highly rhetorically contested ways by seeking to influence diverse audiences with different stakes in remembrance.[19] Three overarching claims drive the present study:

[1] That public memories offer a vital resource for GLBTQ persons, communities, and institutions for shaping public beliefs and judgments and winning political, cultural, and social change.

[2] That the trajectory of this memory work is not exclusively a contemporary phenomenon but rather a long-standing tactical and ephemeral

practice that has recently begun to include more monumental enactments, styles, and forms.

[3] That monumental memory practices in particular, while posing significant challenges to GLBTQ advocates and audiences, will increasingly
offer valuable effects in both heterosexual and homosexual public cul-
ture(s). As such, efforts to refine and make better monumental queer
public memories will be an ongoing and important project.

History, Memory, Rhetoricity, Queerness

For longer than anyone alive can remember, history has been our preferred
means for understanding our shared relationships with our pasts. An old but
still very modern concept, history, in its most colloquial sense, is conceived as
society's record of days gone by. In Pierre Nora's phrasing, it is "a reconstruc-
tion . . . of what is no longer," a "representation" of what has come before
that addresses our pasts in a very specific set of ways. In particular, history
is a means for intellectualizing and rationalizing past times; it is ordered and
structured, giving the hodgepodge happening of previous eras a continuity,
linearity, and exactitude that can be taught and analyzed. Through this process of "intellectual and secular production," we forge *the* narrative of *the*
past, a record of previous moments with "universal authority" that "belongs
to everyone."[20] As a relationship to the past so invested with precision, objectivity, and general appeal that has served society's interests for so long,
history might then seem the best perspective for better investigating and
understanding GLBTQ pasts in this project on several counts.

However, the concept of history is entirely inadequate for examining
the particular applications of GLBTQ pasts. For one, history is increasingly
incapable of connecting people to their pasts as it once did. While history
had relevance within the transition from premodern to modern societies, the
social, cultural, and technological forces battering our contemporary world
have undercut history's appeal. As Andreas Huyssen argues, globalization,
weakened national borders, and the "very real compression of time and
space" that typify our contemporary moment have unmoored history from its
raison d'être. To put it another way, the hierarchical, national, rational, and
totalizing merits of the history model, "no longer work."[21]

Another inadequacy of history is that it is far removed from the "objective and scientific" telling of the past it proclaims.[22] History's façade as a fair
and neutral assessment of the past has now long been exposed. Nietzsche's
critical history called into question the implied "truth" of events described
in historical tomes. Marx gestured to the concealing nature of history in *The
German Ideology*. Marxists such as Louis Althusser have argued that history's
neutrality is more akin to an ideologically infused narrative that ensures the

perpetuation of the status quo.[23] Likewise, Michel Foucault has shown that the metanarratives of history are discursive constructions rather than rational Hegelian steps forward.[24] Such thinkers have been followed by a long line of feminists, materialists, radical socialists, and cultural studies scholars who recognized that when the disempowered and the marginalized put their faith in history, they often only affirm the powerful and become complicit in their own marginalization. GLBTQ people have likewise found significant reasons to doubt history's claims to neutrality. As pioneering gay historian Jonathan Ned Katz remarked in 1983, GLBTQ people rarely appear in history in evident ways and, when they do, they are "mainly of concern to those who wish to be sure that they and their revered others do not fall into the class of the terrible tabooed."[25] Despite progressive work to ameliorate these concerns by some historians in recent decades, the belief that history-writing's function was much more than simply to record the past objectively permeated GLBTQ communities, prompting many groundbreaking gay men and lesbians to attempt to do their own historical work beginning in the 1970s.

Yet, while important and influential GLBTQ historians have now spent decades toiling to free GLBTQ lives from the shackles of history's heteronormativity, even "gay and lesbian histories" have drawbacks. For one, the "gay and lesbian histories" produced to craft sustainable GLBTQ identities and communities during the 1970s and 1980s are often rife with partial and essentializing tendencies. As Scott Bravmann points out, early "gay and lesbian histories" that organize themselves around the unquestioned virtues of events like the Stonewall Riots "continue to imbue the present with meaning and give the past a surplus of signification that is itself in need of critical analysis."[26] Similarly, some aspects of "gay and lesbian history" push singular, transhistorical, unitary metanarratives of *the* gay and lesbian past that cannot represent equitably the full diversity of GLBTQ experiences. In addition, a monolithic "gay and lesbian history" also suggests a standardized set of disciplinary procedures, measures of credibility, and locations of worth by which a "rigorous" past can be (re)constructed.[27] While many of these resources can be useful—including oral history, historiographic methods, and archival work—the belief that the only viable "gay and lesbian history" is one that can be reclaimed from the dust of an institutionally approved archive or relayed by GLBTQ movement elites still permeates much gay and lesbian history.

In contrast to history, I believe *memory* offers a much richer and more compelling way to understand GLBTQ pasts today. As Nora so well points out, memory is the very opposite of history; in fact, history is a past-oriented practice that attempts to account for memory's loss. Unlike history, a representation which seeks "to annihilate what has in reality taken place," memory is a "perpetually actual phenomenon" and a lived and embodied experience. As such, memory is not set and established, nor does it have any need to be. Memories are instead in "permanent evolution, open to the dialectic of remembering and forgetting," regularly manipulated and altered to fit the needs of the "eternal present." In their embrace of evolution, memories are also "affective and magical," often used for the pleasure and interests of a limited group more than for establishing an unchanging meaningfulness for everyone. Memory can be found and celebrated in the everyday and, as such, connects people to their past in ways wildly distinct from history.[28] Given history's ineffectual place in our contemporary societies, memory has returned to prominence as an important and viable way to connect people to what came before in a world in which we often float freely through time. This reanimation of memory has been particularly fervent over the last thirty years. Described variably as a "memory mania," "heritage boom," and "memory boom," this popular reinvigoration of memory seeks to reconnect people adrift in time with their pasts, offering them more meaningful ways to shape their presents and futures.[29]

Within this memory mania, *public memory* has become a particularly powerful alternative to history. To be able to speak of a "public" memory is, in many ways, contradictory to our traditional understandings of memory's possibilities. Indeed, for much of Western civilization, ranging from the education of ancient orators to the modern diagnoses of psychological traumas, memory has been characterized as the exclusive concern of "isolated beings" and their individual minds.[30] However, at the dawn of the twentieth century, scholars recognized that individuals were not only unreliable loci for recording the past, but that they also played a much smaller role in the full experience of remembering than previously thought. As sociologist Maurice Halbwachs now famously argued, people often acquire their remembrances of their pasts—and their very specific interpretative meanings—through social exchanges with others.[31] To explain this common phenomenon, Halbwachs theorized *collective memory* in which individuals and groups who "share their way of thinking" assist each other in recalling and reconstructing the past together.[32] Through such a notion, memory becomes a rich, social experience. Following Halbwachs, a generation of scholars has articulated assorted ways for conceiving of memory beyond the individual. *Social memory*, for example, is characterized by Edward Casey as "memory shared by those who are *already* related to each other, whether by way of family or friendship or civic acquaintance."[33] Similarly, Marita Sturken posits *cultural memory* as "memory shared outside the avenues of formal historical discourse yet . . . entangled with cultural products and imbued with cultural meaning."[34] Likewise, Foucault has coined the term *popular memory* to describe subordinated memory practices outside the dominant view of the past.[35] These modifiers only scratch the surface of the memory forms conceived during the memory boom. However, while drawing distinctions between these varieties of memory is sometimes unproductive, there is, as we will see, particular value in adopting a public-memory approach.[36]

But beyond being another form of shared memory, what is meant by *public memory*? *Public memory* refers to multiple and contradictory memories of the past articulated and debated at the level of the public. A rich topic for interrogation, public memory has been defined by an assortment of scholars in largely complementary ways: Kendall Phillips describes it as "multiple, diverse, mutable, and competing accounts of past events";[37] Casey, as "the external horizon of the public domain";[38] and Carole Blair, Greg Dickinson, and Brian Ott call it "beliefs about the past . . . shared among members of a group."[39] Within each of these definitions is nestled several key dimensions of public memory worth unpacking. First, public memories exist within particularly large groups conceived as publics. Well beyond the scale of families, friends, and acquaintances, public memories address entire communities, whether local, national, or worldwide. Understandably, public memories are therefore commonly expressed in mediums (monuments, media, museums, speeches) which can achieve such lofty circulation. Second, by virtue of their circulation, these memories often help *"narrat[e] a common identity"* for the public.[40] As Jan Assmann states, memories "comprise that body of reusable texts, images, and rituals specific to each society in each epoch, whose cultivation serves to stabilize and convey that society's self-image."[41] In this way public memories offer a shared orientation to or understanding of events in the past from which like-minded remembers can constitute, de-constitute, and reconstitute "identities of many kinds."[42] Since public memories encompass wide-ranging audiences, what Casey calls an "encircling horizon," public memories leave "little in our lives . . . untouched" by their influence.[43] As a result, expressions of public memories, third, produce "profound political implications" commonly contested and debated by members of the public and others. To put it another way, if how we remember the past matters, then people, communities, groups, and institutions invested in particular ways of telling the past will struggle against each other to ensure that their iteration wins the day. On one level public memories' tendency to inaugurate fierce contests over their meanings and interpretations is largely the result of their presence in the *koinos cosmos* and their ability to impact the entire community. However, on another level these contests are also facilitated, fourth, by memory's permanently partial view of the past. Always in "permanent evolution" and always "hovering, ready to be invoked or revised, acted upon or merely contemplated," public memories are ready-made arguments that can speak to nearly any perspective and are therefore useful in the collective negotiation of our shared world.[44] Unlike history, which falsely claims to tell what actually happened, public memories make no pretense of being "objective or scientific" in their account of the past;[45] rather they and their rememberers revel in memory's fluidity and flexibility, welcoming its own manipulation and alteration as warranted. This brings us to the fifth particularly important dimension of public memories: they are always animated by a present exigency. While the subject matter of public memories always concerns our shared pasts, Blair, Dickinson, and Ott show that "groups tell their pasts to themselves and others as ways of understanding, valorizing, justifying, excusing or subverting conditions or beliefs of their current moment."[46] Therefore, like all forms of memory, public memories "reconstruct an image of the past which is in accord, in each epoch, with the predominant thoughts of society."[47]

When taken together, one can make an additional unequivocal statement about public memories: they are inherently rhetorical. The term *rhetoric* refers to what Aristotle describes as "the ability, in each particular case, to see the available means of persuasion."[48] In this definition we recognize many of rhetoric's defining qualities: it is a creative endeavor, one that trades in contingent knowledges and situational constraints to instill meanings and produce enactments in the people it constitutes as an audience. Rhetoric then is a highly communicative act; one which, at its heart, seeks to move audiences to see, act, and be in the world differently. While rhetoric's earliest forms achieved these world-changing objectives through powerful appeals cloaked in public oratory, today rhetoric draws more widely for its "available means of persuasion." Twenty-first-century rhetors, then, are just as prone to invoke artifacts, acts, objects, images, and performances in their suasory undertakings as they are to refer to speeches. Given public memory's public, partial, contested, and exigent qualities, public memories also represent compelling "available means" for shaping the world. As such, by crafting images of the past through a particular perspective in order to produce social, political, and cultural change in the minds of their audiences, GLBTQ people and communities who turn to public memories become powerful participants in the rhetorical tradition.

To understand the public memories at work in GLBTQ pasts, it is important to take the study of memory one step further, to the examination of *queer public memories*. The term *queer public memory* was coined in 2004 by Morris in his essay "My Old Kentucky Homo," in which he considers efforts by Larry Kramer to reclaim Abraham Lincoln as queer in the face of a vicious heteronormative apparatus. In his project Morris defines queer public memory as the "revolution" that was "initiated when public memory and (homo) sexuality collide[d]." It is marked by a "deliberate *turn toward* memory in a culture for which public memory itself," according to Morris, "is defined more by absence than presence."[49] Through this turn Morris posits GLBTQ communities may find vital resources for their collective future. In the wake

of Morris's work, interest in queer public memory and its capacity to mar-
shal pasts for contemporary political and social activism has appeared with
greater interest in scholarly venues and popular forums alike.[50]

However, what distinguishes a public memory as "queer" requires further elaboration. At its most basic level I understand a queer public memory as a memory or remembering practice deployed by anyone who claims
membership in or common cause with the broader gay, lesbian, bisexual,
transgender, or queer community. By doing so I am signaling a broad and
inclusive use of the term *queer* in this particular context. Simultaneously, I
am then not equating queer public memories *exclusively* with the collection
of theories, criticisms, and political orientations popularized in the 1990s
known as "queer theory." Queer public memories in this book are first and
foremost queer because of their subject matter more than their orientation
or execution. This is not to say that "queering" or "queer theory" have no
place in this study, but that, for the most part, when I wish to signal a particularly "queered" person, event, or memory moving forward, I will mark that
meaning explicitly in the text.

Since queer public memory emphasizes the broader commitments of
public memory articulated above—including memory's fluidity, public scope,
and rhetorical possibilities—following Morris in using queer public memory
as the primary term for deployments of GLBTQ pasts is particularly useful.
This, however, is not to suggest that additional formulations for understanding GLBTQ pasts have not been made by others scholars. There are, in fact,
significant points of resonance between memory, time, and queerness elsewhere in extant scholarship. Memory has been broached by an assortment of
queer thinkers in recent years. Indeed, in early efforts to theorize queer theory, Lauren Berlant and Michael Warner directly linked the "queer project"
with making "forms of affective, erotic, and personal living . . . *available to
memory*" in order to combat the insistence that "normal intimacies" are the
only forms of relating to be found in the past.[51] Their theorizing was based
in Foucault's belief that different ways of considering the past might yield
valuable insights about past and present understandings of sexuality.[52] In
the years since, other queer scholars have elaborated the role memory might
play in queer world making. Ann Cvetkovich, for instance, suggests strug-
gling with trauma and affect through memory can revise repressed pasts into
resources for lesbian power and self-understanding.[53] In a similar vein Judith
Halberstam points to "the construction of queer archives and queer memories" as essential for ensuring the ongoing existence of queer culture and
sites.[54] Dianne Chisholm has built upon Halbwachs and Walter Benjamin
to illustrate how urban experiences may connect queer people to counter-
memories of themselves and others.[55] Meanwhile, Christopher Castiglia and

Christopher Reed have identified a "counternostalgia" within gay male and HIV/AIDS cultures that disconnects generations of gay men and proffers memory as a means to counteract this disconnect.[56] These examples only scratch the surface of a concerted queer interest in mobilizing the GLBTQ past in productive ways.

Queer temporality, too, is a recent point of contact with our figuring of queer public memory. Theorizations of queer time or temporality take as their point of departure the view that heteronormativity is embedded everywhere in our society, even within our understandings of time, sequence, and chronology. For theorists of queer temporality, time and its influence in ordering life, particularly as it relates to reproduction and compulsory heterosexuality, are cultural constructs in need of critical interrogation. Therefore, to "queer" time is to question assumptions about linearity and life plans in order to produce alternative ways of experiencing time that valorize different modes of living. Queer scholars from across the academy have located these alternatives in diverse places, including Warner's "repro-narrativity," Lee Edeleman's "death drive," Carla Freccero's "queer spectrality," Elizabeth Freeman's "alternative chronotopes," José Esteban Muñoz's "queer futurity," and Valerie Rohy's "queer anachronism."[57] Within these and other searches for alternative approaches to time, scholars have often turned to memory and queer propensities to live in the past as particularly salient sites for forging new queer worlds. Indeed, as Heather Love rightly claims, "not only do many queers . . . feel backward, but backwardness has been taken up as a key feature of queer culture."[58] The work of these scholars and thinkers offers compelling evidence that queer pasts have been and remain an important preoccupation in GLBTQ and queer thought.

Turning to queer public memory as the primary lens for investigating the snapshots and case studies that populate this book not only brings greater attention to the term but also provides a more nimble approach which can ameliorate several ongoing issues in current ways of studying the queer past. First, by focusing on queer public memory rather than on history, a diverse range of past-oriented practices and productions become accessible for interrogation. This turn to memory is key for GLBTQ examinations of the past in particular since, for much of the twentieth century and before, many of the more traditional forums for historical articulation, such as journals, books, archives, museums, and other traditional media of historical exploration, have often been inaccessible or unfavorable to queers (or only accessible to those willing to closet their sexuality as an act of complicity). Second, instead of privileging a hegemonic notion of a unitary past, the contestable, diverse, and political nature of our shared pasts comes to the fore when memory is embraced over history. Particularly important in this contestation

are tensions not only between heterosexual and homosexual tellings of the
past but also among simultaneous, distinct memories of GLBTQ pasts and
how those pasts are inflected differently by issues of race, gender, and class,
among others. Third, memory allows for more democratic telling of GLBTQ
pasts. As we have seen, history's focus on elites and public authorities to
recount what has come before is one if its major constraints. By privileging
memory instead, the array of subjects capable of articulating pasts extends
beyond elites and the institutions of public authority and public knowledge.[59] This is particularly key in GLBTQ projects for which most of the
initial archival and recovery work was completed not by trained historians
but by diligent amateurs, community organizations, and other marginalized
communities. Fourth, because of the tenuous existence of GLBTQ historical "evidence" and its often traumatic trappings, queer tellings of the past
are highly creative in form and remembered in media different from more
traditional public memory sites. For instance, many queer public memories
are derived from fleeting, nontextual sources. Ephemera (pulp novels, cos-
tumes), myths (queer Greece, the Amazons), and fantasies (sexual or otherwise) hold greater sway and sometimes greater importance than what little
documented proof might exist.[60] In addition, queer narratives of the past increasingly rely more on fictive pasts than their heterosexual counterparts do.
Much of this diversity can be attributed to the assorted group of researchers
and rhetorical producers who did and do GLBTQ historical work, including
scholars, archivists, documentarians, and librarians and also, importantly
(and often most prominently), activists, artists, performers, and amateur
or untrained historians.[61] These producers generate queer memories visibly on bodies, through affect, in performance, or through art more readily
than heterosexual memories. Finally, and most important, by considering
GLBTQ pasts as discourses used in public to shape understanding and exercise power, the rhetoricity of GLBTQ pasts—its social construction, its
publicness, its constitutive nature, its contestability—becomes not simply an
incidental feature but the central focus of this work.

Having firmly established queer public memory as the preferred lens for
examining GLBTQ people's uses of their shared pasts over the last century
and half, it is important to better understanding the shifts and evolutions
that have taken place within those practices. While the ultimate goal of the
present study is to explicate the queer "*turn toward* memory" noticeably
taking root within our contemporary societies, achieving that aim requires
first examining evidence of GLBTQ, homophile, fairy, or other groups' memorial action prior to the present moment. These earlier mobilizations of
GLBTQ pasts may be best characterized as tactical and ephemeral memory
rhetorics.

Tactical and Ephemeral Memories
■

The last three decades have witnessed an emerging era of queer monumentality. The concept of *queer monumentality* refers to concerted efforts to inscribe GLBTQ pasts in forms that offer it greater degrees of durability, epideictic energy, power, and opportunities for expansion linked to the queer "*turn toward* memory" described by Morris. In many instances, this literally means the construction of monuments to gay and lesbian lives of a very traditional sort. However, queer monumentality need not be limited to material or aesthetic factors exclusively. In fact, as an emerging form of GLBTQ activism, the contours of queer monumentality and its limits are not clearly defined.

To begin to articulate queer monumentality more fully requires first considering homophile, homosexual, and early gay and lesbian approaches to memory in the decades that preceded it. Existing scholarship on queer public memory in general largely ignores the fact that GLBTQ people used memories for rhetorical ends prior to 1980. Morris, for instance, pegs the "*turn toward* memory" by GLBTQ communities directly to the traumatic effects of the HIV/AIDS crisis. However, this book argues explicitly that memory has been a vital resource for homosexual, homophile, and GLBTQ activism for more than a century. In this reading, the queer "*turn toward* memory" is not the beginning of the construction of queer pasts but a moment for ushering in a new stage of memory's utility—queer monumentality. This view suggests a very different characterization: the 1980s and 1990s are *not* a unique moment of queer memory work but instead represent a renewed reliance upon memory by queers in historically distinct and culturally important forms. The queer "*turn toward* memory" is really a *queer return to memory* with significant shifts to monumental over tactical and ephemeral forms of memory work. Therefore, by taking seriously the tactical and ephemeral memory rhetorics that existed prior to the queer turn to monumentality, considerable light is shed on how gay men and lesbians and their compatriots used memory rhetorically for much of the last 150 years.

Ephemerality has long been recognized as a common and often essential aspect of queer life. As Muñoz argues, "queerness has . . . existed as innuendo, gossip, fleeting moments, and performances that are meant to be interacted with by those within its epistemological sphere—while evaporating at the touch of those who would eliminate queer possibility."[62] This should come as no surprise, considering that for much of the nineteenth and twentieth centuries any variation from the "normative intimacies" that buttress compulsory heterosexuality were scarcely tolerated at best or rooted out, punished, and annihilated at worst.[63] In such a hostile environment the fleetingness of queer life was essential for the existence of queer life. This logic applies equally to the ephemerality of GLBTQ pasts. Nonheterosexual pasts, if they were to survive, needed to be as prone to evaporation as their chronicler. They could often not be discussed in public without fear of retribution, written down without risk of discovery, or acknowledged without threat of persecution. Instead, queers relied upon ephemeral forms for preserving their past—intergenerational storytelling, tales committed to memory, private and fleeting performances, same-sex attractions masked as homosocial friendships, and the like. In short, queer memory rhetorics for much of human history were found only as hidden and invisible "traces," for the protection of their narrator and the queer past itself. As Muñoz points out, this fleeting quality inevitably demanded "archives of queerness" that were "makeshift and randomly organized," lacking in the "rigor" most heterosexual histories supposedly stipulated. However, in their ephemerality early queer memory rhetorics maintained a historical legacy that GLBTQ people could deploy as needed to advocate for themselves at key moments of crisis.[64]

In addition to being ephemeral in form, early queer memory rhetorics were also tactical in aim. This characterization is resonant with Michel de Certeau's theory of tactics—forms of resistance exerted against an authoritative, strategic power that succeed by turning established sites, acts, and activities dictated from above to their own purposes in the course of everyday life. In his theory of power Certeau claims tactics arise when a set of actors separate from the center of extant power recognize that they do not have their own space from which to act. For Certeau a tactic is "a calculated action determined by the absence of a proper locus. . . . The space of a tactic is the space of the other. Thus it must play on and with a terrain imposed on it and organized by the law of a foreign power. It does not have the means to *keep to itself*, at a distance, in a position of withdrawal, foresight, and self-collection."[65] Facing this structural disadvantage, actors deploy tactics—often reliant upon time, luck, and creative re-use—to exert some form of resistance, if only temporarily, within the realm of the powerful. Exemplary tactics for Certeau include people walking the city outside of its prescribed paths, creative cooking that undermines packaged food's prefabricated uses, and reading texts in ways that defy their authorial intent. Yet, of all the human practices that might invoke tactical iterations, Certeau suggests that rhetoric—as a situational art that can turn arguments on their heads for effective action—is one of the most adept.[66]

If rhetoric, in general, is an archetypal site of tactical action, early gay and lesbian memory rhetorics operate as powerful, specific instances of the (ephemeral) tactics Certeau describes. Denied a proper locus to preserve and share their common pasts in a fiercely heteronormative world, early gay men and lesbians "made do" with the dangerous and disciplining situations in which they found themselves. Rendered from heterosexual history and relayed in ephemeral forms, people with same-sex attractions and gender nonconformity of all kinds frequently generated memories under the pressure of disciplining heteronormative forces to defend moments of queer self-understanding. Turning to the detritus of the "foreign" territory of the heterosexual past, early gay men and lesbians carefully sorted, selected, and renovated this powerful normative history to scrape together queer meanings.[67] To put it another way, if the heterosexual telling of history is key terrain at the center of a supposedly exclusive straight society, early gay and lesbian actors made a life for themselves by violating that terrain and nimbly and temporarily turning it into a queer resource that might deliver them some crucial, if fleeting, victory. Certainly, the existence of such tactical and ephemeral memory rhetorics should not suggest that gay men and lesbians were unable in earlier decades to find sustaining "safe spaces" in which they could nourish their own selves and communities with a sense of the past. Doubtless, such spaces existed, if still only precariously. However, in many cases early gay and lesbian memories were mostly tactical and ephemeral rhetorics—pasts preserved on the fly, enacted in the moment, and derived from the "stuff" that constitutes heterosexual history.

It is when this tactical and ephemeral memory work was practiced in public that it was at its most rhetorical. And the nature of that public is particularly important. If we were to examine GLBTQ pasts put on display before an early gay, lesbian, or queer counterpublic, we would have little difficulty finding countless examples. Indeed, George Chauncey's pioneering work on gay subcultures in New York at the dawn of the twentieth century suggests explicitly that these pasts were present within the discourse and deeply influential in beginning to shape a collective queer imagining. However, gay men performing their pasts for themselves or in front of other gay men does not depict the full extent of tactical and ephemeral memory rhetorics at the time. Rather it is when the queer past was performed, argued, or made visible before heterosexual eyes and ears that the tactical and ephemeral nature of queer public memory reached its apex.

This dual nature of pre-1980 gay and lesbian memory rhetorics, both built from the scraps of heteronormative history and expressed in forms ambiguous and fleeting, can be seen in some of the earliest public acknowledgments of homosexuality. Perhaps, the best-known examples occurred during the trials of Oscar Wilde. The boisterous and outlandish Wilde was a playwright, literary master, and social celebrity in England from the late 1800s until 1895 when he was hauled into court on charges of "gross indecency." The trial was a media spectacle—one that Wilde himself became quite adept

at playing to his advantage in the halls of the Old Bailey. One of the most
noticeable and commented upon aspects of his self-defense is a prominent
example of a tactical and ephemeral memory rhetoric: in open court, in a
manner presaging Robinson's patients decades later, Wilde claimed that
Plato, Michelangelo, Shakespeare, and the biblical David and Jonathan had
all delighted in "the love that dare not speak its name." "'The love that dare
not speak its name' in this century is such a great affection of an elder for
a younger man as there was between David and Jonathan, such as Plato
made the very basis of his philosophy, and such as you find in the sonnets of
Michelangelo and Shakespeare. It is that deep, spiritual affection that is as
pure as it is perfect. It dictates and pervades great works of art like those of
Shakespeare and Michelangelo, and those two letters of mine, such as they
are. It is in this century misunderstood, so much misunderstood that it may
be described as the 'Love that dare not speak its name,' and on account of it
I am placed where I am now. It is beautiful, it is fine, it is the noblest form
of affection. There is nothing unnatural about it. It is intellectual, and it
repeatedly exists between an elder and a younger man, when the elder man
has intellect, and the younger man has all the joy, hope and glamour of life
before him. That it should be so the world does not understand. The world
mocks it and sometimes puts one in the pillory for it."[68]

The description Wilde puts forth to justify his behavior with a string
of younger men who only days before had given testimony against him on
the stand is clearly more in line with a description of pederasty than what
we might consider today to be a GLBTQ identity or same-sex relationship.
However, Wilde's heterosexual audience increasingly believed him to be a
practicing sodomite as the trials unfolded, further aligning his pederastic
relationships with what we think of today as homosexuality than might be
expected at the time. Nonetheless, it is apparent in this quotation that Wilde
sees resources for self-preservation within heterosexual history that he might
use to justify his own position "in the pillory."

But what qualifies Wilde's retort on the stand as a tactical and ephemeral memory practice? Clearly Wilde's speech suggests a kind of homosexual
content and relies heavily on historical imagination. But in what way might
we consider this a tactical and ephemeral form of memory? Wilde's claim
can be characterized as a particular form of such memory rhetorics: bricolage. A term used widely across the academy, many trace *bricolage* to Claude
Lévi-Strauss in *The Savage Mind,* in which he defines the "bricoleur" as
someone who uses "whatever is at hand" to complete a job.[69] Lévi-Strauss's
characterization of the bricoleur has been summarized as someone who uses
"the instruments he finds at his disposition around him, those which are
already there, which had not been especially conceived with an eye to the
operation for which they are to be used and to which one tries by trial and

error to adapt them, not hesitating to change them whenever it appears necessary, or to try several of them at once."[70]

The concept of bricolage has been taken up and elaborated upon by a wide range of cultural critics from Jacques Derrida to Dick Hebdige.[71] Certeau also uses the term, defining bricolage as "poetic ways of 'making do.'" For Certeau it is a way of using content (in this case public memory) for purposes unintended by its producer.[72] Indeed, in a system of cultural production where only those in a position of power are able to make and sustain authoritative objects (or, in our case, texts), bricolage becomes a tactical resource for those on the margins to reappropriate existent culture for distinctly different purposes.

Wilde's reclamation of revered historical figures that he believed participated in the "love that dare not speak its name" is an excellent example of a queer bricolage as a form of tactical and ephemeral memory rhetoric. Because Wilde is not able to produce evidence of GLBTQ pasts that might ameliorate his actions, he is forced to borrow from heterosexual history to defend himself—to "make do"—with what his culture and discourse provide. Wilde's selection of figures in this case is not haphazard; he does not just randomly select figures he views as helpful. It is likely that he is selecting figures of whom there already existed some degree of suspicion, probably within homophile literary circles. But while Wilde may not have been pulling historical figures out of the closet at random, he was certainly highly selective in his choices so as to align himself with figures who both might have practiced same-sex desire and who also already served a laudable function within wider heterosexual culture. After all, Wilde did not align himself with any less reputable historical figures convicted of gross indecency. Rather he chose to identify himself and his actions with those great men who constituted central figures in the commemorative realm of Western civilization, thereby seeking to make him credible and respectable and to nullify his "crime." Thus, by "making do" with the history to which he had access, Wilde relied upon inventive tactical and ephemeral memory rhetorics to make his case.

As we know, despite his insightful use of bricolage Wilde's defense would not be successful. He would be found guilty and spend two years sentenced to hard labor in an English prison. He would be released a visibly older man and with little of his previous joie de vivre. Wilde would die shortly after his release in the year 1900 of meningitis, largely alone and penniless.[73] Nonetheless, Wilde's testimony is an excellent example of how GLBTQ people have long used public memory in fleeting and unexpected ways to defend themselves in public against heterosexual intrusion.

While Wilde's self-defense is perhaps one of the most recognizable examples of this tactical and ephemeral memory work on the part of an individual

with same-sex desires, it is only one example. However, a brief review of
certain historical "snapshots" over the last 150 years reveals similar forms
of bricolage at work among sexual and gender minorities, each making do
with the past(s) they have. For instance, art and art display have long been
a resource wherein collectors may situate historical (or perceived historical)
homosexuality before heterosexual audiences. In many cases this was a solitary joy of the homosexual himself or herself, for both male and female visitors to Victorian museums gazed upon Greco-Roman sculpture and other art
works to fulfill an erotic desire.[74] However, homosexuals themselves sometimes crafted homoerotic displays of the past to imagine a queer present and
future. In particular Whitney Davis has highlighted how the construction
and display of homoerotic art collections from 1750 to 1920 often willfully
combined otherwise nonhomoerotic art pieces in ways that suggested—both
blatantly and discreetly—historical same-sex desire before modern audiences.[75]

Those with same-sex desires also relied on literature to appropriate heterosexual history. One of the most powerful of these appropriations during
the early twentieth century was the collection *The Ioläus*. Colloquially referred to as the "bugger's bible," it was first published in 1917, and, while many
of its essays were not explicitly homosexual in content (its subtitle was *An
Anthology of Friendship*), the assembly of these scattered essays into a single
text framed them in a way that many homosexual individuals found invigo-
rating and assuring. In Chauncey's words, *Ioläus's* "depiction of the nobility
of male affection and love helped readers affirm their own love for men by
encouraging them to identify it—and themselves—as part of an honorable
tradition."[76]

While World War I and World War II provided opportunities for many
inexperienced gay men and lesbians to get their first taste of queer life, the
wars and the situations they made possible required gay men and lesbians
to rely upon tactical and ephemeral uses of heterosexual history to render
themselves powerful in the face of often vindictive heteronormative antagonism. Just as many gay civilians had, gay soldiers, sailors, and Women's Army
Corps members (WACS) used tales of great gay war heroes and heroines
of the past to justify their identity. In some cases similar acts of historical bricolage enabled especially persuasive and patriotic men and women to
win the approval of military psychologists to enlist. However, these tactical
and ephemeral memory rhetorics also served gay men and lesbians well in
the course of battle. If they were ever questioned about their nonnormative
masculinities or their unusual proclivities by heterosexual peers or others
(as well as to shore up their own questioning selves), gay soldiers and sailors could list many similarly situated historical examples (without making
express their connection to homosexuality). Allan Bérubé has suggested that

this inventive work was most common among college-educated soldiers who "carried with them a mythology, developed from reading the classics and in conversation with other gay men." Bérubé highlights "'armies of lovers' such as the 'Sacred Band of Thebes' in ancient Greece, and heroic military leaders, such as Alexander the Great, Julius Caesar, Frederick the Great, and Lawrence of Arabia, who like themselves [in the case of gay men] had had male lovers."[77]

As we have seen in the reports of Dr. Robinson, the fields of psychology, psychiatry, and sexology became not only a prominent space in which homosexuality was described, assessed, accosted, and treated but also a space where GLBTQ patients defended themselves, their sexual practices, and their lives by "making do" with the heterosexual past. While Robinson's notoriety may have made him a compelling target for gay men and lesbians, the practice of citing historical precedent among esteemed figures was common in many doctor-patient interactions and was publicized in reports, books, and conference proceedings. For instance, in an 1883 accounting of homosexual activities documented by medicine, Drs. J. C. Shaw and G. N. Ferris highlighted how a patient of Dr. Richard von Krafft-Ebing named "Dr. G." in 1881 defended his homosexuality as "abnormal, but not pathological or unjustifiable. . . . It was no vice, since they were driven to it by a natural power." In making such a claim, Dr. G assured Krafft-Ebing that "men of his character [have] poetically gifted natures; [he] considers as such Voltaire, Frederick the Great, Eugene of Savoy, [August von] Platen, and many others of the present day."[78] Another young man, seeking assistance from Dr. William Hammond in 1883, reveled in retelling how "he spent the whole of one evening drawing the gluteal regions of the great men of the world, and imagining that he was having pederastic relations with them."[79]

It is important to note that, while gay men frequently relied upon these tactical and ephemeral memory discourses to make their claims to normalcy, women commonly did the same. In an 1895 article in the *American Naturalist* condemning the effects of female suffrage, Dr. James Weir, Jr., reported that many of the "viragints" (strong-willed, masculinized women of many types whose "most aggravated form . . . is that known as homo-sexuality") he had studied aligned themselves with others in history. He suggested that Joan of Arc, Catherine the Great, Messalina, and Queen Elizabeth were strong examples of viragints in the "history of the world."[80] In another account Sarah Edmonds Seelye recalled in 1882 how the cross-dressing style and lesbian tendencies of Fanny Campbell—the "female pirate captain"—inspired her to live a life in drag and serve as a man in the American Civil War.[81] Perhaps the best-known example from psychology, Alfred Kinsey's reports on the private and public sexual pasts of thousands of average Americans opened the floodgates to many individuals who thought themselves alone in the world while simultaneously challenging the assumptions of the homo/hetero binary by popularizing notions of a bisexual norm.[82]

As the gay and lesbian press developed in the early to mid-twentieth century, it also highlighted historical homosexuality in tactical and ephemeral ways in its coverage. In the 1940s and 1950s, if a reader could acquire a national or international newsletter such as *Vice Versa, ONE Magazine,* or those produced by the Mattachine Society (*The Homosexual Citizen* or the *Mattachine Review*) or the Daughters of Bilitis (*The Ladder*), it was quite simple to find allusions to GLBTQ pasts within its pages. Articles discussed the potential homosexual orientations of Hadrian, members of British royalty, and George Washington in the first year of the *Mattachine Review* alone.[83] Sapphistic poems and images of homosocial embraces between women and men were commonly conveyed to the reader in other publications. As the movement evolved, diversified, and expanded, other newsletters, journals, narratives, and images became accessible to a growing GLBTQ subcultural reading public which also diversified such displays of the past. In the 1960s and 1970s *Body Politic, Gay Sunshine, Conditions, Fag Rag,* and *Sinister Wisdom* (to name a few) became popular publication venues for GLBTQ scholars, particularly historians.[84] Meanwhile, small local and regional newsletters, magazines, and newspapers circulated within communities beyond the large metropolitan areas, spreading historical representations to readers.

Art, literature, the military, psychology, and the media—each presented opportunities for a diverse range of sexual dissidents to draw from wider culture to defend themselves from heteronormative invasion. These sorts of tactical and ephemeral deployments of GLBTQ memory rhetorics continued as a primary means of queer argument in the public sphere throughout the last century and continue today in the present. For instance, one could easily conceptualize past-oriented discourses produced by GLBTQ youth navigating the coming-out process as forms of tactical and ephemeral memory rhetoric along the lines described above. In addition, nascent GLBTQ movements in some more aggressively homophobic cultures still rely heavily upon tactical and ephemeral memory rhetorics both to build community and to minimize and question disciplining forces. Doubtless, GLBTQ persons and queers in our contemporary moment continue to face many of the same issues of violence, discrimination, and disciplining that queers of an earlier time faced when they invoked tactical and ephemeral uses of queer pasts more often. GLBTQ people still rely heavily on tactical and ephemeral memory rhetorics to attend to important needs in the community. Nonetheless, monumental rhetorics of GLBTQ historical representation have become a progressively important part of the articulation of GLBTQ pasts.

The Monumental Turn in
Queer Memory Rhetorics

While tactical and ephemeral memory rhetorics constituted the exclusive forms for sharing queer pasts during much of the previous century, over the last three decades GLBTQ communities have gradually turned to a distinctly different form of memory rhetoric. As a response to the fleeting and cast-off nature of earlier GLBTQ memory rhetorics, it is tempting to label this new form of memory discourse as a strategy, in line with Certeau's counterpoint to tactics.[85] However, while strategies are resonant with this new phase of queer memory practice, the label does not entirely fit. For instance, as we will see, the tensions inherent between tactics and strategies in Certeau's schema are not so imbedded between past and present queer memory rhetorics, which often operate in common cause as well as in conflict. Likewise, while queers may increasingly move closer to cultural acceptance, to equate GLBTQ persons as "the center" of society, like other strategic subject positions, is both a post-gay illusion and a vast misrepresentation of equality across all segments of the diverse GLBTQ community. Last, while Certeau casts strategies as powerful and defendable, this characterization lacks an appreciation for contexts in which even the strategic center is ultimately overwhelmed. Given these constraints, in this book a term different from Certeau's is used to characterize a more recent trend in queer memory action, what I label *queer monumentality.*

Queer monumentality may be defined as an ongoing and evolving assortment of efforts by GLBTQ people, institutions, and communities to give their shared pasts a weightiness, timelessness, and grandeur in order to activate collective power and effect social change. Queer monumentality is not merely the creation of material monuments with gay and lesbian subjects; rather it signals a broader shift in how GLBTQ people present their pasts before public audiences that is both evocative of aesthetic displays seen in previous eras yet deeply distinctive from what has come before. Therefore, beginning to understand queer monumentality fully demands a broader introduction to monumentality itself.

Conventional definitions of monumentality highlight several related qualities. Dictionaries typically refer to monumentality as something "exceptionally great" in "quantity, quality, extent, or degree," as having a "historical or enduring significance" or a "heroic scale," or as simply "relating to a monument."[86] But these basic understandings of monumentality have ancient origins. Monumentality—as a concept, style, and approach to memory—has roots in the architectural wonders of the ancient world. As Gretchen E.

Meyers declares, the idea of the monumental is informed by the grand structures of Greece, Rome, and Egypt through which individuals and communities sought to arrest the ravages of time and mark cultural values by erecting
supposedly everlasting symbols in the visual landscape. When eighteenth-
and nineteenth-century European artists, explorers, and tourists encountered the ruins of these great structures and were wowed by their grand,
distinctive, and long-lasting qualities, the monumental impulse took hold,
and more contemporary creators began to consider how they might, in Richard Wagner's assessment, build the equally compelling ruins of tomorrow.[87]
As the invocation of Wagner here suggests, while the basis of monumentality
lies in the material creations and discoveries of architects and archaeologists, an array of interested parties have drawn on monumentality to inspire
their creative projects including composers, artists, performers, playwrights,
historians, politicians, and speechmakers, to name a few. Through their uses
of monumentality in these diverse forms, varied leaders, artists, and nations
have harnessed the imposing features of monumentality to unify communities, inspire sweeping civic accomplishments, and embrace bold visions for
changing the shape of the world. Many scholars point to the great works
of the New Deal in the United States in the1930s as exemplary feats of the
modern era inspired by the rhetoric of monumentality.

But while monumentality has been broadly invoked over several centuries, its defining features are historically contingent and not always so clear.
Indeed, as Alexander Rehding suggests, monumentality is often an experience difficult to describe in words, calling into question whether a "taxonomy" of monumentality is possible or useful.[88] Nonetheless, despite the
simple and ineffable features of monumentality, there are certain meaningful characteristics that resound through time: durability, an epideictic impulse, expansion, and power.

Perhaps most immediately, monumentality is about durability. Monuments are fashioned to anchor something meaningful in time and, as such,
are made of materials or assume forms which will allow them to outlast
their subjects and creators. At a simplistic level this means merely that
most traditional monumental objects are made of sturdy materials: marble
buildings, bronze statues, and the like. But durability is also psychologically
connected to the monument's function to "escape time." As Henri Lefebvre
notes, "the most beautiful monuments are imposing in their durability . . . ;
[a monument] achieves monumental beauty because it seems eternal, because it seems to have escaped time. Monumentality transcends death . . . ;
a monument transmutes the passage of time, and anxiety about death, into
splendour."[89] By outlasting the flesh, monumentality—whether expressed in
a commemorative site, epic poem, or heraldic music—offers its subjects the
capacity to become immortal.

Likewise, monumentality is an epideictic form. Traditionally referenced in classical rhetorical theory, epideictic is defined by Aristotle as a "speech of praise or blame . . . both reminding [the audience] of the past and projecting the course of the future."[90] This telos is even inscribed in the term *monumental* itself, meaning in Latin "to exhort or remind."[91] Undoubtedly, monumentality leans toward the former more often than not; rarely does one encounter a monument to shameful behavior, except perhaps as a warning to others. Therefore, the epideictic quality of the monument is largely about finding praiseworthy and honorable subjects to recognize for their achievements and to mark as models of society's highest virtues. Given the valorizing impetus to most monumentality, the epideictic nature of monuments is often recognized in two ways: content and style. First, monumental content often praises grand achievements, lionizing battles won, barriers broken, roles fulfilled, and esteemed values exemplified. Second, this praise is conveyed in grand style. While what counts as appropriate grandeur varies by culture and time period, its epideictic message is delivered with awe, spectacle, "scale and elaboration," pomp and circumstance, or ornament.[92] Rehding calls this quality "an aesthetic of wonderment" and goes so far as to suggest that monumentality resides in the sublime.[93] In short, it is insufficient for the monumental to simply endure; it must banish death in a grand style which sets its subject matter apart from the everyday, conferring upon it esteem or righteousness suited to its commemorative impetus.

Given the praiseworthy dynamics at work in monuments, it should come as no surprise that monumentality also features expansive instincts. Indeed, a monument that does not spread its message to others so that it might be replicated, matched, or exceeded is likely a failed monument. Expansion gets at the social quality of monumentality; while they might be conceived for the honor of a particular person, monuments are almost always executed for an audience.[94] It is within other people's uptake of monumental messages that their cachet lies. Nor is this expansive quality limited to the content of the monument; monumental forms, styles, and designs likewise are copied, referenced, appropriated, or surpassed by their monumental progeny. Just as the grand ruins of Athens and Rome inspired the powerful civic designs of Washington, D.C., today's newer monuments—from Maya Lin's Vietnam Veterans Memorial to the United States Holocaust Memorial Museum—are iterated across the globe, spreading similar messages in parallel forms.

Finally, monumentality is deeply aligned with power, both in its creation and exertion. Invoking the monumental is no simple undertaking. To create something in monumental terms demands power on a scale far beyond that of most individuals. This is certainly the case with the most traditional form of monumentality: the material monument or monumental building. Erecting a material monument costs significant resources, requires connections to public authority, and demands approval from governing bodies. As the archaeologist Bruce Trigger suggests, there is an implicit connection between the creation and maintenance of monuments and people or institutions with the time, energy, labor, and financial resources to bring them to fruition.[95] As such, monumentality is often best understood as the provenance of the powerful, not the peasants. Similarly, given monuments' ability to be durable, epideictic, and expandable, monumentality has the capacity to assert power effectively after its creation. Indeed, monumentality's rise and fall from 1850 to 1950 can be traced precisely to its ability to influence wide swaths of humanity. The persuasiveness of monumentality was recognized by political and cultural leaders across the globe in the 1800s, spawning investments in grand symbolic gestures, buildings, art collections, and artistic works that would enthrall the population and inspire unity and action. While such projects were not without merit, the exploitation of monumentality in multiple forms by totalitarian regimes in the past (and present) has left monumentality with hefty "ideological baggage."[96] It also explains the rejection of monumentality from many quarters in the decades since World War II (most notably by Thomas Mann).[97] While such blame is undoubtedly misplaced in its entirety, monumentality's "ideological susceptibility" remains its greatest appeal and vice.[98] Still, as a form that marks, instills, and inspires what is valuable, what is worthy, and how one should live life, monuments *can* (though not necessarily, *do*) hold vast power over the communities in which they reside.

Understandably, these features should make monumentality an appealing resource for communities seeking to make an impact in the public arena and to preserve their memories through time (like GLBTQ people). Unfortunately, some of the most prolific proponents of monumentality in the twentieth century did much to tarnish its image. Indeed, Rehding emphasizes what so many other commentators have: "the experience of the Nationalist Socialist years have left their indelible mark on the notion of monumentality."[99] The Nazis' Third Reich—which sought to trace its roots to the great civilizations of the past—and Stalin's cult of personality are perhaps the worst twentieth-century offenders, having taken monumentality's symbolic inducements to unity, power, and eternity too far. In the years after World War II horrific regimes' affinity for monumentality played a significant part in sidelining it as a failed project. Despite some assertive efforts to the contrary, resurrecting monumentality in its traditional form has since been largely unsuccessful.[100] As a result, for several decades monumentality was left fallow.

This is where queers come in. While dominant heterosexual societies had long since depleted their interests in monumentality, monumentality was still a shiny object beyond queer reach by end of the 1970s. As we have seen, tactical and ephemeral memories still emerged sporadically with secretive tales of GLBTQ pasts at the time; but no out GLBTQ person had ever been enshrined in stone, celebrated in song, or recalled with pride on the size and scale of monumentality. The hostility from heteronormative culture had been too great and the implications for GLBTQ people were too much to imagine. Yet, with monumentality cast aside by most heteronormative cultures in the 1950s, GLBTQ people were presented an opportunity—a chance to seize upon an established and historically powerful memory rhetoric now ripe for the taking. Ironically then, the story of queer monumentality begins as an act of tactical appropriation.

Indeed, in many ways monumentality as it existed in the 1970s was perhaps best suited to queer hands. In the eyes of the leading (heterosexual) architects, scholars, and statesmen at the time, monumentality was old, outmoded, not modern, out of favor, and from a different time.[101] Meanwhile queers had a fancy for "objects out of date, past their prime, and in decline," particularly if they could "resurrect them and provide them new forms of attention."[102] For years monumentality has been excoriated for its complicity in the dehumanizing mass murder, oppression, and warfare that characterized the century; but from a queer perspective monumentality was something of value taken far too seriously.[103] Finally, if monumentality was a failed project, one to be quickly swept away by the modern International Style or postmodernity, there was no better community to appreciate it than GLBTQ people. As Halberstam proclaims, "failing is something queers do and have always done exceptionally well." As a queer approach to memory, the monumentality that failed normative culture could be reimagined as a "queer style or way of life" that might "offer different rewards."[104] As such, in the grandeur, splendor, and spectacle of monumentality, GLBTQ people found not only something with purpose, but something highly amenable to their dispositions to the world as well.

In comparison to tactical and ephemeral forms of memory, monumentality has features that offer queers a powerful solution to the many ongoing challenges that face and threaten GLBTQ pasts. In monumentality's durability queers rendered their pasts more permanent, minimizing the regular erasure they faced at the hands of a heteronormative society. By embracing monumentality's epideictic capacity, queers could undermine pervasive characterizations of GLBTQ people as criminals, perverts, threats, and psychopaths. Instead they could make new argument for understanding queers as good, ethical, important, and valuable, for the benefit of generations to come. The expansive qualities of monuments were also alluring, providing queer actors the inspiration and the models to magnify and enhance the struggle for GLBTQ rights. Perhaps most of all, in monumentality queers located a means of accessing power all their own. Queer monuments, early advocates hoped, would not be mere derivatives of heterosexual history but powerful, independent sites of queer activism that might further advance their agenda. In sum, while heterosexuals of all stripes had increasingly turned against monumentality for its unitary, authoritative, bombastic, and mobilizing potential, GLBTQ people identified a powerful rhetorical resource that they began to adopt voraciously.

Yet the feverish adoption of queer monumentality that began about 1980 did not occur overnight; rather, a series of developments both within and external to the GLBTQ community coalesced during this period to make renovating the queer past in a monumental guise possible. For most scholars who have engaged queer public memory and its parallel lines of thought in the last few years, the most important of these events is the HIV/AIDS crisis. Several scholars correctly point out that the traumatic losses of the HIV/AIDS pandemic prompted an especially strong wave of past-oriented practices within GLBTQ communities. Morris, for instance, claims the "memory void" left by the HIV/AIDS crisis and the queer "*turn toward* memory" that followed it are inextricably linked.[105] Likewise, Castiglia and Reed argue that HIV/AIDS was made "an agent of amnesia" that spawned widespread forgetting in the community and justified a new urgency with regard to remembering 1970s sexual culture(s).[106] Sturken even goes so far as to argue that the HIV/AIDS crisis "force[s] a rethinking of the process of memory itself."[107]

While HIV/AIDS undoubtedly was a significant contribution to the rise of queer monumentality, at least three additional factors contributed to making this transition in queer public memory rhetorics possible. One of these is the so-called memory boom. Scholars suggest that this broad cultural appeal of the past (dated to the mid- to late 1980s) emerged for several reasons: postmodernism's questioning of history and grand narratives, the turn of the millennium, the close of the Cold War and its attendant "end of history," among others. Many academics have studied the issue of memory while evidence of the "boom" was found in a myriad of cultural zones: expanding national museums and memorials, the culture wars, textbook debates, reparation payments, truth and reconciliation commissions, speeches of national apology, memory tourism, and a wealth of "memory industries," among many others. Indeed, while this focus has been pervasive, it has not been limited to academic and authoritarian undertakings.[108] Average people see the memory boom reflected in the spread of interest in genealogy, television series that trace family histories, the increasing popularity of historical documentary, and new recording and event-sharing technologies that allow us to better preserve our local pasts. As a result of the memory boom, Gavriel D. Rosenfeld has argued that "memory became virtually inescapable in everyday life."[109] Within this context appeals to the past (and memory, in particular) were not only more viable but encouraged by the social milieu as well.

Another factor is the increased organization (and power) of GLBTQ politics. While homophile activism dates at least to the turn of the century in Europe and to the early 1900s in the United States, the GLBTQ organizing that crystalized in the 1950s and culminated in the cultural upheaval of the 1960s created a new era of GLBTQ power instrumental to the success of the monumental turn. Whereas earlier homosexual political efforts were largely ignored or crushed by heteronormative apparatuses, the various branches and iterations of the post-1950 gay liberation and gay and lesbian rights movements have had immense staying power, greater visibility, and a stronger organizational core. Thus, by 1980 a large cohort of GLBTQ actors had been in play for decades, able to frame and make claims about GLBTQ concerns. Simultaneously, GLBTQ institution-building provided the tools, resources, and opportunities to bring monumental memory rhetorics to fruition. Various GLBTQ institutions and advocates created safe spaces, raised funds, and lobbied leaders to make possible opportunities for strategic planning.[110] Without these resources, gay and lesbian activists would be in no position to erect memorials, build archives, lease space, change zoning laws, and petition government in ways that would make queer memories more enduring.

Finally, an assortment of academic and community projects to recollect and preserve GLBTQ history made accessible the raw materials for this larger turn to queer monumentality. Beginning in the 1970s, a highly political GLBTQ archival movement began to collect GLBTQ historical representations for preservation while simultaneously making their holdings more accessible to the community. Many of these projects began locally in libraries, performance troupes, reading groups, and universities.[111] Thereafter, now-prominent gay and lesbian archives opened their doors, including the Western Gay Archives/ONE National Gay and Lesbian Archives (1971/1986), the Lesbian Herstory Archive (1972), the San Francisco Gay and Lesbian Historical Society (1985), and the Leather Archives and Museum (1991). These early archival efforts were made possible by the determined work and giving of a broad range of GLBTQ persons with little material, financial, or symbolic support and formed the foundation upon which both early and contemporary GLBTQ historical work have been made possible.

In conjunction with this community-based work, academics began the arduous task of discovering, reconstructing, and in some cases inventing GLBTQ pasts. Though late-nineteenth-century researchers such as John Addington Symonds, the "father of queer history," conducted some scholarly work, the researched histories that emerged in the 1970s began to shape decisively how GLBTQ pasts were understood.[112] The first notable historical tome of the period was Jonathan Ned Katz's *Gay American History*, published in 1976. A massive collection of documents related to GLBTQ pasts from

1607 to 1950, the text demonstrated for political and academic observers (as well as for gays and lesbians themselves) that lesbian and gay history "was possible."[113] Katz's first volume was shortly followed by a slew of influential book-length histories tracing GLBTQ pasts through the standard practices of historical research by authors including Michel Foucault, Jeffrey Weeks, John Boswell, Lillian Faderman, Alan Bray, John D'Emilio, Estelle B. Freedman, Paula Gunn, and Judith C. Brown, Martin Duberman, Martha Vicinus, and George Chauncey, among others.[114] Even these monographs were predated by articles and essays in feminist, Marxist, and social-history journals as well as works by dutiful amateur historians and archivists who toiled in anonymity for decades before the academy decided such work was tolerable, if not acceptable.[115] New interests in gay historiography followed in the 1990s while queer historiography became concerned with "how 'queer' might point the way to methodologies that broaden the questions we ask of the lesbian and gay past."[116] Such queer work has pointed toward more complex rearticulations of GLBTQ identity, culture, geography, and history with Leslie Feinberg's *Transgender Warriors* (1996), John Howard's *Men Like That: A Southern Queer History* (1999), and E. Patrick Johnson's recent *Sweet Tea: Black Gay Men of the South* (2008) being three prominent examples.

These factors, when read in conjunction with the real and important effects offered by monumentality, clarify both monumentality's appeal to GLBTQ individuals, communities, and institutions over the last three decades and how the community was able to transition to monumentality from a previous reliance upon tactical and ephemeral memory rhetorics exclusively. But what, at a practical level, does queer monumentality look like? What forms does it take? What strategies does it employ? How is it carried out? Also, what is at stake in adopting queer monumentality? What are its limitations? And what happens to the idea of monumentality when it is queered? Exploring these questions is the central task of the remainder of this book.

Building Queer Monuments, Queering Monumentality

∎

Beginning to understand the exciting emergence of queer monumentality as a modern form of queer public memory and its ongoing transformations requires investigating instances of this rhetoric at work in the public sphere. In the course of writing this book, opportunities for examination have grown immensely, revealing both common themes and genuine instances of innovation. The cases selected herein seek to balance these two imperatives, providing the reader with a broad understanding of the monumental turn. Likewise, these cases have been arranged deliberately to illustrate the era of queer monumentality progressively from exemplary instances to worrisome examples to pioneering new possibilities.

Perhaps the most evident examples for understanding queer monumentality are material monuments to gay and lesbian subjects. Gay and lesbian monuments began to appear as early as 1984 when George Segal's second casting of *Gay Liberation* was placed at Stanford University.[117] Other well-known gay and lesbian monuments followed, including the 1987 *Homomonument* in Amsterdam, the 1992 *Gay Liberation* monument in New York, and the 2008 *Memorial to the Homosexuals Persecuted under the National Socialist Regime* in Berlin. Betwixt and between these most prominent instances, a bevy of lesser-known, explicitly GLBTQ-themed monuments emerged on the public scene worldwide, including in cities as diverse as Amsterdam, Manchester, London, Frankfurt, Vienna, Rome, Sydney, Barcelona, Stiges, Tel Aviv, and Dayton, Ohio. While these material markers of GLBTQ pasts vary considerably in scale and scope, each demonstrates the most poignant appeal of the turn to queer monumentality: the capacity to enshrine GLBTQ pasts in a fixed position and material form that can persist through time with some degree of stability and security. While queer monumentality is most apparent in monuments of bronze and marble, its many virtues are not, as we will see, constrained exclusively to physical spaces and forms. Nonetheless, attention to material monuments to gay and lesbian subjects makes clear queer monumentality's ability to counteract the withering onslaught of GLBTQ people's erasure from history.

An archetypal instance of queer monumentality is the Alexander Wood statue in Toronto, Ontario, Canada, the subject of chapter 2 in this book. Wood was a pioneering Scottish colonist in 1810 in what was then called York when his life was turned upside down by accusations that he was a "molly," after which he was forced to flee Canada or face persecution. Nearly two hundred years later, Wood has been recuperated as a "gay hero" by the Church-Wellesley community of Toronto, a moniker enshrined with the installation of a neoclassical monument in Wood's honor in the center of the city's heavily gay neighborhood. The Wood statue provides an exemplary case study for considering the major objectives of the turn to queer monumentality in the GLBTQ community. In particular, chapter 2 investigates what is gained when a historical GLBTQ figure is remembered in monumental form, as well as the challenges inherent in representing in stone an often complex, transitory, and unstable notion like sexuality. In sum, the Wood statue depicts a compelling (if not perfect) instance of queer monumentality, facing considerable backlash, but still enduring and powerful because of its monumental form.

Important to the exploration of queer monumentality is the question of how queers can do monumentality outside its most traditional form, namely,

material monuments like Alexander Wood's. Given that monumentality's
roots lie in the architectural grandeur of mostly Western antiquity, it is interesting that the nonmaterial dimensions of monumentality have been deployed by a wide assortment of social actors ranging from storytellers to
composers. In these instances monumentality's power often shifts away
from durability toward its other noted qualities: its ability to inspire and
produce change by commemorating great heroes and heroines of the past
with wonderment. Rehding's work on musical monumentality is perhaps the
best recent example of the capacity of ephemeral, nonmaterial subjects to
be addressed in this way. Examining the great musical deployments of monumentality in nineteenth-century Germany, Rehding shows how an experience as fleeting as listening to music can produce in audiences synonymous
feelings of pride, power, and the sublime that rivals the marvelous grand
displays of the German nation. While always conscious of the potential for
musical monumentality to lead its listeners astray into unifying moralistic
adventurism (or worse), Rehding argues convincingly that monumentality's
nonmaterial instantiations are just as powerful and should be taken just as
seriously as its durable brethren.[118]

The powerful possibilities of less-material forms of monumentality are
explored in this book in chapter 3 through the tragic murder of Matthew
Shepard and his public defense by what I label the queer counterpublic.
Shepard was a twenty-one-year-old college student at the University of Wyoming when he was abducted from a bar under false pretenses by two men
who said they would give him a ride home. Instead of taking Shepard home,
the men robbed and assaulted him, tying his badly beaten body to a ranch-
er's fence and leaving him to die of exposure. Though he was found the next
morning, Shepard ultimately succumbed to his injuries a few days later in
the midst of a growing national outcry over hate crimes. Given the divisive
uproar across the nation against protecting GLBTQ people from such violence, Shepard's body was intentionally denied a public physical monument
at the time of his death. Nonetheless, monumentality played a significant
part in how the GLBTQ community remembered Shepard in the days and
weeks following his death. This monumentality took the form not of stone,
but of discourse. Specifically, this monumental discourse was deployed by
gays and lesbians to counteract pernicious characterizations of Shepard far
too common for other victims of antigay violence: that this was an isolated
case, that Shepard had provoked the attack, or that gay men were deserving
of violence. Instead, gay and lesbian voices—enunciated in public speeches,
at political marches, during candlelight vigils, in media interviews, in letters
to the editor, and online commentary—turned to monumental memories of
Shepard that depicted him alternately as a saint, martyr, and common man.
Such appeals relied heavily on the monumental quality of epideictic rhetoric,

heralding Shepard as an exemplary image and often remembering him in un-
paralleled public acts inspiring awe, reflection, and emotional engagement.
As is typical of the turn to queer monumentality, not everyone acceded to
this queer public-memory rhetoric: queer and transgender activists lamented
Shepard's representativeness and the inclusive claims these monumental rhetorics proclaimed. Indeed, the monumentality deployed in the Shepard case
approximates in some ways the incessant and mindless drive to unification,
sameness, and moralism Thomas Mann and other critics of monumentality
deride. Regardless, exploring the Matthew Shepard case demonstrates the
compelling potential for queer monumental memory rhetorics to be effective
above and beyond material markers.

The cases of Wood and Shepard establish the powerful capacity of
queer monumentality to remember queer lives in ways that far outstrip what
could be accomplished through tactical and ephemeral memories alone.
However, queer monumentality, like other invocations of monumentality before it, is not without its limitations. One of these limitations is that queer
monumentality clearly privileges identities, experiences, and representations
of historical (gay) men over lesbians, bisexuals, and transgender people.
Unfortunately, this limitation comes as little surprise. Simone de Beauvoir,
for instance, pointed out as early as 1949 that the myths, legends, and stories that form the basis of how little girls come to see the world invariably
reflect "the pride and the desires of men."[119] Scholars have remarked that
when women are represented in commemorative zones, they largely take
the form of mythical beings or represent shared virtues more than actual
women.[120] More recently Barbara Biesecker has identified the "systematic
exclusion of women," from military history and memory generally.[121] The
dimensions of memory that structure this exclusion are many, including the
privileging of the *vita activa* in the public sphere, the exclusion of women
from the rarified realms most readily rewarded with commemoration (military service, politics, business, and so on), the generic use of women in
commemorations to represent values and ideas rather than real women, and
the reliance on private and public funds controlled by men to make these
commemorations a reality. While it might be hoped that gay men, who have
long experienced similar exclusions from commemorative culture, might
actively seek to remedy these representational inequities, the case studies
in this book largely confirm the relationship between male privilege and
commemoration even in emerging GLBTQ memory rhetorics. As a result,
it is virtually impossible not to fall short in representing the real diversity
of the GLBTQ pasts by focusing on queer monumentality alone. However, attempting to critique these representational failures and suggesting
ways of remedying them will, it is hoped, contribute to ameliorating these
harms.

The limitations of queer monumentality are not confined to representational inequities. For instance, the common casting of the GLBTQ past
in stone or other static forms key to monumentality's durable appeal simultaneously makes representing the fluid and variable identities, attractions,
and desires of diverse GLBTQ communities difficult. Likewise, epideictic
impulses inherent in monumentality, when matched with poor or narrow-
minded representational choices, can easily verge on homornormativity,
making less "safe" members of GLBTQ community unwelcome in queer
pasts and presents. Similarly, queer monumentality often mimics and re-
iterates the mindless appeal to gay pride without actively considering the
important critiques made by gay-shame scholars about commercialization,
antisociability, and historical suffering.[122] Clearly, queer monumentality, for
all its strength, is an imperfect approach to resolving the risks of GLBTQ
oblivion.

Some of the limitations posed by queer monumentality are highlighted
in chapter 4, which takes as its subject the ongoing political battle to teach
the "contributions" of GLBTQ people within public-school curriculums and
textbooks in California. As substantial scholarship has shown, textbooks are
among the most pervasive forms by which children are incorporated into the
ideological systems of their cultures. Worldwide and throughout the twentieth century, textbooks have stood as cultural and political markers for the
expression of identity, nationalism, and performances of citizenship. As a result textbooks and curriculums represent powerful cultural sites in which to
exert queer monumentality, rendering GLBTQ people as important, heroic,
and valuable members of U.S. society rather than as antinational threats.
Such a struggle has been under way in California since the late 1970s and in
the last few years has won critical victories that will see GLBTQ representations in public-school classrooms by the end of this decade. However, the
textbook reform case also illustrates that rarely do cultural victories come
without significant costs. As chapter 4 demonstrates, that is particularly the
case when GLBTQ inclusion in monumental texts such as textbooks is predicated on supporting other, already existent discourses at the center of society. In this case that extant discourse is nationalism, and GLBTQ reformers
made the imperfect choice to equate queer monumentality with nationalistic
ideologies in textbooks in order to gain a more durable, secure, and expandable base in public classrooms. In doing so these reformers made some of
the limitations of queer monumentality clear: the valorization of neoliberal
individualism, the erasure of antiheteronormative politics, and the forgetting
of sex. In the end the benefits of queer monumentality as a rhetorical strategy are called into question, as its limitations are made all too clear.

Recognizing the potential costs inherent in monumentality as it has
been deployed by gays and lesbians over the last few decades appears to put

GLBTQ memory makers in a difficult position: either accept queer monumentality as a strategy for all its virtues and vices or reject queer monumentality and return again to the less costly but more inept tactical and ephemeral memory rhetorics relied upon over the last century. However, such a framing is a false binary. Queer monumentality, like other forms of monumentality before it, may have its drawbacks; however, if how queer monumentality is done can be revised to account for and ameliorate these drawbacks, we may still find in the monumental turn a powerful resource for queer public memory.

The key to doing queer monumentality better lies in queering monumentality itself. By *queering* in this context, I do not refer to a wide swath of GLBTQ experiences or the use of the term *queer* in pioneering, pre-1990 GLBTQ scholarship.[123] Rather I mean a deployment of monumentality that more fully embraces the radical deconstruction project of queer theory.[124] Queer theory emerged in the early 1990s out of the work of gay and lesbian, feminist, poststructuralist, and cultural studies as a theoretical position against "normalization." At the heart of these studies is the belief that cultural forces of power continually seek to normalize human bodies, minds, and actions through discourse that rewards acquiescence and discipline and makes unintelligible those that do not. While previously, such exclusions led some GLBTQ activists and thinkers to see inclusion into the system as the primary means toward individual and/or group liberation, queer theory holds that the subject position of the abnormal commands a valuable power that should not be given up. From these queer positions the normalized center can be interrogated and disrupted, exploding the systemic binaries and definitions that frequently harm those on the margins. As a project that "support[s] forms of affective, erotic, and personal living" by making them *"available to memory,"* queer public memory does important queer work.[125] However, monumentality's homonormative tendencies, male-dominated subjects, overreliance on pride, and rigid expressions of identity, are often ill-equipped to meet the needs of the diverse modern GLBTQ community. Queering monumentality, then, becomes a means to make GLBTQ pasts available to memory while taking the best of the monumental form and supplementing it with more queer-friendly elements.

But how can monumentality begin to be queered? We can initiate this process by adopting a both/and approach to the queer past that emphasizes monumentality's durability, power, expansions, and epideictic qualities, and marries these with the tactical and ephemeral memory rhetorics of both historical protoqueer subjects and contemporary queer actors. Such an approach is well within the impulses of the queer project. By bringing tactical and ephemeral approaches to memory into monumental projects, queers can supplement (without replacing) monumental discourses—celebrating representational triumphs, critiquing (or embracing) failures, complicating more staid images and identities, and introducing a queer flair for irony, sarcasm, and silliness into texts that approach monumentality's moralistic or fascist tendencies. At the same time monumentality's advantages can provide ephemeral queer memories opportunities to be more loudly heard and acknowledged while at the same time limiting their reterritorialization by anti/hetero-normative forces. Likewise, this both/and approach to queer memory represents a more coherent line of attack against heteronormativity. Indeed, I share the conception of power articulated by those such as Foucault, Gilles Deleuze, and Félix Guattari—a power that is not a single entity that contrary forces line up against but rather "manifold relations of power" that are infused throughout the social system simultaneously at various points.[126] These many enactments of power have the ability not only to evolve and change but also to "reterritorialize," or compromise, what Deleuze and Guattari call "lines of flight"—temporary acts against power that offer moments of resistance and the potential for transformation. However, inevitably these supposed acts of liberation are transitory and soon become consumed back into the fold of power.[127] In view of such a conception of power, liberation per se is unlikely and a resistance to that power in hopes of transforming it (no matter how minutely) becomes the goal. The GLBTQ community (broadly defined) must be willing to engage the complex forms of heteronormative power at multiple points and in multiple ways. Adopting a queered form of monumentality moves queer public memory further down this road. In short, by finding ways to renovate monumentality to allow it to ensure GLBTQ pasts while not foreclosing the queer present and future, a revised-queer monumentality may become an even greater asset to political, cultural, and social change.

In an important sense rethinking monumentality away from its classical instantiations and toward a more queer orientation falls well within a broader attempt to do monumentality differently in the twenty-first century. Huyssen has been perhaps the most vocal and influential on this subject. According to Huyssen, despite a rejection of monumentality in the mid-twentieth century, monumentality is still alive and well today in the grand commemorative projects we have seen spawned by the memory boom. Indeed, as postmodernism has left individuals and communities free-floating through time and space, monumentality continues to appeal—even with its flaws—for its ability to tether communities to some sense of a past that is meaningful. Nonetheless, contemporary monumentality is different from classical monumentality. Today monumentality, for Huyssen, is rather "antimonumental."[128] The spirit of antimonumentality recognizes the virtues of commemoration as key features of monuments that people refuse to abandon wholeheartedly. At the same time antimonumentality rejects the "heaviness and permanence" of traditional physical monuments, embracing instead the more ephemeral and transitory appeals privileged in our modern age.[129] In other words Huyssen suggests a synthetic approach to monumentality that can forge "a monumentality that can do without permanence and without destruction, one that is fundamentally informed by the modernist spirit of a fleeting and transitory epiphany, but that is no less memorable or monumental for it."[130] His example of this new rendering of monumentality is the artist Christo's wrapping of the German Reichstag in silver fabric. As a temporary installation the *Wrapped Reighstag*'s effect was fleeting and ephemeral but simultaneously served to highlight the staid monument and its perduring form. Similarly, a queer monumentality that embraces both tactical/ephemeral and monumental forms of memory simultaneously to produce a complex, fluid, both/and approach to GLBTQ pasts has the potential to reinvigorate monumentality in productive ways going forward.

The possibilities for rethinking queer monumentality come to the fore in chapter 5, which shifts focus away from the present and past to how gays and lesbians have directed their energies toward being remembered queerly in the future. The chapter assesses how the relatively mundane processes of an everyday individual's death are deeply inscribed within heteronormativity. As such, it is highly likely that a person who lived a profoundly out and proud life might be constituted as straight by the technologies of death. Also important are strategies by which gays and lesbians have sought to maintain a public gay legacy after their deaths, primarily focused upon the performance and representation of GLBTQ identities within "gravescapes." Two gravescape monuments are highlighted and analyzed in particular, the first the 1986 grave of Sgt. Leonard Matlovich who became one of the first gay men to challenge publicly his discharge from the U.S. military because of his sexuality, and the second a 2004 grave marker created by artist and lesbian Patricia Cronin and her longtime partner titled *Memorial to a Marriage*. In both cases the activists turned to traditional material monuments to mark their gay and lesbian afterlives with durability, honor themselves and their life choices with respect, and situate themselves as role models for others. However, at the same time Matlovich and Cronin and their peers relied upon tactical and ephemeral opportunities to secure their queer monumentality. In doing so, albeit in less explicit ways than Christo's *Wrapped Reichstag*, each memorialist provides insights on how queer monumentality might be done better going forward.

Final concerns are considerations of the work of GLBTQ memory makers for social change and of what the future may hold for the queer past in the decades ahead. Taking as its point of departure the announcement of a new LGBT heritage initiative on the gay and lesbian past by the U.S. National Park Service, chapter 6 sketches the dynamic progress achieved by the queer public memory project to date, considers the value of queer public memory generally, and reviews the challenges and opportunities that lay ahead as the struggle for GLBTQ pasts continues.

CHAPTER 2

A Monument to "a great fag"

IN THE SUMMER OF 2005 A PROMINENT statue with a wry smile, historic dress, and a "gay flair" was unveiled for the first time in the Church Wellesley neighborhood of Toronto (fig. 1).[1] The more than three hundred people in attendance would be the first to see the monument to Canada's "gay pioneer," Alexander Wood, a Scottish immigrant to the small town of York (present-day Toronto) in 1797. A man of means at the age of twenty-five, Wood quickly became engaged in the life of his new home as he rose to the position of magistrate in 1800. By most accounts Wood excelled in his position until a scandalous incident in 1810 that would forever link the name Wood with *molly* (a derogatory term for a homosexual man throughout the period) in Upper Canada.[2] During his time as magistrate a local woman reported to Wood that she was raped. Distraught, the woman had difficulty describing her assailant; however, she believed a scratch she inflicted on his genitalia in the course of the attack could identify the perpetrator. As a dutiful enforcer of public safety, Wood leapt into action. Calling before him several local men of the right age, Wood ordered them to face forward and drop trou. He carefully inspected the genitalia of each man himself determined to seek justice for the victim and return order to fair York.[3]

Or so we might like to think. Shortly after the inspection, the residents of York began to grumble. The examination had revealed no scratched member, and no suspect had been found. Indeed, there were whispers the woman had begun to rescind aspects of her story. There were even rumors that there had been no woman at all. To this day the facts remain unclear. Nonetheless, the magistrate was engulfed by fierce denunciations from all corners of colonial life. Particularly troubling were accusations that Wood fabricated the story to quench his secret homosexual desires. Whether Wood was homosexual is, of course, unclear. As is the case with many historical figures, Wood's sexuality is ambiguous at best; however, the nature of the scandal, his lifelong bachelor status, and his flamboyant character suggested to onlookers that

FIG. I

East-facing view of the
Alexander Wood statue.
Photograph by the
author.

he might be gay. Certainly he was accused of being a "molly" on the street, and rumors about his sexuality swirled in the colonial press.[4] However, while there was and is no convincing evidence one way or the other about Wood's intentions, the accusations eventually became too much. After months of personal anguish, the scandal forced Wood to flee not only York but also the continent, seeking refuge in his native Scotland.[5]

This story of Wood and his monument marks the beginning of perhaps the oddest effort to remember a queer life in the public sphere. At the same time Toronto's Wood statue also serves as an emblematic example of queer monumentality. As we have seen, for much of the last century queer pasts have been constrained by heteronormative forces and erased by historical arbiters, leaving queers reliant upon the most tactical and ephemeral forms of memory—such as gesture, performance, and intergenerational storytelling—to maintain their shared pasts.[6] While more secure forms of memory have emerged in recent decades, they have often been derived from heterosexual history, held up by heteronormative apoplexies, or revised to the point of abstraction. By contrast, the Wood statue represents a prime instance of how public memory can be done differently in the age of queer monumentality. Erected in durable stone in a public square, the Wood statue exemplifies the traditional monumental impulse to imbed the past in glorious and perduring material forms. Commissioned, designed, maintained, and funded in part by the GLBTQ community, the statue likewise situates itself amid and among queer people, independent from the heteronormative forces that regularly patrol access to the past and power as a result. In addition, the statue uses several techniques to highlight Wood's sexuality and his achievements in an epideictic display of pride (one of only a few publicly known memory sites to label their subjects as queer). Indeed, it can be argued that Wood's statue constitutes an official memory sanctioned within both the GLBTQ and heterosexual community.[7] Also, as an image reproduced, recycled, and innovated upon in recent years, the statue helps to inspire expansive queer memorializing beyond itself. In short, there are few examples of queer monumentality as explicit as the Alexander Wood statue. As such, it provides a compelling case study for understanding how queers can disrupt the forgetting and erasure that has so contributed to GLBTQ marginalization.

Of the several monumental dimensions at work in the Wood statue, its durable form as a material artifact placed and observed in the public sphere is perhaps the most consequential. This is not only because such material renderings of the queer past have been so rare; because it is a material and contested public memory, the ways in which both the creators of the statue and its diverse audiences interact with the site are also critical to understanding the statue's meaning. Indeed, Carole Blair and Neil Michel have argued that the viewing practices of diverse kinds of audiences are just as important in understanding the message that is conveyed through a memory site as what is made in/visible.[8] In addition, Blair has demonstrated that contemporary commemorative sites in particular rely on materiality as well as symbolicity in order to shape their memorial rhetoric.[9] Thus, the visual, material, *and* discursive enactments of the Wood statue's rhetoric are of great concern. For instance, how one approaches the statue and in what order its components are consumed inform the meaning that is generated. How one views the statue, either through an extended "gaze" or a series of "looks," contributes to this understanding.[10] The statue's permanence, reproducibility, tactile effect on people, and the way it interacts with other sites in Toronto and beyond also says much about the statue's meaning.[11] In addition, the "image vernacular" which organizes how viewing practices are structured among various communities at different historical moments are central to understanding how the statue is received by various audiences.[12] Taken together with the representational and aesthetic elements, the various ways in which the Wood statue can be read provides fertile ground for rhetorical analysis that can shed light on queer monumentality's virtues.[13] Yet the inclusion of such rhetorics into the queer memory repertoire simultaneously produces unintended consequences for how historical and contemporary GLBTQ identity is conceptualized. How gay and lesbian, queer, and heterosexual audiences respond to these consequences suggests important implications for queer public memory moving forward.

While the Wood statue raises the importance of materiality in the era of queer monumentality, it also serves as a dynamic example of how "gay space" within the city can be created and destroyed through various discursive, visual, and material readings of public memories.[14] Despite suggestions to the contrary, the urban environment has not always been friendly to those in search of same-sex desire. While the fruitful works of Chauncey, Allan Bérubé, Elizabeth Lapovsky Kennedy and Madeline D. Davis, and others have illuminated the possibilities for queer lives in the city, many cities across the globe, including Toronto, have a history of identifying and eradicating gay space.[15] The creation of gay spaces in cities is better thought of as an evolutionary process full of strife and political/cultural activism. Toronto's queer community has been waging such a battle for decades. From its shutting of lesbian bars to the infamous 1981 Bathhouse Raids, Toronto is an example of the dynamic tensions between expanding and shrinking queer sites. On the streets of Toronto, according to John Grube, "change did not happen overnight, nor were gains won without prolonged struggles that still continue." Instead Grube suggests that the GLBTQ community, in line with the turn to queer monumentality, has waged a battle away from a hidden space of homosexual desire toward a "'democratic' gay public space." In using the term *democratic,* Grube names a process of spatial negotiation whereby GLBTQ people (primarily gay men) carve out for themselves geographies often taken for granted by the heterosexual community. The key characteristics of these spaces for Grube are threefold. First, unlike closeted spaces, gay democratic space makes GLBTQ identities visible to heterosexual and homosexual audiences alike. Second, gay democratic spaces promote a form of public sexuality (distinct from identity) where same-sex desire can be out in the open rather than hidden within veiled everyday urban activities. Finally, gay democratic space is fostered when members of the GLBTQ community debate openly and frankly about the rules, organization, and structures of that space. This community dialogue is perhaps the key factor in naming these spaces democratic. It is within these spaces that a different kind of GLBTQ community is formed, one aligned with queer monumentality's lasting and proud aims.[16]

However, Grube's perspective is only one of many possible ways to understand gay space in Toronto. While many in the GLBTQ community have worked to craft spaces that confer stability to gay sites (the Wood statue being a clear example), people from across the cultural and political spectrum have adopted different ways of viewing these spaces to challenge this stability. As tactical and ephemeral memory makers, these people regularly draw upon the statue itself to construct their meanings, subverting its intended message for their own (divergent) purposes. Two prominent viewing positions from which people actively challenge the statue's meaning include the cultural traditionalist viewing position, whose members continue to minimize and destroy gay space, and the queer radical viewing position, whose participants seek to destabilize the meaning of all space. By examining not just the monumental rhetorical messages crafted to express the public memory of Alexander Wood but also the countermemory readings and performances offered by these two viewing positions, the meaning of gay space in Toronto is opened up to diverse visual, cultural, and political interpretations.[17] While these readings are not mutually exclusive or available only to those who inhabit particular identity categories, the contest between these groups of viewers over the meaning of the statue and similar spaces throughout the city is central to understanding the public memory of Alexander Wood and the limits to queer monumentality.

To tackle this complex and multivocal text, it is helpful to analyze the statue by performing three different ways of understanding it. Performing these positions suggests ways of reading the Wood statue that draw upon and inform preexisting ideas of queer representation and public space. Key to this approach to studying queer public memory is Leah Ceccarelli's description of polysemy—"the existence of plural but finite denotational meanings for a single text."[18] As part of a marginalized community, GLBTQ memories have long been devalued and erased in dominant culture's reliance upon limited, heteronormative historical narratives.[19] Monosemic approaches to criticism that privilege the speaker, author, or creator of a text can be complicit in this erasure by ignoring the resistive, creative, and tongue-in-cheek queer voices that permeate some texts below the surface. By embracing a polysemic analysis of the Wood statue, a constellation of readings comes to the fore, allowing the complexity of the text and its nuanced interactions among different audiences inhabiting different viewing positions to emerge. In addition, discourse about the statue in local newspapers and online material is useful in contextualizing both what this statue was designed to do as well as its reception by those who interact with it. Diverse meanings of the Wood statue in different interpretive communities thus emerge through a "close reading of receptional fragments in conjunction with a close reading of the text."[20]

While the meanings of this statue are as diverse as those who gaze upon it, three primary viewing positions emerge: the official democratic memory, which remembers Wood—monumentally—as a valuable contributor to Canadian community; the traditionalist countermemory, which remembers Wood as a criminal who abused his authority and should be shielded from public view; and the camp countermemory, which remembers Wood as a camp figure both insufficient to represent contemporary identities and capable of being altered for more queer purposes. These readings and their interactions in the public sphere implicate particular thoughts about queer monumentality and what constitutes queer public memory.

Visualizing the Official Democratic Memory

■

In the first way of viewing the Wood statue, the official democratic frame, the term *official* designates that the meaning derived from this viewing position is the meaning intended not only by Wood's memory makers but also by the institutional forces within Toronto that sanctioned the statue's creation.[21] Simultaneously, *democratic* in this case suggests a commemorative designation akin to Grube's understanding of democratic gay space: one that makes gay men and lesbians visible, highlights public same-sex desire, and relies on community deliberation.[22] Collectively, both the official and democratic dimensions of this viewing position suggest a very particular way Wood should be understood by audiences.

This understanding relies heavily on the fact that Alexander Wood is remembered in the form of a commemorative site. Wood is not the first queer to be remembered in stone. Rather, the statue is part of a larger effort in recent decades to make GLBTQ pasts more visible and material through public commemorative practices: a period of queer monumentality. However, while the Wood statue shares much in common with its predecessors, it is one of the first queer monuments to be authorized in part by a primarily official institution. This authorization takes three forms: official funding, official sanction, and official endorsement. Unlike many other queer monuments, the Wood statue was not donated or funded by a nonprofit organization. Instead, the Church Wellesley Business Improvement Association (BIA)—an organization of gay and lesbian businesses sanctioned by the city for local development projects funded by city taxes—initiated the statue and funded fifty percent of the two-hundred-thousand-dollar cost of the statue through its own revenue. The remaining half was paid by the City of Toronto.[23] In addition, the city sanctioned the statue through deliberations for city funds, alterations of street zoning to allow for construction, and extensive support and consultation with municipal researchers, designers, coordinators, and experts. Public statements by officials also endorsed the Wood project. Former Toronto councillor Kyle Rae stated: "People who have lived in this neighborhood have known and heard about him over the years . . . but it's never been mainstream. . . . This now becomes part of all of everyone's knowledge."[24] In short, the Wood statue, its design, content, and funding all signify an official stamp of approval by the state on a monumental instance of queer public memory. In this way the Wood statue embodies an official public memory.

The idea of an officially sanctioned queer memory may seem drastically progressive in the U.S. context, but Canadian perspectives on gay and lesbian rights have changed more quickly. In Canada homosexual acts were decriminalized in 1969 with the help of future Canadian prime minister Pierre Trudeau who argued that "there's no place for the state in the bedrooms of the nation."[25] The contemporary Canadian gay and lesbian rights movement emerged soon thereafter at much the same time as its U.S. counterpart, most visibly with mass street protests in response to the raiding of four gay bathhouses in Toronto in 1981. The following years brought great success, including the adoption of the Canadian Charter of Rights and Freedom in 1982, which was later used to grant legal equality for gays and lesbian in marriage, adoptions, employment, housing, and government services.[26] Canadian public opinion polls continue to show that large majorities support full equality for gays and lesbians.[27] In real and visible ways the past few decades have marked a turning point whereby GLBTQ identity has been ushered into the Canadian notion of citizenship and nationality.

The official reading of the Wood statue attempts to make visible a public memory that reifies queer citizenship and recognizes the Canadian queer community.[28] Much of this work draws upon how Canadian citizenship is made manifest in the statue and how a conservative image of homosexuality is made "safe" for public consumption. Visitors to the statue in its capacity as an official memory are expected to read its meaning at face value. Evidence to support the official reading of Wood's memory as the intent of the design can be gleaned from interactions between the BIA statue committee and the artist, Del Newbigging, who submitted two proposals for the statue design: a contemporary design and a traditional design. According to Newbigging in an oral history interview: "For the contemporary idea, we would do five bronze trees and put them on the corner of Alexander and Church Street [signifying Molly Wood's Bush, a colloquialism for Wood's home in the neighborhood], . . . It's a nice idea, but maybe it's a little too contemporary for what the committee wanted."[29] While the committee liked both designs, they ultimately chose the traditional one.[30] By choosing the traditional design over the more ambiguous postmodern design, the committee signaled its determination to establish a straightforward and conventional reading of Wood's memory.[31] The distinction is clarified when comparing the Wood statue to other monuments: "Gay rights monuments exist in Amsterdam, Cologne and New York, but none are large-scale foundry projects in the form of traditional bronze statuary used to celebrate more 'mainstream' historical figures."[32] The Canadian statue is designed to present Wood as a legitimate and important gay man in the history of Upper Canada with no vice attached.

Part of the image that is made evident in reading the Wood statue in this way is the continuity of gay space within the city. It is no accident that the statue is erected on the corner of Church and Alexander Streets just outside the Old City of Toronto, originally known as York. The spot on which the statue stands is located on land once owned by Alexander Wood himself. Indeed, much of the area that constitutes the largest GLBTQ district in the city is encompassed by this historic space.[33] The statue thus serves as a marker in the city of present and past gay space. The statue's creators intentionally articulated the continuity of space. Dennis O'Connor, BIA chair noted: "We wanted to do a public art project. . . . We chose him because he has a connection to our community, and [to] this particular spot."[34] But this continuity is not an assumed fact. Instead the statue visually signals both a past understanding of the space as gay and a present reaffirmation of that fact. While the visualization of Wood himself may signal to some to view the area as a historically gay space, for those unaccustomed to Toronto history the statue makes this connection plain. This is particularly clear in one of the plaques on the pedestal of the statue (fig. 2), which features a depiction of Wood standing in a forest scene. Surrounded by trees, wildlife, and a hidden figure in the distance, this depiction, the viewer should surmise, represents the present space more than two hundred years ago. In each space, both past and present, Wood stands to mark his territory. In this way the statue visually moves readers to consider this space as gay space. To quote O'Connor again: "We're trying to create a sense of place, a sense of history about why we're here. . . . We're pretty lucky to have a link back to the 1800s. How many gay communities can say that?"[35] For those incapable of making the visual jump, another small plaque beneath the wooded scene states clearly that this spot marks the lands of Alexander Wood.

A third plaque plays a central role in establishing Wood, through queer monumentality, as part of the Canadian community (fig. 3). Emphasizing Canadian citizenship was clearly part of the intent of the BIA in creating this statue. As O'Connor noted: "This monument is a monument to a great Toronto citizen, a great Canadian and a great fag."[36] In this viewing position of Wood's public memory Canadian citizenship and nationality are

FIG. 2

North-facing plaque depicting Wood's land in colonial times.
Photograph by the author.

marked heavily. Aside from the constant refrain in the press that he was one
of Canada's first "gay heroes," the long list of Wood's achievements over his
lifetime positions him firmly within the pioneering days of Old Canada.[37]
On the plaque Wood's service as "Militia Officer, Businessman, Public Ser-
vant, Justice of the Peace" is marked clearly, followed last in the list by "Gay
Pioneer." By foregrounding his commercial and civic accomplishments, the
plaque highlights Wood's traditional and exemplary career over his sexuality.
In addition, Wood's deeply Canadian past is highlighted, including his moves
through the territory, his nationalist military service, his ownership of one
of only three stores in the city, and his return to Canada after his scandal
had subsided. The plaque also features a small silhouette that shows Wood's
prominent features. Beyond being a mark of wealth and class, the visualization of such an image in bronze is reminiscent of a coin featuring a prominent national figure. The statue reveals Wood's deep commitment to Canada
and his full participation as citizen. This is perhaps best summarized by the
final line of the inscription on the plaque that quotes the Toronto newspaper
the *British Colonist* in 1844 upon Wood's death. According to the plaque,
Wood was "one of Toronto's 'most respected inhabitants.'"

Beyond the tie to citizenship, the statue also cues a visual heroism specific to the GLBTQ community. Wood's stately posture and elegant dress echo

images of other statues depicting war heroes and leaders. His exploits (beyond the infamous scandal) are outlined clearly on the statue, most notably by the title of "Gay Pioneer." A heroic representation was even signaled in the design of the Wood figure. According to an oral history interview with O'Connor, the committee sought a more heroic image for Wood after early attempts to enlarge the statue from the original maquette revealed lackluster results: "When we enlarged the head . . . he really was ugly. And it wasn't really attractive. So [Newbigging] said, 'I just rebuilt him' . . . and I looked at him and said, 'Wow! He looks like he's a superhero!' And he said, 'He was. He was a superhero.'"[38] In addition, the physical orientation of Wood to his viewers connotes the heroic framing of a gay forefather. Upon the raised pedestal Wood's sculpted body towers over the crowds, forcing their eyes upward in reverence. On a crowded day, particularly during the massive pride festivals that consume the neighborhood each summer, the Wood statue is a marker that is easily visible. But with this visibility also comes a meaning for many viewers. As one observer noted: "This is the statue of Alexander Wood that towers over the village. I'm sure he watches Pride with great approval!"[39] Standing watch over the parade, as if he were a head of state reviewing his proud army, Wood is positioned and understood as a central figure in a transhistorical Canadian GLBTQ community.

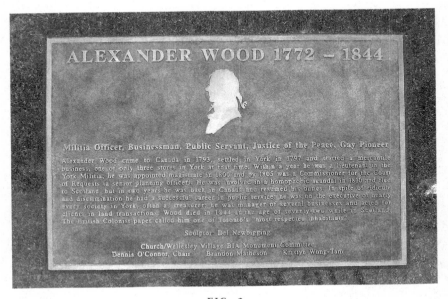

FIG. 3

Plaque featuring Wood's accomplishments.
Photograph by the author.

This public memory also presents a specific (and what some have called safe) version of gay identity. Media and rhetorical scholars have described at length how gay identity can be co-opted in its least transgressive forms to be represented publicly. Among them, Larry Gross suggests: "When [marginalized] groups or perspectives do attain visibility, the manner of that representation will itself reflect the biases and interests of those elites who define the public agenda."[40] Bonnie J. Dow argues that queers are often represented in "poster child politics, in which the attractiveness of an issue is directly related to who represents it."[41] In addition, Helene A. Shugart and Robert Alan Brookey suggest that representations of "safe" gay men in particular are actually means by which patriarchy and other normative structures secure themselves, by reinscribing these more traditional images in new forms.[42] In this way visibility comes with a cost.

However, this safe visibility should not suggest that the statue was designed so that Wood would be read as a heterosexual person. The artist instead made specific choices to signal to the contemporary viewer that Wood was, in fact, visibly gay. According to an oral history interview with Newbigging: "Just look at the curl on his hair that comes down on the front of his forehead; . . . look at the bowtie, . . . the ties around his neck, . . . the frills on his sleeves, . . . the tightness of his pants, . . . the flow of his coat. All of this speaks of a gay taste, I think, and being very stylish and that, as most people know, would be talking about a gay man. I think you can see that in all gay people . . . and throughout history."[43] While it is doubtful that these cues represent transhistorical or transnational markers of same-sex desire, they do play into (sometime stereotypical) expectations of contemporary gay visibility.

Nonetheless, as an official public memory the Wood statue's design does come with significant representational costs. Visually, the image of gay presented is quite safe. Young, masculine, and physically fit, the body size and dimensions of the statue mark Wood as an active man of strength. He exhibits no physical qualities (like a small frame or so-called effeminate hand gestures) that might potentially mark Wood as a "sissy." Wood may be a "molly," but he is a masculine one. His dress is clearly of the period, but it indicates wealth and prestige. This is no average man in a simple ensemble but a magistrate and businessman in colonial splendor. Wood is also gloriously white. As Kirk Savage suggests, "classical sculpture served as the benchmark of whiteness." In sculptural style, facial physiognomy, and position, Wood is the exemplar of the Greco-Roman aesthetic—an aesthetic that has been perpetually used to denigrate nonwhite identities, here locating gay identity within whiteness.[44] This white aesthetic is buttressed with codes of wealth, prestige, and historical Canadian identity. In essence, the Wood depicted in the statue reflects a contemporary gay male habitus likely to be found on the cover of the *Advocate* magazine.[45] Certainly Wood was white, male, and wealthy, and his memory, some would argue, must reflect that. But the embodied classical style of this design was a willful selection between two options presented to the statue committee. It was a choice between a less-divisive postmodern design that may not have deflected the diversity of GLBTQ identity and the statue design that ultimately became a reality.[46] Thus, while some argue there was no way to avoid these issues, the BIA's own design process provided alternatives.

The cost of this choice is profound. By constructing historical and contemporary gay Canadian identity as white, male, masculine, wealthy, and "moral," these images become reified into the public consciousness. The diverse others of the queer community—queers of color, bisexuals, transgender and intersex persons, sissies, dykes, leather daddies, queens, genderfucks, among others who complicate and enrich nonheterosexual life—become marginalized. They remain in the closet of public memory while the safer and more prestigious form of gay (according to contemporary heteronormative culture) makes its grand appearance.

This visual representation of Wood, when read through an official democratic lens, holds important significance not just for GLBTQ identity and citizenship but also for the way in which gay space is constructed in the city. Read with an official democratic gaze, the Wood statue represents perhaps the most well defined democratic gay space within the city and a potentially prominent site within the nation. According to Grube's requirements, the statue can be read as such. First, it clearly makes gay identity visible. Not only is the material marker designated specifically for the gay (and LBT) community, but also the subject is marked as gay in the text itself. By using words such as *homophobic* and *gay* on the statue, the Wood monument stands out as a clear gay identity in the public sphere. Through the official lens of this public memory, the statue reflects the shared past achieved through community dialogue. From discussions among members of the BIA itself, work with the artist, approval from the city council, and even the reaction of visitors to the site, the Wood statue represents a deeply democratic notion of gay space.[47] Thus, the statue marks the Church Wellesley gaybourhood as a primary site of democratic gay space that defies the homosexual spaces so prevalent for much of history.

Visualizing a Traditionalist Countermemory
∎

With the introduction of such a pro-gay text on the public scene, it is not surprising that a traditionalist, antigay countermemory arose to contest its meaning and significance. In the days leading up to the unveiling of the

Wood statue, conservative columnist Rachel Marsden wrote a scathing attack of the monument and public officials' assent to its presence in the *National Post*. Among the accusations, Marsden alleged that Wood should primarily be remembered as a criminal "pervert" not a "gay icon," that Wood could not be sufficiently verified as gay, and that the visible sex act depicted on the base of the statue—Wood inspecting the genitals of a local militiaman—would be damaging to children and other passersby.[48]

Marsden was not the only voice to speak out against the public commemoration of Wood.[49] However, as a Canadian citizen and public figure, Marsden was the most prominent and often cited pontificator of the traditionalist countermemory. Her commentaries were widely circulated in public newspapers and quoted, reproduced, or linked to other critiques. In many ways her perspective represents a central and consistent organizing text of this anti-Wood view.

While some of Marsden's contestation of the Wood statue echoes the typical "issue culture" arguments surrounding antigay rhetorics, she also offers several traditionalist readings against the official democratic memory of Wood that asks viewers not to forget Wood but to remember him differently.[50] First, Marsden remembers Wood as a criminal, above and beyond his sexual orientation. She argues that if we must remember Wood, it is through this primary lens: "One of the monument's plaques reads that Wood 'suffered a homophobic scandal.' Look, 'homophobic' implies that people were scared of this guy because he was gay. In reality, this event had nothing to do with his gayness—only his abuse of authority."[51] At later points in her framing Marsden argues that sexuality is irrelevant to this criminal act. She suggests that any one—homosexual or heterosexual—caught in such an act today would be equally charged and run out of town. While this demonstrates Marsden's unfamiliarity with the shocking history of false charges used against GLBTQ people, it also reveals Marsden's focus on only one piece of the larger statue.[52] This element of the statue is another plaque that dramatizes Wood's infamous scandal, what I label "The Fondling Plaque" (fig. 4). By foregrounding the fondling plaque and minimizing the rest of the statue, Marsden increases the criminal ethos of Wood and his memory.

Marsden seeks to criminalize not only Wood's act but also the representation of it. Marsden argues that the artistic depiction of Wood engaged in his scandalous act in the fondling plaque is essentially public pornography. Through such a reading, a traditionalist countermemory suggests that the act that made Wood infamous should be shielded from public view. Marsden's view of gay visibility is clear: "For kids, that should mean lots of pretty rainbows and purple Teletubbies—not an illustration of something that could pass for a scene out of the Michael Jackson trial. If two people—gay or straight—were acting out this same type of thing in public, they'd be tossed

FIG. 4

■

"The Fondling Plaque,"
featuring Wood in-
specting the genitals
of a local militiaman.
Located on the base of
the statue, facing west.
Photograph by the
author.

in the slammer."[53] Beyond the invective and punditry lies one potentially legitimate means of framing queer memory: gay identity is a sexual identity predicated on a sexual act. As such, this act should be private and representations of this act should be private as well. Thus, Wood the man and Wood the statue are making visual not gay pride but rather an illegal (and immoral) public act.

Second, Marsden argues for undermining Wood's claim to homosexuality. According to Marsden, the statue's representation of a visible gay identity is illegitimate, for Wood's sexuality is ambiguous at best. Citing Councillor Rae in her article, Marsden writes that "'there's no determination that [Wood] was gay.' The evidence was only ever circumstantial. As Rae says, 'out of the event, people felt that he was homosexual. But I don't know if he was homosexual.'"[54] In a separate article Marsden claims that not only is Wood's sexuality in doubt but also the process by which historical sexuality is identified is suspect: "gay history lessons seem to consist largely of combing the books to find prominent male figures who were never confirmed homosexuals—such as former U.S. President Abraham Lincoln, or renowned

Toronto area pervert Alexander Wood—and slapping the gay label on them retroactively."[55] Through this process of destabilizing Wood's homosexuality, Marsden seeks to challenge his legitimacy to public memory. In other words the traditionalist countermemory reads Wood as just another unsexed criminal. He becomes unremarkable and undisciplined and thus unworthy of memory. In no veiled way Marsden is committing an act of mnemonicide.[56]

By virtue of this countermemory reading of the Wood statue, Marsden also offers a counterargument against queer public memory projects altogether. The potential for the Wood statue to reimagine the past to include an official, heroic gay identity is a threat to traditionalist, antigay privilege. Marsden acts against this threat not by recourse to morality and decency but by destroying the grounds upon which queer public memory is justified. With Wood as her representative anecdote, Marsden makes criminal activity a disqualifying feature of public memory, virtually eliminating any historical queers in a world replete with antisodomy laws. Doubting Wood's claim to homosexual identity, Marsden eliminates the remembering of anyone as gay whose sexuality cannot be proven definitively. In doing so, Marsden does not eliminate queer public memory per se but sets the bar so high for making such a claim that almost no queer could meet it. At the end of her framing Wood and all historical queers are no longer valuable enough, no longer gay enough, and thus no longer worth the public's time. The result is the de facto evisceration of queer public memory, leaving in its wake only the traditional narratives of the heteronormative past. In essence Marsden and the traditionalist countermemory roll back the value of remembering queer lives in any capacity. Heteronormativity is defended.

At the same time as it represents a challenge to queer public memory itself, this traditionalist countermemory has some compelling effects on the concept of gay space. In particular, Marsden's equation of the statue with public sex or pornography has material effects on issues of gay space. By equating the representation of gay sex in a public commemoration with public sex, the statue and its subject become outlaws in need of disciplining. Thus it is not surprising that Marsden urges readers to keep their children away from the statue. Based upon the way the public memory of Wood is visualized, it becomes a marker not just of gay space but also of immoral space. Gay space is constructed as deviant with the possibility of having lasting detrimental effect upon those who enter it—particularly children. Through resistively reading the statue as public sex, gay space in Toronto becomes condemned space upon which no one should tread.

While such attacks are biting and brutal, they are not entirely capable of destroying the official democratic memory. This is because of the statue's material form. Marsden and those who see the statue similarly can do substantive damage to the queer past and, if they are successful, potentially limit its expansion and replication in the future. However, at the end of the day the Wood statue remains as a durable form. Its meaning may be challenged, its visitors disappear, and its esteem wither, but at some level— its monumentality—the official democratic memory of Wood can endure in ways that few other queer public memories can claim.

Visualizing and Performing a
Camp Countermemory
■

Most interesting for the study of queer public memories is the countermemory reading of the statue popularized by, but not limited to, members of the queer community themselves. This critical perspective reads the text with the same distrust as the traditionalist countermemory does but with a pleasure and an alternative telos toward destabilizing gay identity and recuperating the queer potential of performance, site, and display. In essence this part of the community confronts the public representation in the Wood statue with one response: you must be kidding!

Essential to this characterization is the assertion that some people perform a resistive reading of the Wood statue as camp. *Camp* is a notoriously complex term that skirts simplistic attempts at definition. Susan Sontag described camp as a "sensibility" that is a "love of the unnatural: of artifice and exaggeration." It has aesthetic qualities related to "bad art" or "kitsch."[57] However, *camp* is almost always understood as being performed. It is an act, a style, a "fervent involvement," an attitude for engaging culture and cultural objects in which the performer *does* camp.[58] Frequently making the performer look foolish, camp is typically directed at others—usually cultural, economic, and political elites—amounting to "a trivialization through parody of the dominant culture."[59] Gays, lesbians, and queers are widely recognized as engaging in camp, though GLBTQ persons need not be considered is exclusive performers.[60] Indeed, camp is increasingly recognized as a necessary critical resource for others in the contemporary mediascape.[61] While none of these characteristics alone is definitive of camp, collectively they suggest a highly visual and material performance in which a failure to be serious is celebrated at the cost of dominant culture, providing a lively mélange of meaning making.

When camp is performed within the realm of memory, certain characteristics of camp come to the fore. First, camp is often derived from the past. It focuses on the out-of-date, on objects past their prime and in decline, resurrecting people, places, events, and memories of the past and providing them with a new form of attention.[62] Sometimes these memories, as raw materials of camp, lack significant preexisting meaning; other times they have been drained of meaning or overly signified. In either case camp's "necrophilic tendencies" work to make the past relevant in ways not seen before.[63] Second, camp is deeply tied into the idea of nostalgia. While some read *camp* and *nostalgia* as synonyms, camp is better understood as an "ironic nostalgia" that relies less upon a genuine longing for the past and a tastefulness that might make that longing legitimate.[64] Third, camp is also a dated phenomenon. Several commentators have suggested camp was primarily a (counter) cultural performance that predated contemporary gay and lesbian political activism.[65] Indeed, some have suggested that camp is now only a moribund aesthetic that has lost its power.[66] However, others claim that camp continues today and thrives in drawing contemporary attention to previous historic periods.[67] For instance, Mark Booth suggests that camp plays with the periodization of history by recreating "idealized versions of the past" and making them "retrograde rather than progressive." In doing so camp "sidestep[s] the onward march of history."[68]

While it is difficult to encapsulate the essence of camp, several techniques of camping can be isolated for our purposes. For instance, simply by targeting Wood's memory, some of his viewers are already engaged in a highly camp style.[69] However, understanding how to remember Wood resistively requires turning to three related camp techniques.

First, camp celebrates the failure of acts attempted in all seriousness. Unlike kitsch or naïve camp that do not recognize their own ineptitude, camp derives much of its pleasure from its willful recognition of artifice and failure. According to Fabio Cleto, "camp certainly debunks seriousness, along with the 'original' intentionality of the camped up object of perception. This is not to say, though, that camp can't envision a horizon of seriousness, or that it simply works through a conversion of the serious into the frivolous; . . . on the contrary, seriousness always takes part in the production of camp effect, and it does so through the self-undermining, queer strategy of its 'transvestic thinking.'"[70] In short, camp is double voiced. It ridicules its target's deficiencies in order to interrogate them, simultaneously making a legitimate point of critique. Thus, Christopher Isherwood's statement: "You can't camp about something you don't take seriously."[71] Second, camp relies heavily on exaggeration to do its critical work. Exaggeration, as part of the camp aesthetic, uses excess to critically mark incongruence in its targets in a visible way. This excess of exaggeration renders its subjects spectacles, making them available for critical assessment. While exaggeration can play out in various ways, the exaggeration of gender (and its cultural markers) is one of the most common and recognized forms, especially in drag.[72] Third, the grotesque: an emphasis on the out-of-control and the outer limits, often directed at the body. Representative of the carnivalesque and frequently visible in camp aesthetics, the grotesque directly challenges the beautiful human (male) form by celebrating bodies that are unstable, leaky, and "unruly" (and often feminine).[73] Transforming an object into something grotesque, a camp performer marks that object (or its meaning) as incomplete, out-of-focus, and marginal, recognizing the "perception that something is illegitimately in something else."[74] Uncontrollable and often repulsive, the power of the grotesque is its ability to complicate the seemingly simple—a deeply queer act.

If camp is consuming or performing culture "in quotation marks," then, from the perspective of the camp countermemory, what does it mean to "remember" Alexander Wood?[75] While visitors to the statue who adopt the camp viewing position might partake in any number of different camp practices, celebrating the statue as a failure and playfully supplementing the statue itself with an exaggerated and grotesque style are key to a camp reading.[76] Collectively, these symbolic and material practices challenge Wood's official meaning, destabilize claims to rigid identities, and indulge tantalizingly sexual imaginings of his queerness.

A common way of challenging Wood's memory is by reading his statue as a campy failure. As Isherwood's definition suggests, at the core of attempts to read Wood's memory as camp are serious concerns about how the statue fails adequately to represent Wood, queer identity, and the Church Wellesley community. Crucially, many Canadian queers do not see themselves in the Wood statue. For instance, the initial reporting on the statue by Reuters described the reaction of one local gay man in Toronto: "'It's nice to have the statue in the community, but I don't think it's well done,' said one area resident, referring to a plaque at the statue's base that outlines the scandal. 'I think it's misleading. The sensationalistic side of homosexuality is not the norm.'"[77] Beyond the spectacle, there is also the recognition that the statue fails to be recognizable with its contemporary audience. Many viewers have not heard of Wood before, or if they have they have little appreciation for who he is. In addition, Wood's dress and appearance mark him as a historical queer—a move that may challenge the way many readers engage with the text given the paucity of images of historical queer identity. Most important is the way in which Wood's race, class, and gender are foregrounded along with his sexuality, making the narrowly defined notion of queer embodied in the statue a serious failure in representing the full diversity of the community. In a very real way for women, queers of color, bisexual or transgender persons, and low-income queers, Alexander Wood is just another wealthy white gay man who means little to their present or their past. This leaves the statue open to a deep and abiding lack of resonance—a lack frequently marked by a camp reading.

To make this point, camp readers of Wood's public memory have become adept at finding failure in a serious consideration of the statue. One way this failure is provoked is through an informed viewership that recognizes that the name Alexander Wood has historically been a joke. Despite the dignified stature Wood attained before the end of his life, his memory in Canada has long been the subject of ridicule. Sometimes this ridicule has emerged from the heterosexual public, but more often the very people who best understood Wood's predicament—his queer colleagues—were his most merciless quipsters.[78] For example, in 1994 there was a popular but limited run of an original musical called *Molly Wood* that was performed in the Church Wellesley neighborhood.[79] The authors described the play as a "naughty Gothic romp," while a review of the play in the *Toronto Star* emphasized its "special attention to double-entendres, effete speech, campy gesture and over-loud bitchiness."[80] Anecdotal commentary by fellow playwright Sky Gilbert put it succinctly: "Was it a drag show or was it a historical drama? And what was it really about? What was the theme? I wasn't sure."[81] Presented as a campy laughingstock, the play did little to enhance Wood's reputation as a serious figure. These previous experiences with Wood's memory predispose some viewers to read the statue in ways counter to the serious meaning intended by the official memory.

Yet, the failure of the statue to denote its original meaning for all readers does not rely solely upon a viewer's lack of prior knowledge. Indeed, another important way in which the camp countermemory reads Wood's statue as a failure is as a strangely juxtaposed representation—a representation made possible by a specific prescribed *"pathway"* that structures how the statue is viewed. Blair argues that commemorative sites sometimes prescribe pathways that dramatically shape their reception by audiences. These pathways— frequently paved walkways or mapped out routes—order sites in particular ways, direct gazes, and highlight different aspects of both the statue and the landscape in which it is placed. In the process they direct how one comes to interpret the meaning of these sites.[82] Situated on a busy street corner in a commercial district, the Wood statue prescribes four particular pathways that mimic the sidewalks and roadways that run from north to south and east to west through the Church Wellesley neighborhood. Three of the four pathways act on the body of the viewer to encourage the official democratic reading of the statue. Important to this reading is not the collectivity of images but rather the order in which the images are read. If the statue is approached from the north, south, or east, the viewer will most likely see the large embodied Wood figure first followed by the two relatively tame plaques on the base. Viewers at that point may choose to continue walking, confident they have absorbed the statue's intent. Others might pause and circle to the western side of the base which features the fondling plaque. When the plaques are read in this order, it is possible for the fondling plaque to serve to visualize Wood's sexuality and society's homophobia. The viewer moves on and an official reading is confirmed.

However, approaching the statue from the western pathway produces a striking disconnect in the mind of a viewer between the fondling plaque and the rest of the statue. As the visitor walks closer to the statue, the stately figure of Wood upon his pedestal meeting most of the preconditioned expectations of official statuary is first to come into view. Yet as the visitor moves closer and the eye strays to the fondling plaque, a moment of visual and experiential incommensurability occurs. Before them, within one representation, camp readers witness a strange union of stately Greco-Roman design and lurid pseudo-sexual imagery. Unexpected in design and unclear in meaning, this jarring juxtaposition instantly sends the viewer into a visual conundrum. While an official-democratic reader would view these images as consistent and a traditionalist reader would focus on the fondling plaque alone, the camp viewer reads the two together, witnessing a representational failure on display. The statue, according to the definitions above, becomes a hilarious put down of one's self and one's culture. Mocking the idea of a democratic gay space, Wood and his statue become camp, not to be taken seriously.

Queers also "camp up" Wood's public memory by embellishing the statue with supplemental commemorations. The act of supplementing a commemorative site—usually by leaving intimate tokens or decorations—has become increasingly important in public commemorations. By leaving objects at these sites individual visitors attempt to alter the meaning of otherwise officially articulated spaces by adding to their preexisting rhetoric(s). According to Carole Blair, these left objects "transmute the commemorative site from a completed text to a context for individual, but still public, memory practices."[83] Individuals in a sense engage in a performance with the statue that "challenges the easy composure of history under the sign of objectivity."[84] Thus visitors supplement the meaning of an existing commemorative site's rhetoric with their own in ways that call into question its previous (official) interpretation.

While supplementing rhetorics do not occur at all public commemorations, Kristin Ann Hass has shown that they are particularly common when sites mark highly unstable memories, "restless" memories where meaning is still largely up for grabs and engaging with them materially can provide visitors ways to move those meanings in particular directions.[85] The Wood statue, as we have seen, is a site where meaning is still malleable. But while others have argued for various meanings through symbolic interpretations of the statue, camp visitors have relied excessively on material acts of supplementation to augment the statue's understanding. However, these visitors have not drawn upon traditional supplements such as photos, flowers, or teddy bears to make their point. Camp readers have instead supplemented the Wood statue with outrageously campy augmentations, augmentations that rely on common camp tactics and ephemera to queer Wood's memory and destabilize the static interpretations of both official-democratic and traditionalist readers.

The first major campy supplementation is drag or, rather, the dragging of the Wood statue. To dress in drag is to perform a role marking the transformation betwixt and between genders.[86] It relies heavily on the exaggeration of gender prominent in camp.[87] While drag does critical work in balls, clubs, and daily life, the exaggeration and artifice of drag in public venues can also do important political work.[88] In remembering Wood, drag is used to contest the radically normative gay-male habitus intended by the official-democratic memory. The dressing and alterations of the Wood statue in left objects that run counter to Wood's represented gender allow camp viewers to critique the stable gay-identity characterizations the statue represents. Performing such a transformation on the statue is not difficult. Already including a cape and tight-fitting clothes, Wood's ensemble is routinely accessorized with beads, costume jewelry, feather boas, and hats. In addition, on more than one occasion Wood's rigid demeanor has been brightened by an array of colorful rouges and lipsticks.[89] Given the diva ballads that emanate from the many gay clubs that line Church Street on almost any night, a passerby might mistake the Wood statue to be a drag queen ready to walk fiercely through the night—a stark contrast to his more official demeanor. Questioning publicly Wood's past gender, camp readers challenge official-democratic discourses that represent past and contemporary sexual identity as stable and rigid.

In addition, graffiti is added to the statue both to challenge Wood's memory as a wealthy white male representative of the community and to render the ambiguous act on the fondling plaque clearly queer. Both critiques are accomplished by transforming the classical statue through camp aesthetics. Wood's body is made grotesque by supplementing its heroic form with very human representations of excrement, waste, and fluid. For example, for several months Wood's cheeks were tattooed with tears dripping from his eyes. At other times a highlighter was used to emphasize the prominent bulge between the statue's legs. Another thoughtful camp viewer used marker to draw a zipper and fly onto Wood's trousers, allowing his flawed body to relieve itself.[90] Perhaps most pointedly, for several months in 2006 Wood's face on the fondling plaque was smeared with an unknown substance. The milky white substance on the infamous plaque unquestionably was meant to represent ejaculate.[91] The revisioning work done to Wood's memory through this particular act of graffiti is powerful: the image of Wood and his young suspect, tantalizingly frozen in an ambivalent moment of potential sexuality, bursts forth into a visual, tactile, and unmistakable sexual explosion. To play on Barbie Zelizer's words, the graffiti destroys the "subjunctive voice" present in the fondling plaque, unfreezing the image's ambiguous sexuality and making visible within public memory queer male-on-male desire.[92] With this act of countermemory the ambiguity of Wood's sexuality—and more important, the sexual nature of his scandal—comes to a conclusion. The Wood monument is transformed from an about-to-be-queer image into an unquestionable portrait of queer lust. Each of these acts deftly demotes the privileged image of the white gay male form. By drawing attention to his grotesque dimensions, the classical figure of Wood becomes less divine and more human—a more fitting representative image for a diverse community that is anything but stable.

Finally, the most common material interaction camp visitors have with the Wood statue is "rubbing the bum." According to BIA chairman Dennis O'Connor, "rubbing the bum" is a local tradition whereby visitors rub the bare buttocks of the young man being groped by Wood in the fondling plaque. Unplanned by the committee, this playful trend evolved on its own and circulates throughout the statue's discourse. Commentary and images of the act are available online but the following description in *OUT* magazine is a good example of the practice: "Afterward, we walked to the nearby statue of Alexander Wood, the legendary testicle inspector that I wrote about yesterday. . . . On one side of the statue there's a sculpted illustration of Alexander doing the actual genital inspecting that made him famous. The soldier's naked ass is right there for all to see and enjoy. Paul told me that it's become a tradition in the 'hood to rub the naked ass and make a wish.' A lot of people must have been making wishes because that ass is already a little tarnished. And it's only been a couple of years."[93] "Rubbing the bum" is yet another way in which visitors add meaning to the statue through campy supplementing rhetorics. Not only is this act supplemental, but it is also contrary to what some on the statue committee hoped would be the audience's reception. Perhaps not surprisingly, Del Newbigging in particular—as an artist hoping to preserve and protect his work—has suggested in oral history interviews that he would rather visitors not "rub the bum" of Wood's inspectee: "If I had thought of that, I would have done something to make it not happen. . . . I'm not thrilled that people are touching the bum."[94] Thus "rubbing the bum" is a deeply supplemental act that contrasts with (at least some of) the original creator's intended meaning of the statue.

However, in this case the supplemental material added to the statue is not a left object but the human body itself. Rhetorical bodies, when engaging commemorative sites, can produce powerful effects. As Blair and Michel suggest, somatic engagements with commemorative sites (among others embodied interactions) can be key to understanding how memory is performed and sometimes altered, beyond what one might see or hear in the site itself.[95] Indeed, one's ability to touch or not touch these sites can dramatically contribute to their interpretation.[96]

Touching the Wood statue in particular generates two prominent rhetorical effects. First, the "rubbing of the bum" reinforces previously discussed supplemental acts to alter the meaning of Wood's public memory. Despite the various reasons one might participate in this act—luck, tradition, peer pressure, play, or an erotic charge—its focus on the buttocks of the young man is not inconsequential. The "rubbing of the bum" in particular, focused on a body part with both excretory and sexual connotations, again participates in the grotesque transformation of the bodies in the statue into flawed human figures. Like the graffiti previously discussed, the rubbing simultaneously unfreezes the static presexual image of the plaque. Particularly when rubbed by a queer man wishing for luck on his date, rubbing charges the image with a queer sexual desire the official democratic memory largely stifles.

However, more important, "rubbing the bum" is also an act of queer world making. Lauren Berlant and Michael Warner have argued that the creation of safe spaces for queer sex, values, and ways of living as alternatives to the privileged zones of the heterosexual couple is key to the creation and maintenance of queer culture. These tactical spaces crafted on top of, in between, or at the margins of heteronormative life are frequently fleeting and unrecognizable as "entrances, exits, unsystematized lines of acquaintance, projected horizons, typifying examples, alternate routes, blockages, incommensurate geographies."[97] Charles E. Morris III and John Sloop have suggested that queers can devise these spaces of queer alteriority by rupturing heteronormative spaces and gazes with tactical, political, and embodied queer displays, such as queer public kissing.[98] Once created, these spaces provide a vital arena in which queer ways of living and "counterintimacy" are affirmed and the politics of heteronormativity can be reconsidered.[99]

As an embodied act, "rubbing the bum" participates in this queer world-making project. Like queer public kissing, the touch of human flesh against sculpted buttocks disrupts heteronormativity by showcasing queer desire in a public venue. However, the act signifies more. Akin to Fiona Buckland's description of queer club dancing, "rubbing the bum" positions the visitor's body as a point which mediates between memories of an event and its present performance in a "theater of memory."[100] While Buckland regularly situates the body as restoring and reinterpreting in the present an individualized memory of the body itself, in this context camp viewers who rub the bum restore to the present not their own memory but a queer memory of Alexander Wood himself. This queer public memory remembers Wood not as an unsexed, victimized hero but as an imperfect, desiring, sexual, queer man. Through the use of their bodies in the present, moving their hands across the bum of Wood's young suspect, camp visitors actualize Wood's queerness in the present: made real not by the statue itself but through the performative interplay between human body and commemorative site. Considered in the realm of everyday life, the hundreds of queers and nonqueers alike who rub the bum every day in an anonymous string of stranger sociability do not simply participate in a tradition but together also construct in public view a new meaning of the statue as a marker of queer life, in both the past and the present. In doing so the material rhetoric of the statue when joined with camp performance contributes to the creation of queer communal space.[101]

Taken together, these three camp tactics offer dramatically different readings of Wood's memory from those proffered by either the official-democratic or traditionalist memories. Simultaneously, the camp memory of Wood also drastically reshapes the way queer space is understood in the city, by both creating and destroying it. First, a camp reading of this public memory can decimate the work of crafting a gay democratic space in Toronto. While Grube offers some useful and productive examples of gay democratic spaces that are visibly marked, the Wood statue takes that concept to an extreme. Identity is not just visible, it is oppressive—reaching into the past and claiming a man as gay whom history records as having had a vague sexuality at best. Evidence of sexual contact is not just obvious but rendered visible in a way that cannot be taken seriously. Gay sex becomes a public joke. Also, despite what appears to be a lengthy process of discussion among multiple groups about the creation and structure of this space, the democratic nature of this discussion is elitist. Designed by an economically entrenched community, approved by the city, and debated within the spheres of the gay business elite and the mostly heterosexual city council, any democratic exchange is far from open and inviting. A camp reading makes these failures meaningful to readers, and the notion of an officially sanctioned democratic gay space becomes destabilized.

Second, while destroying this more conservative notion of gay space, a camp reading points to queer world making as a different process for generating queer space. Once created, queer spaces provide a vital arena in which queer ways of living and counterintimacy are affirmed and the politics of heteronormativity can be reconsidered. Ironically, the failings and appropriation of the Wood statue dramatize the ability of camp to queer even an already supposedly gay space, reinforcing the potential for camp to read almost anything as queer.[102] Thus, queer space can be created in any moment by anyone with a discerning eye for failure and play. Drawing upon traditional notions of queer reading and camp, the entire city is opened up to a process of queer site creation. No site is free or stable and everything is up for grabs. In addition, these queering acts need not been tethered to the sexual uses of spaces alone. The possibilities of queering run deeper in all kinds of spaces, particularly in those where the reenacts of histories exercise a flair for a queer sensibility.[103] In this way queer space becomes diverse, diffuse, and—in a way—more accessible than spaces fostered through officially sanctioned organizations. Visualizing camp moves readers from focusing on solitary queer sites to queer cities, nations, and beyond.

In the wake of these campy supplementing acts and celebrations of failure, what remains upon the pedestal where the statue of Wood once stood is a dramatically different imagining of his queer public memory. The camp countermemory, in making retrograde the previously idealized or vilified memories of Wood, clashes with both the official democratic and traditionalist frame of remembering. Instead of a virtuous and inclusive image of citizenship or a criminal to be feared, Wood becomes a laughable, gender-bending, grotesque, and scandalous queer—a subject unlikely to be welcomed into the fold of heteronormative culture but certainly someone to be celebrated as a camp personality. Of course, as a memory reading reliant upon tactical and ephemeral forms of memory, these camp challenges to the official memory reading are only temporary. Come the statue's next cleaning, a wet downpour, or the absence of visitors, the bodies and residue necessary to camp up Wood largely disappear and the official Wood narrative reasserts itself. Nonetheless, remembering Wood, in the camp countermemory, becomes an opportunity to mark the eccentric and destabilizing value of queer character, while at the same time it seriously challenges efforts to encase a rigid view of sexual identity—in the past, present, or future—in stone.

Conclusion

The positions performed above are not rigid frames for remembering and understanding Alexander Wood. Rather, the discourse of the statue as a whole reveals a strange mixing and evolution of meanings that makes talking about firm frames difficult at best. However, these general perspectives appear frequently and serve as a heuristic by which we can understand the (de-)evolution of his public memory within this environment. Whether an official mark of existence and visibility, a backlash from tradition and heteronormativity, or a portrayal of a campy pervert that generates (critical) laughter across the world, the statue of Alexander Wood speaks profoundly to the power of memory to be crafted and undone and redone by a simple series of looks or creative touches.

As an emblematic example of the turn to queer monumentality, this analysis suggests several important considerations for theorizing queer public memory beyond the specific work of this statue. Perhaps most important, is the recognition that monumentality's traditional reliance on durable forms of materiality to do its work is of critical importance for remembering the queer past. Materiality itself is not a new dimension of queer studies. Examinations of queer lives on display have drawn similar attention to bodies, their parts and byproducts, and their performances that act rhetorically.[104]

Even some critics of the AIDS Quilt have highlighted the material nature of that project in assessing its rhetorical impact.[105] However, many of these examples look past the enduring qualities (that is, monumental) queer material rhetorics can provide a community regularly erased from the past. Discursive recourses to bodies and performance are indeed valuable, but (as highly fleeting forms of materiality) they do not attend to the benefits provided by the more monumental forms of materiality found in commemorative sites.

Perhaps the most vital contribution of queer monumentality's material focus lies in how certain structural forms of materiality (such as statues, plaques, and commemorative sites) provide security and longevity to queer memories that they are typically denied within largely discursive memory practices. Queer memories have often been situated contrary to collective and public remembering. Typically, queer pasts are banished to the closet, positioned as subjugated knowledges—either disguised in history's systemic archive or disqualified as disrupted and unwanted.[106] In addition, as potentially critical texts that can offer alternative ways to conceptualize intimacy, family, and sexual culture, queer public memories have been subjected to "enforced amnesia" and mnemonicide.[107] Thus it should not surprise us that queer pasts are regularly regarded as hidden from history.[108] Structural materials such as commemorative sites offer correctives to these destructive practices. Despite the ever-present recognition that commemorations often authorize us to forget, given the present position of queer memories it might be argued that queers have little to lose. However, it is expressly because so much has been lost, both through systemic practice and (more painfully) through the HIV/AIDS epidemic, that material structures within queer monumentality offer an escape from the drive to forget. While documents disappear, and generations change, material structures of memory "do not fall into silence."[109] Projects such as the Wood statue suggest, by gesturing to the ancient commemorative logics of the monument, that durable material enactments of memory can offer the queer past perhaps the most reliable means to persevere through time. Indeed, that is what the members of the BIA had hoped. Beyond producing a public-art project, they expressed a genuine desire, in an age of expanding gay and lesbian rights and the gentrification of the gay ghetto, to use a monument to mark "Molly Wood's Bush" as gay space in perpetuity.[110]

Yet despite the assurances that queer monumentality's focus on material enactments of memory provide, even monuments and commemorative sites cannot completely prevent the alteration of the GLBTQ past. These alterations may be productive to queer lives or damaging to them. Regardless, the conflicting memory frames applied to the statue of Alexander Wood illustrate that, while queer memories may be better secured through monumental forms, their meanings are not so easily guaranteed. Indeed, queer public memories are highly polysemic, not just when enshrined in postmodern forms but also on account of their very nature as queer forms of memory.[111] If the queer project is to "support forms of affective, erotic, and personal living" by making them, in part, "available to memory," while simultaneously engaging in practices that disrupt norms, explode binaries, and embrace diversity, it seems clear that these queer memories must not only be open to but also demand a multiplicity of meanings. Such a claim is supported by previous work in queer public memories that urges a "queer cultural studies of history" and challenges heteronormative counternostalgias. This polysemic compulsion at the heart of the queer project therefore requires that critics engage queer public memories as texts with hermeneutic depth or risk missing (and potentially disciplining) the disruptive, world-making potential that is queer public memory's promise.

It is apparent that while the meaning and interpretation of queer pasts are always dynamic and contentious elements of public memory, adopting traditional forms of monumentality (such as statues and memorials) that can ensure, at the very least, the continued presence of the queer past in public spaces is a valuable and productive rhetorical approach. However, while grand monuments etched in stone may make the queer past more sustainable and make the eradication of queers from memory more difficult, the past three decades have also shown that the turn to queer monumentality need not rely on physical materials alone to render the past perdurable.

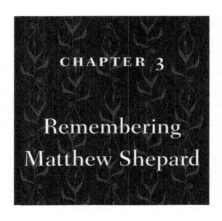

CHAPTER 3

Remembering
Matthew Shepard

MORE THAN FIFTEEN YEARS HAVE PASSED since the brutal 1998 murder of Matthew Shepard, an openly gay college student in Laramie, Wyoming. Shepard was twenty-one years old when he met Aaron McKinney and Russell Henderson one evening at the Fireside Lounge. After a short exchange, Shepard left with the two men, allegedly for a ride home. Instead, McKinney and Henderson drove Shepard to a secluded field outside of town where they robbed, verbally abused, and tortured the young man they had targeted because of his sexuality. After their brutal attack, the perpetrators lashed Shepard—unconscious, cold, beaten, and bleeding—to a cow fence in the cool night air to die of exposure. It was not until the next morning that Shepard was found in a coma, barely alive, by a passing bicyclist—still hanging from the fence, his hands tied behind his back. Shepard died five days later in a hospital bed without ever waking from his coma.

The unprecedented media circus that had developed in the intervening days between Shepard's assault and death soon exploded with public discourse. Television stations and newspapers nationwide spewed a constant stream of information on the attack and its aftermath. Vigils, protest marches, antigay religious demonstrations, statements from the president and national leaders, and interviews of other GLBTQ students and appalled Laramie locals—these scenes were plastered on screens and pages in millions of American homes, renewing an ongoing, but until then often marginal, national conversation about the status of GLBTQ people in American society.

For many GLBTQ people that conversation had felt increasingly to be going their way. Just prior to the dawning of a new century, the GLBTQ community had been reinvigorated by the existential threats posed by HIV/AIDS. In the aftermath of the worst part of the epidemic, GLBTQ people won important political and cultural successes in visibility, government sanction, corporate attention, and commitments to fight HIV/AIDS. Despite harsh rebukes, including the Defense of Marriage Act (DOMA) and "Don't Ask, Don't Tell" (DADT), many gays and lesbians felt that they were on the cusp of acceptance into the American community in ways they had never imagined. By the end of the 1990s GLBTQ persons had begun to risk feeling secure in their lives with real hope for the future.[1] Shepard's death shattered that security, inaugurating contentious debates among all Americans about what his murder meant, how he would be remembered, and how those memories could point to a future for gays and lesbians in this country.

A key dimension of those debates included efforts by various GLBTQ advocates to transform Matthew Shepard, in multiple and often contradictory ways, from an anonymous, everyday person into a monumental (queer) icon of unmatched appeal. Doing so involved more than ensuring that Shepard would not be forgotten like the scores of other GLBTQ people attacked and murdered every year. Rather, given the indelible mark he had left in the public imagination, advocates believed that Shepard's memory could do vital work for shaping social, political, legal, and cultural change. To achieve these ends, advocates and their allies made concerted efforts to make Shepard's memory durable, rich in epidictic appeal, capable of reiteration and expansion, and as powerfully effecting as possible. Shepard's public remembrances are thus further evidence of the ongoing turn to queer monumentality.

However, unlike the Alexander Wood statue and other memorials and commemorative sites, Shepard's monumentality is noticeably lacking in material dimensions. In the years following his murder only a very few material markers commemorating Shepard emerged.[2] Indeed, the most iconic physical marker surrounding the assault—the fence he was tied to after his attack—was unceremoniously removed by the property's owners only a few months after the incident.[3] In addition, given the spectacle of the case, the Shepard family, who scattered their son's ashes out of public view, went out of the way to ensure that his final resting place remained secret and private.[4] Nonetheless, memories of Shepard were given a potent sense of monumentality even without a formal material marker. First, Shepard was remembered alternately as a martyr, saint, and common man. Through these particular frames of memory, Shepard was made to embody the epidictic values of GLBTQ and heterosexual communities, to be held up as a heroic figure worthy of emulation, and to empower GLBTQ people within a society that had sought to limit and overwhelm them. In these ways remembering Shepard echoes a monumental rhetoric similar to that of Alexander Wood. However, second, Shepard was also rendered monumental by giving his memory durability through a distinctly different, nonmaterial means. Specifically, through an embrace of malleability, emphasis on his affective appeal, and iteration of his memory through an incessant stream of rhetoric within and between the GLBTQ community and the wider public, Shepard was given a lasting foothold in eternity that we can still point to more than a decade after his death. Therefore, remembering Shepard is an occasion to illustrate queer monumentality's complex and diverse means for achieving its ends.

While numerous GLBTQ activists and their allies circulated monumental memories of Shepard to assert themselves and to counter trivializing, hateful, and judgmental discourse from within the wider heteronormative public, not all GLBTQ people agreed to remember Shepard uniformly. In fact, significant queer and transgender voices from within the GLBTQ community claimed that the rhetorics of inclusion and identity embedded within Shepard's monumental memories were highly problematic and in need of interrogation. Fearing Shepard would become the new white male wealthy cisgendered poster boy of GLBTQ rights and concerns, some queer and transgender people positioned themselves outside the more conventional discourses over Shepard's memory. From this counterpublic space these critics actively circulated contrary public memories of Shepard and bias crimes rife with intersectionality and division to undermine Shepard's monumental commemoration. While these critiques show little evidence of having significantly diminished Shepard's monumentality today, the tensions within the GLBTQ community illustrate yet again the multiple and conflicting stakes in queer public memory and the propensity for self-identified queers to deploy tactical and ephemeral memory rhetorics against queer monumentality.

To examine these complex frames for remembering Shepard among competing voices in the GLBTQ community as well as within the wider public requires a complex text for analysis. Since no single text can fully account for the veritable explosion of interest in Shepard after his death, I have selected representative "fragments" of discourse from diverse sources within and outside the GLBTQ community to form a text from which we can glean important aspects of the debate over his public memory.[5] The foundation of this text is Shepard's coverage in the *Advocate* magazine, the longest running and one of the most widely read GLBTQ print publications in the United States at the time of the murder.[6] Shepard was an important subject of the magazine, cited more than three hundred times in its pages from 1998 to 2009. In addition, the *Advocate*'s broad selection of writers, editors, and images that represent many facets of the community make the magazine a suitably multivocal text. To represent the scope of the community more fully, I have supplemented my analysis with statements from major GLBTQ organizations, websites, blogs, speeches and comments from several memorial services and vigils for Shepard, and references to previous scholarship on the televisual, filmic, and imagistic elements of Shepard's memory. Clearly, this assortment of memory shards is not exhaustive, but collectively these fragments represent a range of voices across the GLBTQ community's discourse expressing diverse opinions and using divergent appeals.

It is also important to characterize monumentality above and beyond its physical manifestations and to examine the relationship between publics and counterpublics who take up these monumental memories through discourses. Examining popular fragments of the community's discourse teases out the conflicting ways Shepard is remembered, oscillating between publics and counterpublics as well as among counterpublics themselves and helps to suggest several implications for queer monumentality, counterpublic memories, and the queer *"turn toward* memory."[7]

Nonmaterial Monumentality and Counterpublic Memories

■

Elements within the GLBTQ community, recognizing in Shepard a powerful representative anecdote, worked aggressively to remember him through several distinct yet monumental frames of public memory. As we have seen, queer monumentality is distinguished from earlier tactical and ephemeral memory rhetorics, in part, by its ability to endure through time against the various forces that seek to erase not just the past but queer pasts in particular. Thus far, materiality—which can be defined as an object's existence in a physical state of matter—has proven an excellent means for granting queer pasts this durable quality.[8] However, the Shepard case occasions an opportunity to expand our view of queer monumentality to suggest that durability need not be derived exclusively from materiality.

Without question, casting memories in material forms has long been an ideal method for achieving monumentality's aim to preserve pasts from time immemorial. Stone tombs and bronze statues' ability to withstand political crises, plagues, economic ruin, environmental degradation, invasion, and cultural annihilation makes them relatively reliable options for satisfying humanity's eternal compulsions.[9] This logic is borne out by the countless material monuments, many still standing, that can be traced to ancient civilizations around the world—even if those civilizations did not have a word for monumentality itself.[10] At times such abundant examples have led scholars to argue that monumental architecture (that is, material memories) should be a prerequisite to considering any society meaningful.[11] Although this is an imprudent claim, human beings' regular adoption of material forms to transport their names and values through time demonstrates how effective tangible commemorations can be.

Yet even early human civilizations recognized that there were other means to procure perpetuity besides stone and chisel. Epic poetry, for example, could record great heroes' and heroines' names in time not through physicality but through the scope and grandeur of the tale and the length of its telling.[12] Similarly, Hannah Arendt suggested that the Greeks (and their progeny) believed great "works and deeds and words" worthy of eternity could secure the doers of these deeds "their place in the cosmos where everything is immortal except themselves."[13] Likewise, more modern thinkers identified nonmaterial avenues for monumental durability. The eighteenth-century artist Johann Georg Sulzer, for instance, claimed that writing—having only limited materiality itself—was actually the most basic monumental form, adept at keeping the past "perpetually sustain[ed]."[14] Music, too, can retain monumentality's longevity despite the fleetingness of its experience. The structure of a piece, its loudness, transformations, and skill at inciting the sublime in the audience—rather than its recording— often guaranteed a composition's place among the greats of history.[15] Even photography and the Internet have been pointed to by contemporary theorists as monumental exemplars with durability but without hardened substances.[16] Hence, it seems that monumentality's claims to durability need not be reliant on physical form to fulfill its promise.

The question then becomes: In what ways do memories of Matthew Shepard gain durability (and thereby enhance his monumentality) without resorting to materiality? There are three answers to this question that can be used in conjunction to remember Shepard in particular. The first is malleability. As we know, one of memory's greatest appeals over history is its embrace of alteration, manipulation, and evolution. As Pierre Nora reminds us, memory is never static but "remains in permanent evolution, open to the dialectic of remembering and forgetting." That memory is a "perpetually actual phenomenon," and "unconsciousness of its successive deformations," is, in fact, part of its traditional appeal.[17] Malleability is also one of memory's great advantages at the level of the public. By virtue of their capacity to grow, evolve, and change to fit any given situation, public memories are highly rhetorical phenomena, effective at engaging public issues, and extremely useful to public actors. However, public memory's malleability is also wrapped up with its durability. Because, by their very nature, public memories can shift in meaning and interpretation through time, public memories have the capacity to outlast time's constraints. In other words, memory's malleability gives its subjects a powerful defense against oblivion. We see examples of shifting and supple memories regularly in scholarship. For instance, Barry Schwartz points to the transmutation of Abraham Lincoln by every successive generation to fit the demands of their own time as a key reason to explain his durable place in American memory.[18] Charles E. Morris III has confirmed this account through his ongoing project to queer Lincoln, according to which the president's memory has profited not only from "longevity by inertia but in its durability through malleability."[19] Shepard's memory likewise gains a queerly monumental durability by being articulated with malleability by GLBTQ advocates. In fact, public memories of Shepard have proven so malleable that he has regularly been remembered in multiple, simultaneous, sometimes contradictory ways over the last decade and a half.

Another way in which Shepard's memory gains durability through non-material means is by emphasizing the affective qualities within his public memories. Blair, Dickinson, and Ott have recognized the importance affect plays in memory, particularly in giving memories "durability over time . . . in a particular context."[20] What affect means is not, however, always entirely clear. Brian Massumi, one of the leading scholars of the affective turn, defines affect at one point as a *"power* (or potential) to affect or be affected."[21] Although Massumi's is a concise definition, it does not elucidate the particular valence within affect that Blair, Dickinson, and Ott suggest is key to answering the question "How do memories 'stick?'"—another way of asking about durability. What Blair and company offer is the Aristotelian notion of *philia,* or affiliation, as a more precise point of departure. In their description affiliation characterizes "people's modes of attachment or sense of belonging" to collectives. To think of this another way, affiliation is like Burke's notion of identification, however with a particular emphasis on elements beyond the rational. Therefore, through "affective intensities"—such as pride, shame, guilt, or gratitude—directed at certain individuals or subjects, people can come to feel a sense of belonging with them and others. Within this affective attachment, memories activate a connection that helps ensure a particular kind of durability.[22] Given his gentle demeanor and the horrifying nature of his death, memories of Shepard are rife with affect, particularly guilt, shame, fear, anger, pride, and familiarity. Indeed, Jennifer Petersen has argued that "public feelings" about Shepard played an integral role in shaping public responses to the crime.[23] While I leave Petersen and others to enunciate the particular affective qualities at work in the Shepard case, the frames of memory examined below illustrate how Shepard's memory succeeded and persisted, in part, by playing up qualities of his that were relatable and affiliative with diverse public audiences.

Yet, as Blair, Dickinson, and Ott remind us, communities do not just have affective responses out of the blue; rather, effective and lasting public memories are constructed in particular ways that emphasize opportunities for affiliation between the subject and its audiences. In other words, "affiliative investment is elementally rhetorical, in the sense that it is produced (and legitimated) by and among discourses, objects, events, and practices and the ways in which these are taken 'to matter.'"[24] To characterize this point beyond reference to affect alone, it can be said that public memories are made "to matter" as persistent texts when they are thoughtfully crafted so that they might prompt the creation of publics and counterpublics.

To speak of publics in this way means more than Habermas's influential distinction between the private sphere and the "bourgeois public sphere"—private people who come together to petition public authority over issues of shared concern.[25] Rather, I mean a more complex and "actually existing" way of considering public discourse constituted between the public sphere and smaller, multiple, "subaltern" publics known as "counterpublics." Counterpublics exist alongside and in opposition to a dominant public sphere, often representing the worldviews and opinions of marginalized or minority communities. From this outside perspective, counterpublics skirmish with the public sphere in order to define reality in particular ways.[26] This dynamic struggle for collective meaning making is often labeled public world making.[27] However, world making conflicts are not limited to the public sphere and various counterpublics; such competitions can occur between competing counterpublics as well. As Robert Asen suggests, if scholars are really interested in understanding the "actually existing" stakes involved in public controversies, they must be willing to reject binary approaches to understanding publics and counterpublics.[28] Picking up this point, Phaedra C. Pezzullo demonstrates that clashes among counterpublics over how best to represent an alternative worldview of a given public issue occur with important consequence.[29] In the Shepard case, conflicts in world making—as a point at which durability is assured in public debates—have been waged between both the heteronormative public sphere and queer counterpublics, as well as between queer counterpublics themselves.

However, key to understanding how world-making struggles can render a public memory in nonmaterial perpetuity is the role that texts play in public/counterpublic action. Texts of all sorts, including public memories, are actually crucial to establishing any given worldview in the realm of the public. This is because, as Michael Warner has shown, texts are essential ingredients for calling a public into existence. According to Warner, when particularly powerful texts (appealing in affective, affiliative, or other ways) are created and begin to be circulated among strangers, these texts begin to draw people into a group. As the text circulates further, it continues to hail more people, constituting readers or viewers into a public or counterpublic. Therefore, preexisting publics do not typically adopt texts; instead, texts constitute and reconstitute publics, driven by a compelling "stranger sociability."[30]

It is through this understanding of publics and counterpublic that we can identify a third way in which public memories—as particular kinds of texts—can access durability: perpetual (re)circulation within and between publics and counterpublics. Historically, many kinds of texts (particularly speech) have been characterized as fleeting and ephemeral; they are experienced in the moment and have clear and finite beginnings and ends. As a result these kinds of texts can be seen as incapable of having durability or monumentality. However, Warner claims that understanding public discourse as "conversation[s] or decision making" with finite end points is a "misleading ideologizatio[n]." Rather, Warner believes that public texts can have (though may, in fact, not have) "an ongoing life." He continues: "It's the way texts circulate, and become the basis for further representations, that convinces us that publics have activity and duration."[31] The key to this discursive perpetuity are texts embedded in a public or counterpublic that gain a long-lasting recirculation, in effect, having the potential to outlive generations. As long as a text—which can be elaborated on and expanded—continues to circulate, the public it spawned will also continue to exist, further circulating the text and giving it a form of imperishability. If, by contrast, the text stops circulating, the public, too, can cease, and oblivion becomes a distinct possibility.

A durable text may seem abstract to imagine, but consider the Bible as an example. First conceived as a series of fragmented, outsider texts, the Bible has since called into being a sizable public which has succeeded in circulating and recirculating this text at the heart of its affiliative community for thousands of years; and it does not seem likely to cease circulating in the near future. In this way we might think of the Bible as a text with durability, a monumental tome. Public memories of Matthew Shepard obviously do not reach the scale of the Bible; however, as we will see, particularly compelling memories of Shepard have been essential to calling affiliative counterpublics into being. Likewise, the reiteration and recirculation of these memories within the counterpublic and beyond have given those memories a lasting fortitude. Therefore, the ongoing circulation of public memories within and between publics and counterpublics provides a different, nonphysical way pasts can attempt to outlast time's ongoing march.

Malleability, affect, circulation—these three dimensions essential to public memory generally provide powerful recourse for particular memories to persist with durability despite never taking on a material form. These three need not constitute the entirety of nonmaterial endurance; certainly other dimensions are in play in different memory debates. Yet within the public debates spawned by Shepard's tragic death, these three elements have helped secure his past with a powerful durability. For many GLBTQ advocates who found Shepard an appealing subject for rhetorical acts, bringing this durability to his public memories is not just useful but necessary as well. Contrary tellings of Shepard's memory, from the wider heteronormative public sphere and critics of inclusion and identification within queer communities themselves, launched powerful attacks on these rhetorical undertakings that tactical and ephemeral memories could not withstand. Yet when put in conjunction with appeals to power, expansion, and epideictic energies, Shepard's monumental renderings demonstrate the impressive range of queer public memory beyond material monuments alone. What follows is an analysis of GLBTQ discourse highlighting several monumental frames for remembering Shepard and the ways in which those memories are challenged by queer and transgender counterpublic memories.

The Public and Counterpublic:
Victim of Violence
■

The initial reports of the attack on Matthew Shepard sparked immediate attention in both the GLBTQ community and the wider public sphere. Just what garnered that attention when so many other acts of antigay violence escaped public scrutiny remains unclear, but some have suggested that the gruesome violence of the crime played an important part.[32] Indeed, the violence was so gruesome that it can be understood to have ruptured the sense of American community. While such violence leaves many speechless, it constitutes for Stephen H. Browne a chance for intervention—wherein rhetoric can stitch back together a lost sense of community.[33]

Shepard's death generated public discourse from many quarters. Although within the wider public sphere these voices varied in detail, scholarship on the rhetoric of Shepard's death suggests that he was remembered in one primary way: as the victim of an unfortunate but isolated act of violence.[34] For Brian Ott and Eric Aoki, Shepard's violent murder highlighted a pattern of victimization "through the expulsion of difference." But in classic Burkean style, according to Ott and Aoki, Shepard's murder "transferred the public's guilt onto McKinney and Henderson" who themselves became victims for social purging, releasing society of responsibility.[35] This transfer of guilt took many forms. According to John Lynch, popular representations of McKinney and Henderson often attempted to detach the two from the public by "making their actions appear unnatural and inhuman."[36] Susan J. Balter-Reitz and Karen A. Stewart argue that Shepard's death was justified and even demanded in news coverage by visual appeals to the mythos of the rural Western landscape.[37] In each case the wider heterosexual public sought to escape culpability for Shepard's death. This did not mean that average Americans did not recognize horrible acts could be perpetrated against gay men (and lesbians) or that they did not feel that such acts were morally wrong. But it did indicate that major public remembrances of Shepard within the public sphere functioned to frame that violence as a private incident involving three individuals. In other words Shepard's death was presented in a way that did not evoke a strong affiliative response between Shepard and some heterosexual audiences. Because of its distinctive and private nature, Shepard's attack and murder were not culturally sanctioned, and the average American had no responsibility for their having taken place.

The wide adoption of such a view by the public at large, if left unchallenged, would have marked a missed exigence—an exigence in which the GLBTQ community might argue for an alternative meaning of Shepard's death productive for the community's social, political, and cultural aims. If, as Browne (citing Richard Leeman) argues, the construction of violence and its response can "reorder collective commitments and shared meanings" within a culture, Shepard's death was a rare opportunity for skilled queer rhetors to constitute the violence he faced as a worldview associated with culture at large. Once established, the rhetor could present that worldview to an audience, critique it, and articulate a contrary worldview calling the original into question. If the new worldview was adopted, it could realign the politics of society and reconstitute community.[38]

Drawing upon the opportunity presented by Shepard's violent death, the GLBTQ community deployed an alternative way of remembering the college student as a victim that challenged the narrow reading provided by the wider public sphere. This alternative counterpublic memory was highly critical of the systemic nature and invisibility of antigay violence, assuming a strong queer style to disrupt the "regime of the normal" that perpetuated such violence.[39] To challenge the memory of Shepard as an isolated victim, the queer counterpublic circulated memories of Shepard that sought to turn him into a symbolic victim of antigay violence while minimizing opportunities for public guilt to be scapegoated onto others. To put it another way, rather than permit the heterosexual public to obscure its responsibilities for Shepard's death, the queer counterpublic endeavored to "affect" the wider public by placing guilt, shame, regret, and responsibility for his murder squarely on the shoulders of society's systemic violence and heterosexual people's complicity with it. As a symbol, Shepard's memory was capable of calling attention to public disavowals of responsibility, raising awareness of the pervasiveness of antigay violence, and marshaling coalition building for GLBTQ protections. Without this symbolism, the violence of Shepard's death could become individuated and marginalized, losing its potential as it had in much of the wider public.

In order to craft the disruptive violence of Shepard's murder into a symbol, rhetorical work was needed. According to Browne, "to the degree that such violence was publicly performed and culturally sanctioned, it took on symbolic dimensions that might in turn be construed to the [rhetor's] advantage."[40] Thus, to rearticulate antigay violence and make the memories of that violence rhetorically potent, the queer counterpublic needed to publicize the violence of Shepard's death and situate that violence within the wider public's sanction, thereby giving it monumental durability.

Publicizing Shepard's death was the most immediate priority of queer activists; however, drawing attention to the violence of Shepard's death posed two challenges for queer counterpublic remembering. On one hand, the violent act of Shepard's murder was largely consigned to the activities of the private sphere. Sequestered in a field on the outskirts of town, McKinney and Henderson had ample opportunity to privatize their violent acts. Unlike the atrocities of war, lynching, and other bias crimes, Shepard's death was not suffered in public view. In Christine Harold and Kevin DeLuca's language, it was not "witnessed," at least not personally.[41] Such privatized views of violence are more difficult to frame as culturally sanctioned and thus make scapegoating of a death like Shepard's far easier. On the other hand, to the extent that there was publicity within the public sphere of Shepard's (private) death, it publicized his experience of violence differently from the way in which the queer counterpublic would choose to do so. By and large the popular press covered Shepard as a gay man who died in a solitary incident of violence. But such a view was contrary to Shepard's own experiences of violence and those faced everyday by other GLBTQ persons. The queer counterpublic had to renounce these views of Shepard's violent death if his potential as symbol was to be realized. To overcome this challenge, the queer counterpublic took two steps: it aggressively reiterated and recentered violence to enable its public witnessing, and it recast the characterization of antigay violence in discourse.

The queer counterpublic reiterated over and over again in graphic detail the violence Shepard faced, rendering his attack not just a "beating" but a monumental and meaningful murder. More so than the popular press, the queer counterpublic focused attention on the description and framing of the violence of the crime, transforming the private act of violence into a public argument. In its first appearance in the *Advocate* on November 10, 1998, the "savage killing" of Shepard was rehearsed in all its terror: "Shepard, 21, was bludgeoned with the butt of a gun, burned, tied to a wooden fence and left for dead."[42] In another story he was described as "abducted," "beaten," "tortured," and "lashed." One article speaks of his "battered, unconscious body." Elsewhere in the article Shepard was described as "pistol-whipped . . . with the butt of .357 Magnum and then left to die."[43] At a memorial vigil for Shepard, his brutal death was reiterated: "They did not dump Matt's battered body in some ditch hoping the snow would hide it until next spring. They strung him up on a fence. . . . This display was an attempt to intimidate and subjugate Wyoming's gay community and send the message that all gays and lesbians deserve such violence."[44] One caption in the *Advocate* noted graphically: "Tied to a deer fence for 18 hours, Shepard was so brutally beaten that the bicyclist who discovered him at first thought he was a scarecrow."[45] Through repetitive mention and graphic details that stoked public feelings,

Shepard's death became a historic, transformative event not to be forgotten or ignored.

Beyond reiteration, the queer counterpublic publicized violence by revealing that Shepard's attack on the night of his murder was not a unique moment in his life. Matthew Shepard had been attacked before. Indeed, for many GLBTQ persons, antigay and antitrans violence is not a discrete single incident but rather an ongoing part of everyday life.[46] By repetitive descriptions of violence, queer memories of Shepard altered how his murder should be understood. In the *Advocate* Shepard's mother, Judy, reported that her son had been the victim of a sexual assault in Morocco three years prior to his death.[47] The *Advocate* detailed a separate incident the previous August in which Shepard was punched in the face by "a bartender turned off by his advances."[48] In a speech at the Washington, D.C., vigil, Shepard's friend Walter Boulden that stated Shepard had faced repeated harassment and name calling throughout his life.[49] Thus while both the queer counterpublic and public sphere remembered Shepard as a victim of violence, the queer counterpublic memory reflected and publicized not the solitary, private experiences of violence but rather an ongoing violence that stifled everyday GLBTQ life. Shepard's memory in the queer counterpublic centered publicly a new notion of violence in its articulation—violence on a grand scale demanding attention.

In addition to publicizing the violence of the crime, the rhetorical reframing of the experience of violence by GLBTQ persons served the second strategy needed to frame Shepard as a symbol: demonstrating that the violence he faced was culturally sanctioned. Unfortunately, Shepard's experiences were (and are) not unique. The levels of violence gays and lesbians have faced, historically and contemporarily, cannot be understated. According to the FBI, 1,488 bias crimes were committed against gays and lesbians in 1998.[50] An increase from earlier years, this number does not adequately conceptualize the violence gays and lesbians face on a daily basis. As Frederick M. Lawrence argues, the FBI figures are based on voluntary reporting by local law enforcement which "has not yet reached an optimum, nor even representative, level." Equally important, gays and lesbians have been less likely to report bias crimes due to historical animosities with the police and doubts that such charges would be taken seriously.[51] In reality, the violence, harassment, and abuse of gays and lesbians is significantly higher than any official tracking figure would indicate. By reframing Shepard as someone who faced violence throughout his life, McKinney and Henderson could be understood as only the most recent perpetrators of antigay violence against Shepard in a culture in which GLBTQ people were not welcome. However, other strategies were used more widely within queer counterpublic memories to demonstrate that a culture of violence indeed existed and that heterosexuals across the nation should be affected by the nation's inadequate response to date. Primary among these was identifying Shepard with other victims of violence.

Remembering Shepard in connection with other bias-crime victims enhanced the likelihood that such violence would be seen as systemic rather than rare. These comparisons took place on several levels. Many in the GLBTQ community began comparisons with other well known gay victims, particularly Harvey Milk, Allen Schindler, and Scott Amedure. Each was murdered in part because of his sexuality, and each was mentioned in connection with the reporting of Shepard's death. Others in the queer counterpublic drew identifications between Shepard and James Byrd, Jr., a disabled African American bias-crime victim who was dragged to his death a year earlier in Jasper, Texas. Community leaders, the press, and hate-crime legislation made the Shepard-Byrd connection clearly, "impl[ying] for perhaps the first time that gays are no different from other minorities targeted for hate crimes."[52] By creating this affiliative bond between Shepard and other well known victims of violence, the queer counterpublic made it increasingly difficult for this incident to be ignored or forgotten.

More compelling than Shepard's affiliation with other famous victims was his identification with a much larger number of unknown gay and lesbian victims of violence. In queer style, "reminiscing" about one's own experience with antigay violence became an important part of remembering Shepard.[53] Often gays and lesbians would volunteer these reminiscences for the counterpublic. In the wake of Shepard's death the *Advocate* received letters to the editor and news reports describing the violence GLBTQ victims had faced.[54] A seventeen-year-old boy named Daniel drew connections between Shepard's death and his own attack and attempted suicide in a speech at Shepard's D.C. vigil.[55] Advocacy groups relayed similar stories of violence. In a GLBTQ media interview the Lesbian/Gay Rights Lobby of Texas argued that Shepard's case was reminiscent of the murder of a deaf and mute gay man whose attackers were acquitted through a self-defense plea.[56] Connections were also made between Shepard and other gay and lesbian bias-crime victims through the GLBTQ press and supportive heterosexual journalists. The *Advocate* credited the attention of the Matthew Shepard case with prompting newspapers in several U.S. cities, including Philadelphia and Denver, to revisit previously overlooked bias crimes across the country, including a murder dating from 1960.[57] Still others pointed to the likelihood of Shepard's attack in this culture by sharing their concerns that they could become victims of violence in the future. "It could have been me" was a refrain echoed throughout the queer counterpublic.[58] To remember Shepard became an occasion for many GLBTQ bias-crime victims to air publicly their own stories of violence, thereby indicting a culture that saw itself as free from blame.

An additional resource for the queer counterpublic in demonstrating the cultural responsibility for antigay violence was derived from the state-sanctioned crackdown at the event designated the Matthew Shepard Political Funeral and Protest. On the evening of October 19, 1998, four to five thousand gay men, lesbians, and their supporters marched through Manhattan to protest Shepard's murder. Hastily arranged without a city permit, the march was violently broken up after several blocks of progress by the New York City Police Department. Described as "halting traffic and causing chaos" in a short article in the *Advocate,* other queer texts rallied around the incident as further evidence of queers' dangerous position in society.[59] For instance, ACT UP New York suggested that "Mayor Giuliani's police state broke out in full force, escalating violence, with people injured by police brutality and with 136 people arrested and held in jail for 30 hours." The organization further noted that "more people saw firsthand just how this mayor and his police force are running the city."[60] While Habermas reminds us that the state is not always synonymous with the wider public, ACT UP implied that it was possible to read the bloody shutting of the Matthew Shepard Political Funeral and Protest as just another example of antigay violence in America—violence which had been allowed to persist for far too long.[61]

By publicizing in detail the violence of the Shepard murder and linking that violence not to individual perpetrators but to cultural sanctions implicitly supported by many heterosexuals, remembering Matthew Shepard became a means to confront the narrow worldview of people within the wider public sphere. In challenging contrary public memories that freed the public from culpability in the murder, the queer counterpublic offered an alternative worldview of bias-crime violence and the public's responsibility for it. In so doing they simultaneously helped assure that Shepard would not be forgotten and that his public memory would persist. However, while gays and lesbians collectively found countering heterosexual memories of Shepard's death productive, the community was more splintered when considering its own deployments of Shepard memories.

Counterpublics: Secular Saint/Common Man
■

While aspects of the GLBTQ community employed queer counterpublic memories of Shepard to contest the meaning of and responsibility for violence within the wider public sphere, at the same time alternative and conflicting memories of Shepard emerged within the community itself. Some of these memories (what I term "gay and lesbian counterpublic memories") challenged the marginalizing moves of the wider public sphere and articulated Shepard as a "queer fiction of the past" in an effort to solidify a distinctive gay identity and integrate that community into the wider public sphere in terms consistent with the turn to queer monumentality. Meanwhile, other parts of the community, rather than challenging the public sphere more broadly, undercut the gay and lesbian counterpublic. Assuming a critically queer perspective, these queer counterpublic memories sought to disrupt rhetorics of identification and inclusion by their gay and lesbian counterparts, instead arguing for a complex, intersectional, and counter form of queer identity. Two primary frames in which these views were contested were memories of Shepard as a Secular Saint and as a Common Man. While the inconsistency—even counterintuitive nature—of these simultaneous frames of memory might seem as if it might ultimately harm Shepard's memory, the malleability these tensions reflect tells another story. Indeed, Shepard's ability to be remembered as different things to different people (with both positive and negative valences) actually did more to ensure the durability of his memory rather than to encourage its erasure.

The Secular Saint

In the opening remarks of the trial of Aaron McKinney in the fall of 1999, McKinney's defense launched an all-out offensive on the "myth of St. Matthew." In a familiar pattern of blaming the victim known as the gay panic defense, they attacked Shepard's conduct, lifestyle, sexual experiences, morals, and anything else that might sway the jury from convicting the accused.[62] The gay panic defense argues that discrimination, mistreatment, and violence against gays and lesbians are forms of self-defense justified by a psychological "panic" in the "victim" as a result of unwanted same-sex interaction.[63] To be effective, this strategy must construct the gay man or lesbian as aberrant, immoral, and unnatural. Few judges or jurors could logically justify attacking a good person without provocation. But some could justify attacking a social pariah. Indeed, many jurors had previously done so. For McKinney's trial team, the goal was clear: for McKinney to be exonerated, Shepard had to be seen as deviant. Thus for McKinney's lawyers the greatest threat to their defense was an emerging public memory of Shepard as a valued, respected, and likeable person—a secular saint.[64]

It is important to clarify here what the term *saint* means. Indeed, *saint* rarely appeared in the discourse, and, when it did, it had no stridently religious implication.[65] Instead the saint frame signaled Shepard's transition from an everyday person to an extraordinary symbol—a symbol with the power of a religious icon situated within the nonreligious cultural world of social movements. In other words to label Shepard a saint is to cast him as a monumental figure. Drawing upon Émile Durkheim, the sociologist Barry

Schwartz suggests that societies attenuated by "collective excitement" struggle for meaning by endowing otherwise everyday objects and ordinary people
with collective values, thus making them "sacred." In this way "mundane
objects and undistinguished people come to be respected or revered." After
the assassination of the unpopular Abraham Lincoln, Schwartz argues, his
memory was filled with sacred (but secular) veneration, providing meaning
to the confusion following his death and motivating social action.[66] In Shepard's case the previously unknown and unimposing gay man came to embody
the suffering and pride of gays and lesbians across the country, processing
their grief and fear and urging cultural and political change. Remembered
as a saint in the secular realm and filled with the collective epideictic values
of the GLBTQ community, Shepard became a valuable rhetorical tool—a
discursive monument for the gay and lesbian cause.

The sacred qualities that become key to this framing of Shepard emerged
within the larger rhetorical process of making him a martyr. The creation of
martyrs has been a productive area of inquiry across the academy.[67] While
martyrs have historically been most important to religions, social movements
have relied heavily on their own victims of the cause to achieve their ends.
These martyrs of choice—men and women who give themselves willingly to
the cause—can easily acquire rhetorical potential.[68] Shepard, however, did
not fit this profile. He held no political position in any GLBTQ organization,
nor was he a willing victim for his attackers. Rather, Shepard was targeted
for his identity during a routine bar visit. Thus to remember Shepard as
a martyr required greater rhetorical effort. As an individual who "through
chance and circumstance stumbled upon death," Shepard became an "accidental martyr" through the careful choreographing of his mourning.[69] By
examining Shepard's emergence as an accidental martyr within the gay and
lesbian counterpublic, his sacred, or "saintly," frame becomes clear.

According to Richard J. Jensen, Thomas R. Burkholder, and John C.
Hammerback, three steps must occur to sanctify an accidental martyr: the
blunt marking of the martyr's dead body, the transformation of the martyr's
soul from the body to the "spiritual" or sacred realm, and the martyr's identification with the secular cause.[70] Shepard's death was ritualized through
this process, marking the discourse with recirculated fragments of martyr
making.

First, Shepard's death had to be made a reality and the focus of communal attention through the marking of his dead body. According to Jensen,
Burkholder, and Hammerback, "because the mourners' physical relationship
with the deceased has been permanently changed" the rhetor must "rhetorically alter the relationship [with the audience] by acknowledging the
death in a straightforward, almost blunt, fashion." This is usually done, they
argue, through the presence of a coffin or body at a public funeral.[71] While

one thousand people attended Shepard's funeral, most of the day's attention was drawn instead to threats to picket the event from right-wing Christian groups.[72] However, the rendering of Shepard's death was solidified in other ways to maximize symbolic effect. Shepard's violent and highly publicized murder transformed him into a dead body in the public mind. The rehearsals of Shepard's death in the GLBTQ press, films, and images all aided in this transformation of relationship. In addition, the five-day media "death watch" between Shepard's attack and his passing marked this transformation. As Ott and Aoki noted, "that Shepard lay comatose in a hospital for several days while people around the country prayed and stood vigil for him functioned to heighten the public's investment in the story."[73] When daily updates of Shepard's condition were broken by the announcement of his death, there was little surprise that Shepard was indeed dead. Along with contemporaneous vigils across the country organized by the gay and lesbian counterpublic to maximize public attention of Shepard's suffering and death, these discursive fragments show the symbolic transformation of Shepard into a dead body.

More rhetorically potent and compelling was the second step of creating Shepard as a martyr: endowing Shepard's memory with sacred qualities. It is through this rhetorical act that "the myth of St. Matthew" emerged that so threatened McKinney's defense. In the view of Jensen, Burkholder, and Hammerback, endowing the memory of the dead person with a sense of sacredness requires that "human frailties" of the deceased be "forgotten" while virtues and accomplishments are highlighted.[74] Shepard's memorial discourse within the gay and lesbian counterpublic aided this process by putting his virtues and accomplishments on display. The virtues most commonly associated with Shepard were his gentility and his qualities as a good friend. The first mention of his name in the *Advocate* appeared in the headline "The Good Shepard."[75] In an article by Jon Barrett, Shepard was called a "gentle young gay man" who "by all accounts . . . was a . . . fun-loving person whose slight build (5 feet 2 inches, 105 pounds) and ebullient disposition made people feel protective toward him, not threatened by him." Shepard was described as "loved" and "a great success" in life in GLBTQ public-service announcements.[76] His friend Jim Osborn said Shepard "always has a smile on his face."[77] Dennis Shepard, Matthew's father, in a letter to the readers of the *Advocate* described him as "sensitive," having a "quick wit," and a person who could "meet people and make instant friends." Mr. Shepard solidified a perception of his son as a "loving, sensitive, intelligent person" who was proud of who he was and would be remembered as a gentle soul.[78] In highlighting the virtues that Shepard had in life, the gay and lesbian counterpublic memory constructed an image of Shepard endowed with "saintly" appeal in a place of sacred honor that could serve rhetorical purposes beyond those afforded by the creation of a martyr alone.

Third, because Shepard was an accidental martyr not directly engaged in political action, his memory underwent the greatest renovation in order to suggest that he died serving a higher cause—gay and lesbian rights. Key to that perception was the frequent, repetitive invocation of Shepard's political and activist work generally. There were documented reports of Shepard's political involvements, especially in some local campaigns.[79] In addition, he was actively seeking a career in social justice and political science.[80] Shepard was also remembered as wanting to change the world. The *Advocate* declared early on that the "young man's death shakes the nation. It is how Matthew Shepard would have wanted it."[81] This thought was echoed by Boulden at the Washington, D.C., vigil: "Matt once told me that someday he was going to be famous and that he was going to make a difference in the area of human rights. . . . I have to think he had no idea how true that statement would be."[82] Later *Advocate* coverage continued: "If he had to die a tragic death, he would have wanted it to make the country a better place for all of us, and maybe it will."[83] In addition, despite the fact that Shepard had no affiliation with GLBTQ rights groups specifically, GLBTQ advocates made explicit efforts to link him to the cause. In a 1998 article Shepard was referred to as "something of a gay activist" at the University of Wyoming.[84] He was remembered as a new member in the university's GLBTQ organization and as looking forward to the campus's Coming Out Day events that took place a few days after his attack.[85] Later press reports established that Shepard had left a planning meeting for the University's Coming Out Day activities just prior to his fateful encounter with his attackers.[86] The gay and lesbian counterpublic continually emphasized his commitments to the community and to GLBTQ life, positioning him as someone fighting for the cause of GLBTQ equality.

Two major effects emerged from this complex rhetorical project. First, the transformation of Shepard into a "secular saint" as part of the martyrdom process aided the gay and lesbian counterpublic in challenging (in both court and public opinion) the gay panic defense. Anticipating this strategy, the gay and lesbian counterpublic leveraged Shepard's sacred memory aggressively, delivering these constructions into the wider public sphere through press releases, news reports, and speeches.[87] A telling indication of their success emerged at the conclusion of the McKinney trial. With the two memories of Matthew Shepard—the Saint and the Sinner—face to face in a Wyoming courtroom, the memory of "St. Matthew" won the day. McKinney was found guilty of murder in a clear rejection of the gay panic defense; he later plea bargained for life in prison without parole.

More broadly, in constructing "St. Matthew" as a martyr, an image of a united gay and lesbian community was formed. As the creation of a martyr is a eulogistic process, one of its major goals is the construction of an identifiable community in the wake of violence. As Browne suggests, violence can tear community apart while a fitting rhetorical response can reconstitute it.[88] Eulogistic processes, like public memorialization, excel in this "constitutive rhetoric."[89] The creation of a martyr within a social movement adheres "the members of the organization together."[90] Kathleen Hall Jamieson and Karlyn Kohrs Campbell concur, suggesting that speakers in eulogistic situations must attempt to unite the community and minimize advocacy that might divide it. In eulogistic settings rhetoric that "reknits the community" is generically demanded.[91] Thus, remembering Shepard as a martyred saint would allow people to "understand the event and share in a renewed sense of community."[92]

Many within the gay and lesbian counterpublic argued that just such a community had been formed or reconstituted through the ascendance of Shepard in counterpublic memory. Rebecca Granato, quoted in an article in the *Advocate,* believed Shepard's believed Shepard's murder "showed us how a community can come together."[93] Jeremy Kinser described the murder in the *Advocate* as a key moment for a "people joining to become a 'we,' not just an 'I.'"[94] According to Cathy Renna, media director of the Gay and Lesbian Alliance Against Defamation (GLAAD), "Matthew made our community, for better or for worse, very real."[95] In some cases the unity of identity forged in the early days of remembering Matthew Shepard seemed lost. Asked what it would take to unify millions of gay people into solitary action again, National Gay and Lesbian Task Force (now the National LGBTQ Taskforce) president Matthew Foreman said that "movements have to keep being reinvigorated. . . . I think this time it's going to be another Matthew Shepard."[96] While the events around Shepard's martyrdom reconstituted a gay and lesbian community, the incorporation of those events into a collective memory became an occasion for identity building as well. As Chauncey has suggested, the reclamation of collective gay pasts aided in defining a distinct community to assert "a collective identity in the present."[97] The community sanctified certain moments to give gays and lesbians their pasts, generating identification and affiliation among the disparate groups of people who constitute the GLBTQ community.[98] Shepard's martyrdom was such a moment for many community members. Writing to the *Advocate,* Larry Drane suggested that Shepard's death was "like Stonewall" in as much as it changed lives. The *Advocate* featured Shepard's death prominently in its historical narratives as the most important event of 1998 and key to the decade, with Shepard as a hero of the movement.[99] Similarly, members of the gay and lesbian counterpublic made an impressive concerted effort to make Shepard *TIME*'s Person of the Year.[100] For advocates of remembering Shepard as a sacred figure, to remember Shepard was to participate in an act of identification—reinscribing the GLBTQ community from the violence that had shattered it. It is the effect of this construction that allowed Michael Gross to report, in a clear sign of this rhetoric's contribution to durability, that "five years later, Matthew Shepard still matters."[101]

However, while few objected to the defense of Shepard as a valued person, other GLBTQ persons were not so keen to remember Shepard as a monumental symbol of a united gay and lesbian community. For these individuals the elevation of Shepard did not signify a community coming together but pointed instead to what little was left of a community falling apart. These dissenters constituted a queer counterpublic in opposition to the gay and lesbian counterpublic. Engaging the semiofficial gay and lesbian counterpublic, the queer counterpublic utilized their memories of Shepard in a very different way.

Queer Counterpublic Memories of Intersectionality

A central dissociation in remembering Shepard for the queer counterpublic emerged from their queer orientation and complex notion of identity. While constructing Shepard as a prominent person heralded a coming together for the gay and lesbian counterpublic, the critical view of identity taken by the queer perspective saw it otherwise. Instead, the queer counterpublic remembered Shepard as the poster child of white middle-class cisgendered gay men, at the core of the representational power in the GLBTQ rights movement, yet again centering itself and whitewashing the diversity of the actually existing community. Such a practice amounted to what Judith Halberstam has called a "'representative individual' model of minority history."[102]

At the heart of this queer counterpublic memory was what Bravmann has termed the "queer cultural studies of history." Located within discourses of gay and lesbian identity, such projects aim to recognize "race, gender, class (among others) antagonisms 'within' that identity."[103] A queer cultural-studies critique then labeled as "fiction" gay and lesbian counterpublic memories of Shepard for failing to recognize diverse, coexisting dimensions within GLBTQ identity. Instead of being valued as an intersecting mix, GLBTQ was flattened into a singular, hegemonic notion of gay and lesbian identity. While traditional cultural-studies projects focus on the dimensions of gender, race, class, and nationality, GLBTQ discourses around Shepard were largely mute on class and nationality.[104] As such, race and gender took on critical prominence in queering Shepard's memory, provoking an "outcry over other hate crimes against people of color and transgender people."[105]

Race was the most conspicuous issue to draw attention in queer fragments. Little thought was given in the first days after Shepard's murder to his racial status beyond his resonance with James Byrd; however, as Shepard's memory gained cultural cachet, critics actively articulated the community's whiteness. Writing in the *Advocate*, former executive director of the National Gay and Lesbian Task Force (NGLTF) Urvashi Vaid argued that the GLBTQ rights movement was "playing politics with some core principles" by failing to recognize corresponding violence against racial, gender, and political minorities.[106] Jasmyne Cannick echoed this statement a few years later: "If my memory serves me correctly, the world stopped because white gays across the country made Shepard's death a nationwide issue."[107] Out lesbian actor and activist Rosie O'Donnell pointed to racial concerns in gay and lesbian memorial practices as a reason for not attending and speaking at vigils for Shepard.[108]

Gender issues also drew commentary from the queer counterpublic but little in regard to the masculine-feminine binary. Instead, queer criticisms focused primarily on how transgender people were made invisible by remembering Shepard. According to Richard Juang, in "conventional discussions of rights and equality" transgender persons have been "excluded . . . as aberrant cases." This is particularly true in the area of bias crimes where the "multilayered" relationship between recognition and violence suggests that transgender victims deserve violence, makes those crimes invisible, leads to dismissive attitudes by authorities, and encourages transgender people to feel that violence against them is inevitable.[109] Meanwhile transgender persons have a substantially higher risk of repeated violence and harassment, often with higher levels of injury and greater likelihood of death.[110] Ironically, transgender people received relatively less attention in bias-crimes discourse with Shepard as the focus of a gay and lesbian sense of identity and community. Indeed, the first several iterations of federal hate-crimes legislation prompted by Shepard's murder left unclear whether transgender victims would be protected or not.[111] As part of the queer counterpublic, transgender activists were keen to raise inequities in discussions of violence, sometimes using Shepard as a point of comparison. One such event was a protest of Judy Shepard at a 2008 Human Rights Campaign (HRC) event by transgender activists who were angry over transgender exclusion from Democratic nondiscrimination legislation. In the question-and-answer period after her speech, Judy Shepard defended the work of HRC and Congress, for which she received an unusually high level of criticism. Describing her actions as "cowardly and indefensible," one transgender activist remarked: "I remember when Judy Shepard was a friend of the T community, but no longer."[112]

While many of these queer counterpublic memories were instigated by queer elites, everyday queers took up the argument as well. Readers and viewers of GLBTQ texts expressed similar critical concerns for identity formation by critiquing Shepard's memory. Such sentiments were expressed vividly in letters to the editor in the *Advocate*. One example was a letter entitled "Past Tense," by Mark Walcott: "Thanks for reminding us that the phrase GLBT community is a fucking oxymoron. Two black transgendered women

(Bella Evangelista and Emonie Kiera Spaulding) were murdered in Washington, D.C., less than a month before your September 30 issue hit the stands. Another transgendered woman was shot and seriously hurt. You reported on all this recent outrage in less than a page [*Nation*, September 30] yet in the same issue devoted no less than eight pages to the topic of a Caucasian gay male (Matthew Shepard) who was killed five years ago. You call yourselves *The Advocate*. Need I ask for whom?"[113] To draw attention to these representational deficiencies and raise awareness about the broader notions of identity unacknowledged by privileging Shepard's memory, queer counterpublic memories often attempted to link Shepard's name with GLBTQ people of color and transgender victims of bias crimes. Cannick situated her critique of Shepard's memory in relation to the murder of a black gay man named Michael Sandy. In remembering Shepard, Cannick argued: "Why didn't Sandy's death merit the same response?"[114] Some GLBTQ rights groups offered Pablo Zuniga as an example of a Hispanic man who was similarly attacked but given little attention, in part because because he was deaf, mute, and nonwhite.[115] Transgender activists often used the 2002 murder of transgender woman Gwen Araujo to connect Shepard's memory with a more easily assailed victim and as a counterpoint to Shepard's prevalence in gay and lesbian discourse. To quote one transgender blogger after an appearance by Judy Shepard: "I'm obviously sorry for her loss, but the T community has seen many losses in the ensuing years that were as blatant and vivid as hers, perhaps more so. Gwen Araujo's mother would have been a much better choice."[116] Countless other victims including J. R. Warren, Billy Jack Gaither, Angie Zapata, Jesse Dirkhising, and Lawrence King were mentioned in conjunction with Shepard to disrupt a singular focus upon him as the symbol of community and a rallying point for gay and lesbian identity.

To date, such criticisms of Shepard's reified memory have done little to alter the memory industry that has sprung up around his death. That Shepard remains today the "saintly" face of both bias-crime advocacy and the GLBTQ community illustrates just how successful the gay and lesbian counterpublic has been at casting Shepard as a durable monumental symbol. While it has been widely acknowledged even within the gay and lesbian counterpublic that "this is not just about Matt," Shepard's whiteness (and with it his class, age, gender, ability, gender-identity, nationality, and the like) remained largely unmarked, leaving unrecognized the profound violence faced by queers with more intersectional identities and making suspicious claims of unity in the aftermath of Shepard's death.[117] While queer counterpublic memories of Shepard continue to challenge such flattened notions of what it means to be gay, it was not the only identity controversy to result from the Shepard case.

The Common Man

Simultaneously with the monumental memory rhetorics of Shepard's death as an exceptional event for understanding gay and lesbian identity, other gays and lesbians were framing his memory in ways that linked him directly to average, everyday heterosexual Americans. In short, Shepard was remembered as a common man. Such an everyday appeal bears little resemblance to monumentality's preoccupation with epideictic greatness, grandeur, and the heroic. However, the common-man frame does resonate with queer monumentality's other dimensions: durability (through affect and affiliation), expansion, and power. Indeed, a common-man appeal can excel at connecting an everyday hero to the masses so that his life might be emulated and his struggle carried on. For instance, Schwartz highlights how Lincoln's "eulogists politicized common traits" to enshrine an affinity for him in the memory of the "common people."[118] Jamieson, speaking of mediated images, notes that "traditional arguments . . . have been replaced in American political discourse by staged dramatizations that identify the politicians with us and associate them with images that we approve or disapprove of."[119] Richard Sennett echoes Jamieson, pointing to the significance of the personal in connecting with public figures.[120] Burke's conceptualization of identification is also central to this common connection. Burke draws upon Aristotle's common topics to argue for rhetoric's basis in identifying shared experiences with the audience: "You persuade a man only insofar as you can talk his language by speech, gesture, tonality, order, image, attitude, idea, *identifying* your ways with his."[121] Thus, the advocate divided from her "common" audience may invoke a strategy that demonstrates a common touch while still adopting a monumental embrace.

Because "you couldn't even make up a more sympathetic victim," elements of the GLBTQ community took up Shepard's monumental memory to link him specifically to the wider public.[122] In doing so they hoped to connect explicitly gay and lesbian and straight identities, creating an affiliation through shared affective relationships and wiping away the divisions made visible in Shepard's murder. The gay and lesbian counterpublic reinforced the memory of Shepard as the common man by relating his life story through various fragments. Media accounts, narratives, and reminiscences of friends and family within the gay and lesbian counterpublic that extended far beyond the events of Shepard's murder and its aftermath pointed to a counterpublic memory geared more toward describing who Shepard was as a person rather than as a victim or a symbol. What causes did he believe in? What were his likes and dislikes? How did he spend his time? While these were not necessarily the expressed objectives of some fragments, these humanizing insights into Shepard's personality emerged often and repeatedly whenever he was discussed.

Stories about Shepard from his friends and classmates helped to craft this common-man frame. In the hours and days after his death Shepard's friends became reliable targets of media interviews and speakers at memorial events, circulating ample personal anecdotes into the counterpublic sphere and shaping a convincing image of Shepard's common touch. One friend noted that Shepard was a "marathon shopper."[123] Others discussed his predilection for books: "Matt read a lot—the Old West was his favorite." Friends perpetually remarked upon his small stature that earned him the nickname Little Matt.[124] Boulden spent a significant amount of his speech at the Washington, D.C., vigil "help[ing] people understand who Matt was." Among the details Boulden related were Shepard's smoking habit, his interests in world affairs, and how appalled Shepard would be that people attended his vigil in street clothes rather than "brand new suits."[125]

At times Shepard's friends called into question his exceptionalism, in an effort to make him more identifiable. In an interesting example of how different frames of remembering Shepard were often malleable and contradictory, Shepard's close friend Romaine Patterson denigrated the "myth of St. Matthew" in an effort to embrace his common-man persona: "The media really made [him] this saintly character, this martyr for the gay community. In reality, Matthew had struggles; he dealt with issues around drugs, and he dealt with issues around depression."[126] As Patterson illustrated, remembering an individual's flaws can make that person more typical.

Besides friends and classmates, others had important information to contribute to the common-man frame and enhance the affiliative bonds between gays and lesbians and heterosexual individuals. The most compelling of these portraits of Shepard emerged from interviews and editorials by his parents, Judy and Dennis Shepard, who played a major role in shaping the memory of their son after his death. They pictured Shepard's life in the most "normal" of circumstances. He had a strong way with people that made him well liked.[127] He cared deeply for his family. He had a typical American childhood, except for the time in high school he spent abroad with his family. Even his sometimes strained relationship with his father reinforced Shepard's averageness. His way with people, strong family bonds, and demeanor all made Shepard out to be a typical U.S. college student.[128]

The Shepards' rhetoric framed their son, and by association all gays and lesbians, as "normal" children. In a poignant essay in the *Advocate* addressed to other fathers of GLBTQ youth, Dennis Shepard related mistakes he made with Matthew, encouraging other fathers to "accept their kids as kids." Mr. Shepard's frequent refrain was "Matt was not my gay son. Matt was my son who happened to be gay."[129] In other words, Dennis Shepard argued that Matthew was just like any other child, gay or straight, and framed sexual orientation as a common part of American life. In tandem with interviews of his wife Judy, Dennis Shepard reassured everyone that, despite being gay, Matthew was "still the same person we loved and raised."[130]

In conjunction with portrayals from significant people in his life, other everyday gay men and lesbians strengthened Shepard's common-man status through acts of identification and affiliation. Men and women related to Shepard's life regularly in the *Advocate*. Some, like Lee Thompson, expressed grief, noting that he felt like he was "having a conversation with Matt" after Shepard died.[131] The *Advocate* itself called Shepard "the lost brother who [we] were suddenly united [with] in a devastating grief."[132] Others found commonality in shared traumas. One friend noted how Shepard had been "called 'faggot'" like many GLBTQ people, while others commented on how what he experienced was "a familiar sight."[133] Some expressed directly how much of an everyman Shepard was. His friend Jim Osborn stated in an interview that Shepard "could have been anyone's gay son."[134] The *Advocate* noted that Shepard was "a middle class college kid Americans could really relate to."[135] For the gay and lesbian counterpublic, Shepard was regularly framed and reiterated as an appealing and familiar common man who could be easily identified with his peers in the wider public sphere and thus could serve as a bridge toward promoting greater rights and understanding.

Queer Counterpublic Memories of Division

Just as Shepard's "saintly" commemorations splintered views of identity within the GLBTQ community, framing him as a "common man" failed to signal a moment of identification and affiliation with heterosexual America for all GLBTQ persons. Instead, Shepard's death strongly reinforced the divisions between the GLBTQ and the straight worlds. These divisions were especially sharp for those who had felt that they had become part of the wider American community prior to the murder. Charles Kaiser suggested that, with the "sharply dropping shock value of being gay," many deeply believed that the "nation's old ideas of tolerance and inclusiveness would finally expand to include what had long been its most hated minority."[136] Shepard's murder shook these wishful notions, symbolizing that gays and lesbians had not, in fact, "arrived."[137] For these queers, remembering Shepard was a wakeup call, not a celebration of a shared GLBTQ-straight identity.

This wakeup call was reflected in the public queer remembering of Shepard. Rather than argue for what was held in common by GLBTQ and straight Americans, remembering Shepard became an occasion for the queer counterpublic to emphasize that much difference remained. In this emphasis queers again disrupted simplistic notions of identity, this time across the hetero-homo binary. These differences primarily diverged along lines of geography, generation, and complicity.

Recognizing regional differences in the acceptance of GLBTQ people was an important way of remembering Shepard's death in the queer counterpublic. Balter-Reitz and Stewart demonstrate how the rural landscape played a key part in how Shepard's death was framed. For them, Henderson and McKinney were "agents of the land" that "purified the landscape by eliminating the disruptive influence personified by Shepard." Removing human agency from the murder, their argument signifies a sharp distinction between rural and urban life and the appropriateness of GLBTQ people within them.[138] The GLBT community's detached experiences in Middle America contrast noticeably with those of GLBTQ persons on the supposedly liberal, urban, and gay-friendly coasts. Marchers in New York felt this distinction clearly: "There was a sense, I think, in the gay community, particularly living in a certain segment of it in New York City, that we can live in a kind of bubble and feel relatively safe and feel as if we've arrived."[139] For this marcher, living in a gay mecca had blinded many GLBTQ people to the divisions that remained in the rest of the country. Ironically, sometimes queers used the belief in the purity of rural America to emphasize geographic differences. Explained Jim Plogger: "Because it happened in rural, small-town America illustrates [sic] that no one is immune from potential hate crimes."[140] Shepard's death was therefore more heinous because it took place in the rural value system rather than in the city. However, this was a minority view as the discourse reveals that rurality was believed to enhance divisions of queers from nonqueers, making them more likely targets. By emphasizing the urban-rural elements of Shepard's death, the queer counterpublic articulated that liberalizing views of GLBTQ rights were not equitably disbursed. While some GLBTQ people in particular places may have been closer to identifying with heterosexual America, those in Middle America were still outsiders and deviants.

Many of those most keenly awakened to their separation from mainstream America by Shepard's death were GLBTQ youth. Born at a time when many of their gay and lesbian predecessors were marching in the streets and dying in hospital beds, these young GLBTQ people in their twenties and teens had experienced a very different relationship between GLBTQ and straight cultures. For many of them, to be gay or lesbian was intelligible, familiar, and acceptable.[141] Accepted by friends and families at a higher rate than had been the case years earlier, this GLBTQ generation had faced less discrimination, hatred, and isolation. The inclusion was most noticeable on the street. After a decade of radical activism, former Queer Nation spokesman Jay Blotcher recalled, "We were looking to younger people to pick up the mantle and it wasn't really happening. . . . A new generation came of age and said: 'I don't have to be a gay activist, I'm just a gay person. It doesn't have to be an issue.'"[142] The murder of twenty-one-year-old Shepard was a threat to this generational vision of equality.

Interviews with and news stories about GLBTQ youth revealed the shock brought on by Shepard's death. In a submission to the *Advocate* twenty-two-year-old Shawn Harden acknowledged that the murder "instilled fear and grief in all gays and lesbians . . . especially on college campuses."[143] Colleges, in fact, became the loci for similar remembering frames as "Shepard could have been any of the hundreds of thousands of other gay and lesbian students." Despite feeling no homophobia at his school in Tennessee, twenty-year-old Chad Hughes told the *Advocate* he had to change his actions: "Right after what happened [to Shepard], I was a little more cautious, and I think a lot of gay people were." Twenty-one-year-old Amy Warren corroborated this feeling, thinking of Shepard at college in northern Arizona: "We were all in shock after the murder, and for a long time I think people were afraid and careful of their actions in public."[144] These young GLBTQ people used this newfound sense of division to take action. Students on college campuses raised awareness, started organizations, came out, and took to the streets. For example, Jared Roper, after dealing with the fear resulting from Shepard's death, came out of the closet "to provide resources and support for anyone who needs them."[145] A marcher in New York, while not surprised that many older gay friends were present, observed enthusiastically that "there were lots of young people at the rally on Fifth Avenue."[146] In remembering Shepard, many queer youth recognized for the first time that they were not quite the same as their heterosexual peers.

Along with generation and geography, the queer counterpublic also fired warning shots about complacency, highlighting the need for recognizing division after Shepard.[147] After the height of the domestic HIV/AIDS crisis, the radical and vigilant edge of the GLBTQ community had gone dull. Implied in such inaction was the belief that identification with the wider public had been achieved and, along with it, an emerging security. In the wake of Shepard's death, queers recognized that complacency had settled into their everyday lives. Marchers remembering Shepard in New York echoed this idea: there was "a sense that gay rights are there, that we are so much a part of the mainstream in so many ways, so visible, with so many role models on television. It's a bit of an illusion." One marcher, Thomas Rubble, also expressed this view in a *New York Times* interview: "Sometimes, in our little gay lives in the middle of America, I think we have forgotten that they kill us. . . . They hate us."[148] A complacent community had forgotten that real divisions between GLBTQ and straight people existed. They had lost their queer vigilance, and Shepard had died as a result. Even Shepard was framed as someone who had forgotten this division. Shepard's friend Kurt Scofield recalled in the *Advocate* that Shepard "was a very wonderful person who thought everybody was as pleasant as he was."[149] Boulden echoed this rhetoric of security in identification: "Matt told me how happy he was to be back home, how comfortable he felt in Laramie, and how safe he felt there compared to the big city. I was so happy to hear that because I had encouraged Matt to come home."[150] Implicit in these statements was the reality that everyone was not "pleasant"—that, in fact, a great deal of bigotry and hatred still existed in society. In failing to recognize this bigotry—at the core a sign of the division between the gay and straight worlds—Shepard lost his life. Whereas earlier, gays and lesbians had been aware of their separation from mainstream America and had thrived on it, GLBTQ people in the 1990s had too easily embraced a false identification. Shepard's murder was only one brilliant example of how forgetting divisions could be destructive; remembering him in the queer counterpublic became an occasion to place those continuing divisions front and center.

Conclusion

∎

On October 28, 2009, the Matthew Shepard and James Byrd, Jr., Hate Crimes Prevention Act was signed into law by President Barack Obama.[151] Almost eleven years after his murder and twenty-three years after the U.S. House of Representatives held its first hearing on antigay violence, public memories of Shepard had a persuasive effect on the state, yielding political results.[152] Yet, beyond laws, how Shepard was divergently remembered in the GLBTQ community has much to tell us.

Shepard's rememberings illustrate that queer monumentality need not be understood solely as a material phenomenon. While our study of Alexander Wood emphasized material markers as a key tool in the era of queer monumentality, Matthew Shepard's case demonstrates that durability can be achieved through other means. In Shepard's case the multiple and contradictory memories of Shepard shared in the public and counterpublic realms gave Shepard's memory greater attention, not lesser, assuring that he would not be forgotten or ignored. Similarly, foregrounding public guilt and shame about antigay violence and creating affiliative connections to heterosexual audiences placed Shepard's memory deep within the public consciousness, where it persists, by and large, today. Finally, persistent and reiterative remembering rhetorics within and between publics and counterpublics provided and continue to provide a form of eternity to Shepard's life. Queer monumentality's possibilities above and beyond the physical manifestations of the past hold great potential, but only if they are undertaken with vigilance.

Likewise, Shepard's remembrances as a victim of systemic violence, a saint, and a common man affirm the complex set of dimensions that constitute monumentality, generally, and queer monumentality, in particular. As Rehding makes clear, undertaking this kind of work with a strict monumental taxonomy is often more hindrance than help. Investigating monumental creations with a rigid check sheet can often obscure these rich texts, missing the joy monumentality can cultivate despite its weighty transgressions. However, when we substitute the study of *monuments* (object) for the study of *monumentality* (concept), durability and its material enactments can obfuscate monumentality's complexity. By contrast, discursive and symbolic approaches to monumentality in the Shepard case sidestep this issue, directing our attention to the other dimensions of monumentality that enrich queer public memory. In Shepard's case, in particular, the use of power, the heroification of the individual, and efforts to make his life before his murder inspirational and worthy of emulation all come to the fore as key ingredients to making Shepard a monumental figure. These other emphases do not denigrate durability's place in the queer turn to monumentality but enrich it, allowing us to glimpse with greater insight this newly evolving approach to the past.

Finally, queer monumentality's potential for prompting social change is noteworthy, but it also reminds us that this relatively new undertaking brings with it significant costs and limitations. In both the Wood and Shepard examples, these costs and limitations are meaningful. Holding up an individual white cisgendered gay man in the past as representative of a diverse and ever changing GLBTQ community in the present has evoked critical laughter and valid concern. Enshrining these individuals in static forms or affiliative gestures worries some GLBTQ people that the fluidity, effervescence, and dynamism at the heart of much of queer culture and life are at risk. Perhaps most disconcerting, monumentality—and its tendencies toward moralistic judgments, unification projects, and imperial dreams—has revealed uncomfortable impulses in its queer form to collapse valued and meaningful divisions between heteronormative society and GLBTQ life. Such concerns should give us pause. Luckily, in each case queers, transgender people, and others have managed to slow down, critique, and stupefy queer monumentality's more worrisome compulsions. Given the durability of queer monumentality's undertaking, such efforts have not been demobilized; nor should we necessarily reject monumentality's vital potential out of hand. Indeed, as we will see below, queer monumentality can succeed only if other approaches to queer pasts can keep the impulses to grandeur and eternity open to criticism and a bit humble. Nonetheless, as the era of queer monumentality grinds forward, opportunities to restrain its excesses may become fewer and the ability to mitigate its darker desires may wane. Therefore, we turn now to an important question: At what point do the costs of the turn to queer monumentality begin to outweigh the benefits?

CHAPTER 4

Imagining
GLBTQ
Americans

AT FIRST GLANCE, TEXTBOOKS APPEAR far removed from the monumental aims of memorials, commemorative sites, or texts circulating among publics in the modern media. When taken as individual artifacts, textbooks seems minor, trivial, everyday, prone to deterioration, and quickly outdated. Yet, when considered from a broader perspective, the millions of textbooks deeply embedded within our public-education systems have acutely monumental qualities. Produced for a consolidated market by a few major companies that cater to standards set by local, state, and national governments, public-school textbooks reiterate a limited set of perspectives on the human experience to countless students every year. Textbooks present authorized knowledge of who counts, what matters, and what is true with profound certitude, not just recounting but constituting a cultural epideictic that powerfully shapes our children's sense of reality. While any single textbook may have a relatively short lifespan, the rhetorics the books espouse and circulate to successive generations often change minimally, ensuring in near perpetuity ideological status quos that have stood the test of time. In short, textbooks have been and continue to be among the most powerful monumental forms of the last century. Because this is so, GLBTQ reformers have worked assiduously to include GLBTQ lives, for better or worse, within these rhetorical texts as part of the ongoing turn to queer monumentality.

However, marking GLBTQ lives within public schools and their attendant curriculums is much more difficult than it appears. Schools, in particular, are for Therese Quinn and Erica Meiner, "deeply, compulsively, heteronormative spaces."[1] Like heteronormativity generally, the heteronormative compulsions and obstacles erected in public education are multiple and variegated. Charles E. Morris III has recently elaborated some of the most pernicious of these challenges, including "interanimating" forms of violence, "copious silences," administrative hostilities, the equation of teaching with "recruiting," and a conscious and unconscious unwillingness to investigate the intersectional stakes of difference. In addition, Morris reminds us that even "strong commitments" to GLBTQ justice by educational advocates can often crumble in the face of "thresholds and inducements" that serve as a countervailing force against "rhetorical enactment."[2] Among these other challenges, textbooks—which play a key role in patrolling the borders of American identity and regulating the inclusion of marginalized groups within wider culture—present difficulties all their own. While many of these difficulties are resonant with apprehensions raised in other chapters of the present work, there is another different and particularly troublesome rhetoric already deeply entrenched within textbook's monumental forms: American nationalism.

The study of nationalism has been a prominent part of twentieth-century historical, political, and cultural thought. The international studies and nationalism scholar Benedict Anderson defines nationalism as "an imagined political community—and imagined as both inherently limited and sovereign."[3] In other words, Anderson conceives of nationalism as the creative and productive (that is, rhetorical) forces by which people come to "imagine" themselves as part of a large, contained group of persons, sharing a limited and specific set of characteristics and experiences, especially a common past and/or culture. In his germinal work *Imagined Communities* (1983), Anderson traces the development of nationalism during the eighteenth and nineteenth centuries and its subsequent circulation and alterations around the world in ways that highlight its rhetorical nature. Monumentality has been a key tool for securing nationalism in these contexts. Indeed, it is not coincidental that as nationalism grew in the nineteenth century, monumentality spread as well. The grand, heroic, and unifying dimensions of monumentality have proven invaluable to nationalistic projects, which found and constructed texts to hail, demarcate, and bind the once disparate people of a nation together. Nationalism and monumentality have been deeply intertwined for centuries in memorials, commemorative sites, flags, songs, parades, heritage celebrations, rituals—and school textbooks and curriculums.[4]

However, across the globe, while textbooks have regularly remembered heterosexual individuals at the center of national imaginings, they have also actively forgotten GLBTQ lives within those same national borders. This dynamic of remembering and forgetting is integral to how rhetorics of nationalism function. As numerous scholars have illustrated, memory has long been a key means for rhetorically constructing national imagining. Indeed, the construction of "Americanness" has been a formative dimension of interdisciplinary and rhetorical work in memory studies.[5] Likewise, forgetting has recently come into its own right as a highly rhetorical force for shaping public understanding of the nation. Anderson suggests that both forgetting and remembering are necessary for the successful imagining of a national community. As Anderson so well points out: "All profound changes in consciousness, by their very nature, bring with them characteristic amnesias. Out of such oblivions, in specific historical circumstances, spring narratives."[6] The rearticulation of national identity is one such "change in consciousness" ripe with fruitful forgettings. Rhetoricians studying the rhetorical construction of the nation have echoed this dynamic. M. Lane Bruner, for instance, suggests in his rhetorical analysis of national identity construction that "all forms of identification and the narratives that accompany them simultaneously create a field of absence, an Other, and/or forms of forgetfulness."[7] Likewise, Bradford Vivian forcefully argues that what he labels "public forgetting" can free communities from troublesome or traumatic pasts, allowing them to "begin anew." For Vivian public forgetting is "an equally rhetorical phenomenon" when compared to public memory, one that can "coin a *novel public idiom* with which the community's relation to its past, present, and future would be configured anew, or at least in profoundly altered ways."[8] In these assessments each articulation (or rather rearticulation) of national identity brings with it simultaneous erasures that make these new articulations consistent, viable, and believable. In this way we tend to insist upon stories of national identity, character, and culture that maintain what Walter R. Fisher labels "narrative rationality."[9]

While remembering/forgetting is vital to how nations are constructed, central to the process is who is doing the remembering and the forgetting. In the case of GLBTQ persons the fact that remembering and forgetting have almost exclusively been within the purview of heterosexual individuals is consequential for the way GLBTQ persons are understood within contemporary society. Returning to Fisher's narrative rationality, the most prominent narratives of the American nation told by heterosexual culture would put much unquestioned privilege at risk by acknowledging the full extent to which same-sex desire, homosexuality, and homosexual persons have been an important part of the past. In particular, "questions of consequence" may emerge, highlighting the benefits that accrue to people who adhere to the normative telling of the story.[10] Heterosexual history is rife with heterosexual adherents whose many privileges are made possible (consciously and unconsciously) by the forgetting of homosexual individuals from historical narratives. These privileges include: financial and material rewards for heterosexual couples based upon the assumption that heterosexual married relationships are and have always been the norm; privileges of leadership and power that can easily dispense with challengers who might identify otherwise; feelings of moral superiority and religious piety when homosexuals are marginalized as a few passing sinners; permission to assault and even kill sexual nonconformists that might threaten the logic of heterosexuality; and security that one's own sexual practices and identity are stable and secure. This list does not exhaust the privileges afforded to public heterosexual figures by forgetting GLBTQ people, but it points to just how dangerous and threatening disrupting this already existing narrative might be.

By the same token, given the way history is presented within ideological texts, including GLBTQ people in the monumental pasts described in school textbooks and curriculums is not just an act of historical correction; it may also bring with it cultural consequences. While some publicly heterosexual individuals have vigorously contested these consequences, GLBTQ advocates have suggested that the inclusion of their public memories in textbooks would have life-enhancing effects for both the GLBTQ community and heterosexual community alike. Among these benefits are increased self-confidence in gay and lesbian youth, broader appreciation for diversity and greater understanding by heterosexual students, a more accurate historical image, a decrease in bullying and harassment of gay and lesbian students, a decrease in hate crimes, increased support for same sex-marriage, reductions in the always high teen suicide rate among gays, lesbians, and transgender persons, and a more just and equitable culture.[11] Certainly, even many within the GLBTQ community are suspicious that textbook reform itself is capable of doing so much; however, such doubts have not assuaged certain GLBTQ advocates from making ongoing commitments to target textbooks regardless.[12]

With the stakes so high, GLBTQ reformers have actively undertaken efforts to rewrite the nationalistic rhetorics embedded in public school textbooks to make it possible for new generations of Americans to imagine their GLBTQ peers as part of their shared community. Nonetheless, inclusion into these monumental zones is not so easily achieved. This situation is largely because the nationalism at the center of most textbook rhetoric has principally defined GLBTQ people as antinational figures. As such, mere inclusion of GLBTQ people in textbook discourses—while promising productive outcomes in line with the aims of queer monumentality—is impossible without either dislodging nationalism from these texts (which is nearly impossible and would result in the continued abuse of historical homosexual figures) or compromising on which kind of GLBTQ lives are made recognizable in these monuments. Thus GLBTQ reformers find themselves caught in a double bind, forcing them to select among a variety of highly constrained and sometimes compromised rhetorical choices or face oblivion. This is not surprising given the way in which GLBTQ and other marginalized groups are positioned within hegemonic culture. As Lester C. Olson points out in his analysis of traumatic styles: "Advocates exemplifying traumatic styles [such as gay, lesbian, bisexual, and transgender people] have made risky decisions in negotiating multiple double binds understood as lose-lose options. . . . Whichever 'choice' speakers and their audiences may make in response to

unwelcome messages concerning yet another sexual assault, yet another violent act, yet another of the homicides affecting one of 'us'—however 'us' is
understood—the decision entails significant losses."[13] Making such choices
is not unique to textbook debates but is rather a reoccurring challenge faced
by GLBTQ actors in the turn to queer monumentality. As the oft quoted
Audre Lorde reminds us, "the master's tools will never dismantle the mater's
house," and monumentality, however refined, camped, or queered, will always retain some vestiges of its master status.[14] In the instance of textbook
reform, nationalism is one of those vestiges that bring to light the very real
constraints faced by queer monumentality. Exploring what drives these compromised choices and how the attendant losses of those choices influence
our move toward queer monumentality is of crucial importance.

   To explore these questions, it is useful to examine the choices made by
an evolving coalition of GLBTQ advocates in California from 2006 to 2012 to
counter heterosexual culture's forgetting of GLBTQ lives and communities.
These GLBTQ reformers are neither the first nor the only advocates to undertake GLBTQ-affirmative textbook reform; however, the currency of their
campaign, the reputation of California as a "laboratory" of democracy, and
the reformers' direct efforts to grapple with nationalism make this a powerful
case study for analysis.[15] The texts at the center of this undertaking are the
monumental rhetorics within public school textbooks, curriculums, and instructional materials, and a central question is how they might be reformed
to represent GLBTQ people in meaningful ways. Textbooks and related materials are a deeply understudied set of artifacts by rhetorical critics; nonetheless, they remain a vital arena for constructing nationalism that is both
highly rhetorical and critically important to explaining how GLBTQ persons
do or do not enter the national imagination.

   Foundational to the study of elements of the wider movement for
GLBTQ inclusion within the California public school curriculum are fragments of discourse collected from public speeches and remarks, statements,
press releases, publications, and media coverage of the campaign. While
representational claims might be more ideally described by examining the
textbooks and curriculums that resulted from this advocacy movement, it is
important to note that no part of the movement described herein has been
fully realized at the time of this writing. Nonetheless, the rich discourse
reconstituted here represents the rhetorical imaginings of different voices in
this effort in ways that telegraph their shared and divergent rhetorical wishes
sufficiently for critical analysis.

   Before proceeding it is important to note that, despite this book's focus
on public memory, the preoccupation of the California advocates seems to
be on the distinctly different issue of history. Because this is true, an examination of history textbooks in public schools might seem to suggest that

memory has little place. However, as Pierre Nora noted, it is because history is so "problematic and incomplete" that memory's role becomes entirely necessary.[16] While gaps in history can result from limitations of access, archives, and understanding, many of history's absences (generally and within public school textbooks) are also a result of intentional erasures, misrepresentations, and forgettings in favor of supporting the privileges of dominant culture—those, incidentally, usually doing the history writing. Thus in certain key ideological zones within culture (such as schools), history's incompleteness is a rhetorical choice, not a disciplinary necessity. If this is true, it is possible to use memories to complete or at least to supplement the already incomplete history we teach our children. This is what GLBTQ advocates in California have done: attempt to state in public their shared memories of GLBTQ people both to draw attention to the forgettings foisted upon public school children and to ameliorate history's incompleteness with a different way of imagining of the past.

Textbooks as Tools of the Nation
∎

Over the last one hundred years textbooks have become pervasive, highly rhetorical texts capable of broadly influencing public perception. This has not always been true. For centuries textbooks were rarities in many classrooms and, when they were available, issues of printing, cost, and distribution gave textbooks only isolated effects on reading publics.[17] However, during the twentieth century, as efforts to create greater conformity in public education gained momentum, textbooks became an important tool for consistently educating tomorrow's citizens within large national contexts. Today the ten-billion-dollar-a-year textbook industry is a vital component of the American public school system.[18] Given their pervasiveness and ideological character, textbooks are also a contentious front in the culture wars for shaping images of American identity and society.

Several factors contribute to making textbooks highly rhetorical texts. One key to textbooks' suasory power is their implied position of authority within the cultural institutions of the classroom, the community, and the nation. According to David R. Olson, textbooks "are taken as the authorized version of a society's valid knowledge."[19] Those who read and teach textbooks situate their information as certain and characterize textbooks as places where answers to questions can be found with great reliability. This belief is common because textbooks are generally not seen as political texts. Because the selection of textbooks is often made by administrators, school boards, and others within government who are generally viewed as having less overt political motivations, textbooks' rhetorical imaginings can be easily overlooked by the average consumer. Consequently, textbooks are often read

with less critical thought than other media, such as magazines or newspapers.[20] These rhetorical stakes make the way information is presented within
textbooks even more critical.

In addition, textbooks actively engage in rhetorical acts. Like all texts,
textbooks deploy various rhetorics to shape how their content is understood
and interpreted by the audience. Textbooks present content in specific ways,
giving them "rhetorical forms" that influence how they are used and interpreted by students and teachers.[21] As Kenneth Burke has suggested, a text's
success can rely on its ability to structure an argument that allows audience
members to feel as if they are "creatively participating" in the author's argument. Examples of textbook forms vary; however, many history textbooks, in
particular, utilize the formal rhetorical device of climax to craft a Hegelian
understanding of the past as perpetually in progressive forward motion.[22]

While the inclusion of certain rhetorical forms can make textbooks more
appealing to users, the books can simultaneously contain invisible or unnoticed ideologies in need of critical attention. Consider the use of visual images within textbooks. While the inclusion of photographs can aid in making
text more understandable to readers, who is or is not represented in those
photographs and how those individuals are represented can have a profound
effect on the interpretation of textbook content. For example, an empirical
analysis of American government textbooks in 2000 found that visual representations of the poor and impoverished disproportionately represented them
as African American, reinforcing a false stereotype within the wider culture.[23]
Similar charges have been made against popular public-speaking textbooks
that promote values of inclusion, diversity, and equality in written discourse
but contradict those claims in their nonverbal messages, particularly their
photographs.[24] Common rhetorical devices such as absence/presence, invisible metadiscourses, representative anecdotes, terministic screens, and the
like not only shape the interpretation of topics but can also erase certain people and events from history. One of the most prominent invisible ideologies
in textbooks is American nationalism.

Textbooks have long been favored tools to construct and reconstruct
the nation. Writing in the 1980s, John C. Reynolds argued that "the nation
is the most consistent unit of political organization in human affairs at the
present time and textbooks are the most consistent means of maintaining the
elements of nationalism for future generations."[25] The narratives, memories,
and images presented in textbooks highlight for students integral ways of
considering and imagining the nation. Textbooks fit securely into what the
Frankfurt School has labeled the "culture industry," which shapes a unified,
ideologically infused mass culture to perpetuate the status quo (that is, capi-
talism) at the expense of the consumer.[26] This connection is clear from Louis
Althusser's description of schools as institutions that teach "know-how" in

"forms which ensure *subjection to the ruling ideology* or the mastery of its 'practice,'" including national and state ideologies.[27] For the rhetorician Michael Calvin McGee, classrooms are powerful means of interpolating people into these ideologies, because they are the "very first contact most have with their existence and experience as a part of a community." In classrooms we encounter "ideographic touchstones" as epideictic experiences, preparing us to act and make judgments as members of our community.[28]

In concert with this critical orientation to textbooks, numerous academic analyses illustrate the overwhelming persuasive force of these artifacts in the public school system. Jean Anyon details how textbooks are particularly adept at passing on conservative values about the nation in discussions of social and economic ideas.[29] Textbooks can clarify who is a part of the national community and who is outside of it; they also dictate who can be recognized as a worthy contributor and who bears additional burdens to claim any space or recognition.[30] Images and maps in textbooks are decisive for visualizing what nationals look like and who makes up the nation's imagined community.[31] The literary theorist and critic Terry Eagleton notes that what is stated and what is unstated in these books is crucial for reflecting national values. He claims: "These absences—the *'not said'* of the work—are precisely what bind it to its ideological problematic: ideology is present in the text in the form of its eloquent silences."[32] Because this is so, textbooks are a critical component of any nationalist agenda, and textbook content has been a common topic for controversy in nationalist debates.[33]

Among other topics, sexuality has been a source of ongoing controversy in textbook reform. While the California textbook debates of the 2000s are an important turning point for GLBTQ representations in education, they are not the first cultural clashes to take place over the topic of sexuality in public curriculums. As the rhetorician Robin E. Jensen has demonstrated, debates over how to teach people about sexuality and protect them from disease and unwanted pregnancies have extended at least back until the late 1800s.[34] And more recent debates about the topic of homosexuality in education specifically have generated noticeable controversy.

While little scholarly attention was paid to GLBTQ textbook representations prior to 2000, there has been some quantitative work in this area completed by scholars in education. The vast majority of these studies focused on GLBTQ representations in college-level textbooks. For example, a 2007 article revealed limited discussion of gays and lesbians as "'another' structurally disempowered group" in the seventeen top-selling "Introduction to U.S. Politics" texts.[35] Meanwhile, in April 2008 a textbook analysis in "Foundations of Education" classes revealed that while GLBTQ issues were discussed in all introductory textbooks in the state of California, the textbooks generally further pathologized the GLBTQ community as understandable only as victims of abuse, violence, and discrimination rather than, more precisely and accurately, pathologizing the publicly heterosexual individuals who act in such damaging ways toward others.[36] Analysis of elementary, middle, and high-school textbooks is virtually absent, because there are very few such representations to be analyzed.

Despite limited representations of GLBTQ people in textbooks to date, clashes over their inclusion have occurred frequently in the last thirty years. A key site of controversy between GLBTQ activists and textbook gatekeepers has been health and human sexuality textbooks. According to an article surveying the conflict over issues of sexuality in education in the *New York Times,* "chief among the targets [of conservative activists] are sex education programs that include discussions of homosexuality."[37] The health implications of same-sex sexuality (and sexuality in general) have long been a dispute in the culture war. Particularly with the emergence of HIV/AIDS the need for and limits of sex education in public schools grew as a contentious topic of debate. Principal among these concerns (along with safe-sex practices, condom use and distribution, premarital sex, and so on) has been what, if any, commentary such courses should make on issues related to same-sex desire. This debate was heightened further in 2000 as the administration of President George W. Bush took an extremely conservative view of sex education, encouraging abstinence-only sex-education programs, many of which were discredited by independent groups for their vast mischaracterization of the reasons for and consequences of nonheterosexual practices.[38] It seems that many supporters of this policy (primarily within the Republican Party) seemed quite content to restrict access to information on sexuality in public schools, simultaneously mobilizing voters who shared their ideology and doing great harm to a generation of children unprepared for and unaware of the real joys and dangers in sexual activity.

A similar debate relating to GLBTQ representation in textbooks emerged in the realm of college admissions. In late 2005 the University of California rejected the high-school credits of several applicants who had attended the private Calvary Chapel Christian School. The basis of their rejection was that the textbooks the school used in many of their classes had a slanted or inaccurate view of certain subjects, particularly issues related to science and sexuality. An often cited example was the textbook *Biology for Christian Schools* which argued that any scientific "fact" that did not conform to the teachings of the Bible was wrong. Another frequently noted example was the textbook *United States History for Christian Schools* which argued that some social movements were "less legitimate" than others, particularly the gay and lesbian rights movement. To quote the textbook: "One of the worst [of these illegitimate social movements] was the 'gay rights' movement, in which homosexuals tried to remove legal protections to their immoral lifestyle and to gain recognition of homosexual 'marriages' for purposes of adoption and the like."[39] This highly problematic characterization of gays and lesbians reflects how deeply ideological educational instruction can be and was very disconcerting for many institutions of higher learning.

These previous controversies demonstrate that GLBTQ representation in textbooks has been and continues to be a pressing issue in the contemporary American culture wars. However, these previous debates differ from the controversies examined below because they revolve around certain characteristics markedly different from the California textbook debate's uniquely nationalist contours. In part, these differences emerge from the long history in which publicly heterosexual Americans and institutions defined gays and lesbians as de facto "un-American," "traitors," and antinationals within American discourse.

Rhetorics of Gays and Lesbians as Antinationals

As Kenneth Burke has noted, collective identities are often formed by resonant identifications among group members and also by active rhetorical moves that divide these collectivities from others who are labeled different.[40] Nations and national identities are perhaps the most recognizable examples of these identifying and dividing groups, drawing lines both along geographic, cultural, and historical boundaries and between persons to constitute and maintain their distinctive characters. Those who find themselves separated from the nation are often situated as scapegoats, symbolically endowed with the deficiencies of the community and sacrificed and/or punished (sometimes violently) to restore the community's unity.[41] Within the American context GLBTQ persons and their various precursors have often been among the most useful groups of people to serve the national project as scapegoats.

Early documents of the republic demonstrate that defining what it meant to be American was often achieved at the exclusion of sexual minorities akin to contemporary gays and lesbians. As Jonathan Ned Katz's pioneering work in GLBTQ history establishes, early conceptions of the American nation characterized sodomites not just as immoral or illegal but also as corruptive antinational figures. Quoting a 1782 edition of the British newspaper the *Whip*, Katz reveals how early Republican sodomites were not accepted as bona fide native-born Americans but rather were seen as "foreigners" sullied by European (particularly French) ideas: "These 'horrible offences' are 'foreign to our shores—to our nature they certainly are—yet they are growing apace in New York.'" In Katz's interpretation, "American nationalism was constructed at the expense of foreigners, including foreign sodomites. Acts of sodomy, *The Whip* suggested, were alien to American's 'nature,' another early version of the idea that sodomites' psyches differed substantially from those of ordinary men."[42] Katz goes on to claim that Walt Whitman encountered similar assertions about the "foreign" nature of same-sex desires several decades later and actively tried to counter them.[43] Framing sexual minorities as antinational is not a uniquely American undertaking. The historian George L. Mosse has demonstrated that comparable descriptions of homosexuality, sodomy, and so on have been defined as antinational acts and identities in several European historical contexts.[44]

However, while gays, lesbians, and their various precursors have been cast as contrary to the nation since the beginning of nation states, the twentieth century saw those divisions take on new degrees of explicitness and fervor. Indeed, the last century clearly established just how self-serving and delusional these discourses could be in order to maintain the façade and privileges associated with the heteronormative ideal. For instance, George Chauncey notes that the bohemian men of 1920s Greenwich Village were "regarded as unmanly as well as un-American" because of their decided disinterest in getting married and making money, coupled with their deep interest in art, long hair, and colorful clothes.[45] Such dramatic disconnects are frequent not only in American history but also in the history of other nations, illustrating just how quickly nationalist discourses can turn on GLBTQ persons who seek to protect and ensure the nation. One powerful example is Alan Turing, a British gay man, unmatched code breaker, and father of contemporary computer science who recently gained renewed attention as the subject of the 2014 Oscar-nominated film *The Imitation Game*. Given his significant contributions to science and the war effort, Turing became a national hero in the years following World War II. However, in 1952, just a few years after the end of the war, Turing was prosecuted for "gross indecency," stripped of his security clearances, and chemically castrated after admitting to sexual acts with other men. Turing would commit suicide shortly thereafter, in 1954.[46] It would take nearly sixty years for Turing to win a full pardon from the British crown.[47] Nonetheless, his case demonstrates compellingly the lengths to which heteronormative privilege will go—even to illogical and inconsistent extremes—to protect its supremacy. Similar shocking and degrading examples relating specifically to American constructions of GLBTQ persons as threats to the nation have been prominent in recent decades, particularly in national-security debates and the response to HIV/AIDS.

Perhaps the first profound interaction between sexuality and American nationalist discourses in the twentieth century emerged during the Cold War. In a period of heightened nationalist feelings and demands for public displays of patriotism (particularly during the McCarthy Era), GLBTQ people were often maligned in political and popular discourse as anti-American. As

Alan Sinfield suggests: "The Cold War made it especially necessary to control sexual dissidence for, even more than battle conditions, it depended on the ideological—spiritual, moral—determination of U.S. people. . . . Queers . . . undermined family values and the frontier vision of the manly man."[48] As primary domestic targets, gays, lesbians, and other "sexual deviants" were often accused of un-American activities by Cold War principals such as FBI director J. Edgar Hoover, Senator Joseph McCarthy, and U.S. attorney George Morris Fay.[49] While little evidence suggests that gays and lesbians were more prone to being traitors than heterosexuals, such characterizations of the GLBTQ community served a vital purification purpose for a paranoid and suspicious nation. One way in which this purification process becomes visible in American discourse is the myth of the homosexual traitor.[50] According to this construction, GLBTQ persons were adept liars, kept bad associations, were ungodly, and were easy to turn against the nation of their birth because of their many secrets. A popular case used by antigay activists, politicians, and government officials to support this myth is the Martin-Mitchell Affair.

William Hamilton Martin and Bernon Mitchell were two National Security Agency (NSA) code breakers who became infamous in 1960 for defecting to the Soviet Union. A major act of international espionage and treason (and a public embarrassment for the United States), Martin and Mitchell's betrayal was repeatedly justified by government and political leaders as springing from the men's (homo)sexuality. In particular, a 1962 report by the House Un-American Activities Committee suggested that Martin was "sexually abnormal; in fact, a masochistic," and that Mitchell's psychiatrist had testified that he "has had homosexual problems."[51] The report labeled the men "sexual deviants" (that is, homosexual) despite their public statements in a press conference in Moscow that they had defected for ideological reasons. Evidence for the government's belief about the supposed connection between homosexuality and traitorous activity emerged in its response to the scandal: soon after Martin and Mitchell defected twenty-six National Security Agency employees would be forced out because of potential "perversions."[52] Followed by a wave of firings at the State Department, the case was a leading reason for major revisions to national-security protocols and recruitment practices. The goal of these revisions was simple: to eliminate antinationalist "deviants" from accessing the U.S. government in the future. Nor were politicians alone in this antinational framing. Major newspapers and media of the day (including the *Los Angeles Times*, the Hearst papers, and *Washington Confidential*) reaffirmed and circulated these beliefs to a wider audience, often fanning the flames of hatred and suspicion. The case became the representative anecdote for conservative politicians, military leaders, and intelligence officials that homosexuals could not be trusted. Perhaps ironically, an exposé by *Seattle Weekly* in 2007 revealed that an internal CIA investigation at the time of the Martin-Mitchell affair found no evidence to support the claim that the two men were homosexual or lovers.[53] Though less blunt in style, these rhetorical characterizations persist in the present. Even today many U.S. security institutions remain highly suspicious of, if not openly discriminatory against, GLBTQ persons, despite more recent efforts to attend to this unequal treatment.[54] Because this is true nonnormative sexuality can remain a major red flag in obtaining national security clearances. At stake in continuing such policies are potent forms of heterosexual privilege, including access to classified information and assignments, as well as power, prestige, benefits, and the ability to use the levers of government against GLBTQ persons through isolation, surveillance, and suspicion. Ironically, even GLBTQ people who manage to win access to the ranks of the privileged often find themselves forced to choose complicity, hiding their identity to advance and thereby contributing to the erasure of GLBTQ people from nationalist memory.

In addition to the Cold War, the HIV/AIDS crisis played a prominent part in shaping antinationalist views of the GLBTQ community. During the 1980s characterizations of HIV/AIDS as "the wrath of God on homosexuals" and "nature's revenge on gay men" shaped perceptions of GLBTQ persons as deeply antireligious. Though religion may not be aligned with all forms of nationalism and national identity, a Christian religious piety is the cornerstone for some influential narratives of American nationalism. Another distinct but similar discourse is civil religion—"a collection of beliefs, symbols, and rituals with respect to sacred things and institutionalized in [the particularly American] collectivity"—which is also a pervasive resource within American rhetoric and politics.[55] This has been particularly true in the contemporary Christian Right. According to Anatol Lieven, "the meetings, propaganda, and rhetoric of the Christian Right [have] always been suffused with nationalism and national symbolism."[56] This connection between religious devotion and American nationalism was deeply rooted in the Christian Right when it came to power in 1980, just prior to the visible beginnings of the HIV/AIDS crisis. These fervently religious imaginings of American identity were espoused most prominently in the civil-religion rhetoric of President Ronald Reagan and reflected in the administration's response to the HIV/AIDS crisis.[57]

During the height of the epidemic the Reagan Administration remained publicly silent about HIV/AIDS and privately worked to enforce this silence, particularly during the years when the primary victims of the disease were gay men—going so far as to instruct the press not to ask questions concerning the disease during press conferences. C. Everett Koop, the Reagan administration's surgeon general, characterized the politics that drove this active silence in the White House: "I knew that telling the truth about AIDS, the truth, the whole truth, and nothing but the truth would not be well received in some places. One of those places would be the White House, at least in those offices where ideology would be the main concern. . . . A large portion of the president's constituency was antihomosexual, antidrug abuse, antipromiscuity, and antisex education; these people would not respond well to some of the things that would have to be said in a health report about AIDS."[58] As Tina L. Perez and George N. Dionisopoulos demonstrated, the White House, for expressly political motivations that included an antigay agenda, engaged in a rhetoric of "presidential silence" that enabled "the belief that 'somehow people from certain groups, deserved their illness' . . . to continue unchallenged from the great moral bully-pulpit that is—or should be—the Oval Office."[59] While silence itself need not necessarily label the largely gay male victims of HIV/AIDS as un-American, the president's neglect even to acknowledge these victims' existence and his decision actively to avoid presidential discourse on the matter suggested that the administration did not consider HIV/AIDS victims Americans or citizens. If this was the case, President Reagan may have felt that, despite personally knowing gay men who died of HIV/AIDS, he had no responsibility to these people.[60] Thankfully, others disagreed. Not surprisingly, many of these critiques came from the political left. For example, Representative Henry Waxman (D-CA) attacked Reagan's lack of response to HIV/AIDS in an editorial in the *Washington Post* in 1985: "It is surprising that the president could remain silent as 6,000 *Americans* died, that he could fail to acknowledge the epidemic's existence. Perhaps his staff felt he had to, since many of his New Right supporters have raised money by campaigning against homosexuals."[61] However, after years of silence in which 20,000 Americans died of the disease and 1 to 1.5 million others were infected, the administration's silence was finally broken, but not by the president. In 1986 Surgeon General Koop, against administration orders and without approval, released a thirty-six page report on the disease at a news conference.[62] In the ensuing days Koop managed to successfully shatter the silence of the administration, eventually leading the president himself to speak out, though with minimal comment.[63] While no one in the administration expressly characterized the overwhelmingly gay male victims of HIV/AIDS as un-American (and therefore unworthy of assistance), the blatant inaction of the federal government and its supporting institutions in the face of such a destructive public-health crisis inspired such a belief among many GLBTQ people, HIV/AIDS victims, their allies, and supporters. HIV/AIDS and the Cold War both significantly contributed to defining GLBTQ persons as outside of the American nation in the twentieth century.

This short review demonstrates the complex political situation advocates of textbook reform faced in their challenges to rethink the California public school curriculum. Textbooks served as a representational hinge upon which active critiques of nationalist ideologies continually opposed to GLBTQ inclusion could be made. Recognizing this opportunity, GLBTQ educators and allies in California embarked on this critique beginning in the 1980s by seeking to demonstrate both that the GLBTQ community consisted of worthy people and that the nation had wrongly mistreated them. Largely embracing a tactical and ephemeral memory approach which sought to enshrine criticism of heteronormative American nationalism into the public school curriculum, gay, lesbian, and bisexual activists achieved some success. This was particularly true after the emergence of the HIV/AIDS crisis when "factual, substantiated discussion" about homosexuality for middle and high school was made permissible in California health classes. Materials were also made available for voluntary individual usage, and gay, lesbian, and bisexual books in public school libraries were increased.[64] Nonetheless, early gay, lesbian, and bisexual activists saw little progress in regard to their broader goals of GLBTQ-affirmative historical representations in curriculums. Heteronormativity prevailed and the GLBTQ past remained hidden to school-aged audiences, both heterosexual and homosexual. Recognizing that this was the case and turning their organizational strength elsewhere, curricular reformers let their efforts ebb by the late 1990s. It would not be until almost ten years later that a different approach to revise textbooks and curriculums would be undertaken—with greater potential for acceptance but also posing greater risk to queer public memory.

The Bias-Free Curriculum: 2006–2012
■

A few years after the earliest efforts to reform California textbooks and curriculums, GLBTQ rights movement advocates shifted focus to other issues of concern in the new millennium. This remained the case until the issue of same-sex marriage rocked California in the middle of the first decade of the twenty-first century. With same-sex marriage legalized (at least for a time in California), the prospects of GLBTQ-affirming social change seemed unlimited, and interest in further refining historical representations of GLBTQ people in California public schools regained momentum.[65] At the behest of and in coordination with the nonprofit group Equality California, a wave of reformers more fully and publicly engaged the debate. Indicative of this movement, in 2006, S.B. 1437: "The Bias-Free Curriculum Act" came to the floor of the California legislature. The bill, written and introduced by openly lesbian state senator Sheila Kuehl, sought to prevent discrimination against GLBTQ people in public school curriculums and activities, as well as teaching materials, and mandated that all instructional material, particularly textbooks, "portray the contributions of people who are lesbian, gay, bisexual or transgender to the economic, political, and social development of the state and the country."[66]

Since earlier groups had found little success in previous efforts to in-clude GLBTQ people explicitly within the California curriculum, Kuehl, Equality California, and other advocates pursued their reforms on a differ-ent rhetorical track. Like earlier reformers, contemporary advocates believed that including GLBTQ figures in the state's curriculum and its supporting materials would be a net-positive achievement; thus their approach fell well in line with the turn to queer monumentality. However, this same approach largely foreclosed criticisms of the curriculum that had been so central to the more tactic-heavy movement of the 1980s. Instead contemporary advo-cates focused their attention on aligning their vision of the GLBTQ past with the monumental rhetoric of nationalism already deeply inscribed into the ideology of public school education.

Several scholars have noted the key role rhetorics of nationalism play in defining the center of American society. Most specifically, Laura C. Prividera and John W. Howard III have argued that, in conjunction with masculinity and whiteness, nationalism "define[s] group membership and rank accord-ing to their location relative to an elusive 'ideological center.'" Drawing on the work of Raka Shome, they suggest "the further one is from the "ideal" (or archetypal) national, the more foreign, impure, and, ultimately, untrust-worthy a person becomes."[67] Thus being labeled a national brings with it a powerful set of discursive resources that enhance an individual or group's power, access, and respectability with significant social and political conse-quences. However, being labeled a national also requires participation in a series of intertwined rhetorics that reaffirm the established power structure, often at the expense of those labeled as marginal or other. For GLBTQ advo-cates efforts to participate in the rhetoric of nationalism were extremely risky and presented a troubling double bind. On the one hand, they could par-ticipate in the rhetoric of nationalism and gain a degree of visibility despite the fact that this visibility could be costly and representationally damaging and could further affirm the hegemonic status quo. On the other hand, not participating in this rhetoric would likely be met with the same failure earlier confrontational reform efforts had experienced; advocates also believed that textbook invisibility would further perpetuate a worrisome rise in violence, bullying, and suicide for GLBTQ youth. Making a difficult choice, the ad-vocates embraced a rhetorical imagining that sought to represent historical GLBT people as aligned with and in support of American nationalism. Key to this effort was constructing compelling "rhetorics of contribution."

Rhetorics of National Contribution

∎

Rhetorics of contribution are pervasive within GLBTQ advocates' discourse about S.B. 1437 and its subsequent iterations. In almost every accounting of the bill, the language of "contribution" appears prominently, in print media, on television, or online. For instance, the *Los Angeles Times* said the legislation would "require that the historical contributions of homosexuals in the United States be taught in California schools."[68] The *Washington Times* reiterated this point: "a bill . . . would require public schools to teach students in all grades about the contributions homosexuals, bisexuals, and transsexuals have made to society."[69] A *San Francisco Chronicle* headline reads: "Senate OKs bill on gays in textbooks, Emotions run high about teaching their contributions."[70] The *New York Times,* the *Advocate,* and coverage on MSNBC and Fox News all echoed the legislation's contributory sentiment, often quoting the bill directly.[71] Therefore, from the very first reporting, mediated discourses about the legislation pinpointed the language of contribution as central to comprehending the debate.

The language of "contribution" essential to the legislation was so critical, not just because it was the pivot point upon which these debates hinged but also because it illuminated two different dimensions of what the advocates hoped to accomplish. First, "contribution" signaled to everyone that, if passed, the legislation would require GLBTQ people to be highlighted positively and affirmatively rather than in negative ways. Clearly, the bill's authors recognized the overwhelmingly negative characterizations of GLBTQ people in most dominant historical representations, particularly with regard to nationalism. By emphasizing that the bill would require teaching GLBTQ people's "contributions," advocates hoped both to halt and to preempt discussions of GLBTQ people or their predecessors that might reinforce earlier negative views. In short, if this legislation passed, advocates argued, it would mean the queer past could only be discussed as "good," "valuable," and "important." The reformers made this intent plain in their discussion of the legislation. For instance, Kuehl suggested that her bill would make clear to schoolchildren, in many ways for the first time, "the fact that somebody who did something good was a gay person."[72] Elsewhere, she argued, "acknowledging that lesbian, gay, bisexual, and transgender people have made valuable contributions" to history was crucial.[73] Other reformers echoed this claim, encouraging students to learn "about the accomplishments" of GLBTQ people in the past.[74] These accomplishments would do important rhetorical work in an otherwise desolate representational vacuum. To quote Kuehl further, if schools are "silent about the diversity of talented people who were important in California, the impression is that only white, straight men did anything important. That leaves virtually everyone else in school believing their talents may not be sufficient."[75] However, while this change would be a representational victory for reformers, simply requiring that school materials not discriminate against GLBTQ persons would do little to further the aims of the reformers. The change served only to prevent more blatant assaults on GLBTQ people in the curriculum—a feat in itself but not a means of advance for the cause of GLBTQ rights and equality.

In a second and more important dimension of the discourse, the language of contribution emphasized that GLBTQ people would be represented in history as willing and active participants in the national project, aligning them with the monumental rhetorics of the wider public and potentially earning them a degree of representation and power. This assumption reflected in the language differed significantly from those of earlier tactic-oriented critics who, while advocating for recognizing and recovering the achievements of gay, lesbian, and bisexual individuals, did not necessarily position those achievements as supportive of the status quo of American power. By contrast, the way in which contemporary advocates attempted to represent their vision of the GLBTQ past implied a significantly more circumscribed view, favoring those individuals in the past with palatable historical achievements as their preferred choices. These choices then factored heavily into shaping GLBTQ people of the past as active contributors to American nationalism. Two prominent rhetorical approaches made the largest impact in this regard: narrowing the range of worthy GLBTQ representations and aligning GLBTQ people with other minority identities.

Textbook reformers heavily circumscribed the range of GLBTQ people worthy of public remembrance in their public statements about the legislation to recall and represent only those figures of prominent "American" identity.[76] While earlier calls to revise the curriculum foregrounded a diverse and international assortment of gays and lesbians as exemplary figures to be included in public school instruction—including the Aztec leader Montezuma II, the Japanese author Yukio Mishima, and the Spanish poet Federico García Lorca—by contrast, contemporary advocates specified U.S. citizenship as the benchmark of representational significance. This narrow perspective is reflected in the fact that every example reform advocates offered in public remarks could claim American nationality, in line with the precise mandates of the legislation. Any other approach would promote historical GLBTQ people who might be antithetical to American values. Consider the figures mentioned above, offered by advocates in the 1980s: Montezuma was an indigenous American who stood in the way of colonial "progress"; Mishima led an attempted coup d'état in 1970 to restore the Japanese emperor deposed by the United States during World War II; and Lorca was a Spanish nationalist with complicated politics. As interesting historical GLBTQ people, each man fits the bill; however, their nationalistic allegiances were disqualifying, further illustrating how ideologically driven textbooks really are. To avoid similar problems, the textbook reformers of this century largely omitted sexual minorities with international and transnational qualities from the discussion. Instead, by limiting their focus to American figures, contemporary reformers were able to align their envisioned curriculum with the nationalist project implicitly, circumventing challenges that might arise.[77]

Reformers also attempted to align their exemplary GLBTQ figures to be included in the new curriculum with other ethnic-identity groups who had won inclusion into the canon of American nationalist heroes. Such an effort has been a regular rhetorical approach in American political discourse. Several scholarly analyses of memory and nationalism highlight how racial and ethnic minorities sought to incorporate themselves into mainstream civic nationalisms.[78] Meanwhile, the historian Jonathan Zimmerman, commenting on the S.B. 1437 controversy, reminds us that "in the 1920s, when antiimmigrant sentiment was at its zenith, a wide range of ethnic groups fought to insert their own heroes into America's grand national narrative. Polish Americans demanded that textbooks include Thaddeus Kosciusko, the Polish nobleman who aided our revolution; Jewish Americans pressed for Haym Solomon, a merchant who helped finance it; and blacks celebrated Crispus Attucks, the first American to die in it. . . . German Americans wanted textbooks to include Molly Pitcher. Why? You guessed it: she was German! Her birth name, some said, was Maria Ludwig; and eventually, thanks to German pressure, the textbooks said so as well. Germans also claimed Abraham Lincoln as one of their own."[79] John Bodnar's account of "remaking" America echoes this claim, detailing how a diverse range of immigrants in the early part of the twentieth century urged and created "programs that praised both immigrant contributions to America and immigrant heritage" as part of "a more subtle strain of Americanization."[80] GLBTQ reformers found California particularly amenable to a similar strategy since state laws had guaranteed the inclusion of racial, ethnic, and religious minorities (among others) in their textbooks since the 1980s.[81]

However, because GLBTQ communities have not always been characterized as an ethnic identity akin to Latino or Irish individuals, adopting a similar rhetoric proved challenging. Certainly, some GLBTQ people understood their community in exactly this way. According to the sociologist Steven Epstein, "gays in the 1970s increasingly came to conceptualize themselves as a legitimate minority group, having a certain quasi-'ethnic' status, and deserving the same protections against discrimination that are claimed by other groups in our society."[82] Indeed, this view persists as a basic assumption underlying some gay and lesbian politics today. Nonetheless, for numerous people on the political left and right same-sex desire, gender nonconformity, and the cultures that surround them are something profoundly different from an ethnic identity. Many social conservatives believe that homosexuality is a decision or lifestyle; meanwhile, many self-described queers reject static and "essentialist" identities in favor of fluid wants and desires. As different as these views are, both sides were more inclined to see sexuality as less inherent and more transient. As a result, if GLBTQ advocates sought to bring their community into line with other Americanized identities, they would have to build a case for those parallels. Advocates did so by making analogic connections between GLBTQ people and other identity groups in their public comments.[83]

This move is frequently visible in accounts of the controversy. In an article in the *San Francisco Chronicle* it was noted that when critics raged against GLBTQ inclusion, "supporters countered that textbooks should include the contributions of gays and lesbians just as they are required to contain those of other minority groups."[84] An interview with Geoffrey Kors of Equality California in the *Los Angeles Times* linked GLBTQ movements with other social movements: "If you're teaching social movements in schools, and you talk about the United Farm Workers and Cesar Chavez, and you talk about the civil rights movement and Martin Luther King, and you talk about the women's suffrage movement, to leave out the gay rights movement seems glaring."[85] He added to this logic in another interview in the *San Francisco Chronicle*: "This is simply adding the LGBT community to the groups that the state has said must be included in the curriculum; . . . there's nothing special or different."[86] Even examples of previously remedied absences in textbooks were used to align GLBTQ people with other nationalized minorities. According to coverage of the bill by *MTV,* "Kuehl and the bill's supporters said that current textbooks are vague on the contributions of gays and lesbians in the same way they were once silent about those of African-Americans and other minority groups."[87]

Reflecting the ingrained nature of this essentialist rhetorical approach, conservative critics of the new legislation participated in this rhetoric as well, engaging their GLBTQ interlocutors on essentialist terms. In an interview, Benjamin Lopez, a lobbyist for the Traditional Values Coalition, noted that "you're talking about elevating a practice, a lifestyle, and putting it on par with the struggles of blacks, women and (other) minorities. . . . As a minority myself, that's tremendously offensive."[88] A *Los Angeles Times* article covering opposition remarks on the bill characterized statements of state senator Bill Morrow in similar terms: "Sen. Bill Morrow . . . called the bill 'dangerous' and 'insidious' because it lumps sexual orientation—something he said was a 'cultural or behavioral lifestyle'—together with race and sex, which are biological."[89] Though clearly demonstrating the skewed understanding of sexuality shared by many of the most socially conservative politicians in the United States, Morrow and Lopez demonstrate—through their insistent opposition—just how similarly advocates had positioned historical GLBTQ people with other, already protected minorities in the American nation.

Yet, while advocates claimed their legislation would enhance celebrations of American diversity in the classroom, the reformers choices often

eschewed the many real differences within GLBTQ communities so as to
not ruffle any feathers. Despite Kuehl's assurances to the contrary, GLBTQ
people imagined in the legislation did not reflect GLBTQ communities' many
rainbow colors. Rather by framing GLBTQ people as another (read: separate) ethnic minority, they would be represented as a static, homogenous
group similar to but sharing none of the same characteristics as the other
minorities. Washed away in this narrow characterization of American diversity are most clearly GLBTQ people of color and non-U.S. nationality. Yet
by rhetorically separating these identities, it was possible for reformers to
suggest that they, too, had been contributors to the national project much
like their ethnic-minority peers.

By situating GLBTQ representations in the past as ethnic-like minorities seeking inclusion in the greater society and emphasizing their contributions to the American nationalist project, GLBTQ reformers crafted a
specific public memory that they hoped would place them at the center of
U.S. society and history. However, these rhetorical additions to earlier memory projects would be insufficient by themselves to gain access to the center
of American identity. Certain key aspects of the GLBTQ past would have to
be forgotten to make this access complete.

The Forgetting of GLBTQ Pasts
■

Though contemporary GLBTQ reformers found within "rhetorics of contribution" a means for making GLBTQ persons recognizable in dominant
culture by aligning them with the monumental nationalism that organizes
cultural acceptance in American society, this choice had consequential costs
and effects. While there would undoubtedly be significant benefits for both
heterosexual and homosexual youths to see in their curriculums positive representations of GLBTQ people as leading, thoughtful, valued members of
the national community, these inclusions would require sacrificing certain
aspects of the GLBTQ experience in the past that could be viewed as damaging to American nationalism. Just as heterosexual individuals' forgetting of
GLBTQ people has been essential to ensuring heteronormativity a vital position in culture and society for centuries, the things GLBTQ advocates were
willing to forget about their GLBTQ forefathers and -mothers were crucial
to making the prescribed image of homosexual people in California textbooks "work" in ways that could be accepted by national institutions and heterosexual audiences. Though costly, reformers, it seems, felt that the choice
was merited given the continuing high number of GLBTQ youth who were
harmed, committed suicide, or faced violence on a regular basis, often in
public schools. Because of these circumstances, these representational costs
were viewed as a necessary adaption to secure a measure of safety—an initial

victory in a much larger struggle that had little to show for its work over the last twenty years. Similarly, representational sacrifices have been noted in earlier chapters of this book, further confirming the complex tradeoffs between the perfect and the possible in representing the GLBTQ past. Yet the California textbook and curriculum case is different in two vital ways. First, in the examples above, failures in queer monumentality were publicly challenged and critiqued by tactical and ephemeral voices outside the formal process. In the California case these voices have thus far been less vocal or successful. Second, in earlier cases, elements of the GLBTQ past sacrificed in the turn to monumentality have largely been at the expense of the diversity of GLBTQ persons and queer attitudes. However, in the California case study, the very core aspects of what fostered the twentieth-century gay and lesbian rights movement are on the chopping block. Surrendered in the name of inclusion—in hopes of creating a durable, powerful, and epideictic queer monumentality—GLBTQ reformers (either actively or by default) advocated for forgetting several fundamental parts of the GLBTQ past that were critical of the rhetorical underpinnings of American nationalism. As a consequence, their choices expose some of the real limits of queer monumentality and ultimately raise questions about its value.

Forgetting Harms

Perhaps the starkest contrast with earlier efforts to include GLBTQ people into California curriculums was the willingness of later reformers to forgo highlighting the specific and structural harms done to GLBTQ people by the wider American culture. Unlike many advocates in the 1980s who placed a premium on making present, recognizable, and visible both GLBTQ identities and the oppression heterosexual culture had imposed on them, later reformers actively minimized those aspects of history in favor of exclusively positive representations of GLBTQ people.

To be fair, educational reformers in California during this period had already done some work to address GLBTQ harms. In 1999 Senator Kuehl sponsored legislation in the Assembly preventing discrimination in classrooms against gays and lesbians that would later become law.[90] However, this law alone has been inadequate in much the same ways that feminists have argued that nondiscrimination policies are an inadequate response to systemic gender discrimination. For dominant groups that have reaped the benefits of discrimination for centuries, such laws are appealing in that they demonstrate a supposed deference to the historically marginalized—a recognition that the prior situation was unfair, inappropriate, or immoral. However, conscious or not, this appeal to end discrimination is often a façade. For while outwardly appearing to address issues that disadvantage marginalized groups, these policies only address future discrimination without putting at risk the benefits—wealth, power, prestige, control—that the center has accrued on account of historical discrimination. Without a historically informed understanding of discrimination (and other coordinated means of addressing these harms), newly appreciated minorities retain their outsider status because they have to start life's race by digging out of a representational and material hole, further postponing the dominant culture's need to grapple with its own actions.[91] Thus GLBTQ people still pay a substantial price by failing to demonstrate these harms in historic representations, even if the present law may limit some of their effects in the future.

Forgetting the harms committed against GLBTQ people was a necessity if reformers wished to see themselves included in the heroic center of American community. This is primarily because an emphasis on harms was critical of American ideology and challenged American values. It is difficult to imagine a nationalist rhetoric in which the nation was perpetually under attack. However, such would be the requirement if GLBTQ reformers insisted that the discussion of harms be included in textbooks. Thus, the critique of heterosexual culture in American society fell out of the textbook-reform discourse during the 2000s. Doubtless, many of those who supported this approach were unaware of earlier work that had taken a critical stance, did not recognize the incumbent costs, relied upon others to do this work, or made an informed choice, with the hope that such harms could be addressed later after the initial concerns for visibility had been achieved. In so doing they followed a long line of others in marginalized communities making similarly difficult decisions in the realms of textbooks and public memory generally. For example, textbooks that should have described conquistador imperial violence against Native Americans remained mute on the subject.[92] Likewise, planners of the U.S. bicentennial used their American memory projects to emphasize national unity and to forget the violence committed against members of the citizenry by the government during the 1960s.[93] Certainly discussions of violence in public education come with age-appropriate constraints that limit when such harms might be discussed. But this would not seem to prevent the discussion of harms at all levels of K-12 education. Nonetheless, GLBTQ advocates emphasized their contributions over potentially anti-American criticisms.

While the absence of harm is not something discussed commonly in discourse over the legislation, identifying this forgetting is done prominently in a particular discursive fragment: historian Jonathan Zimmerman's influential editorial on the legislation in the *San Francisco Chronicle*. In his editorial Zimmerman argues passionately against the bill not because he fears GLBTQ inclusion in the curriculum but because he thinks it will distort critical thinking about the conditions of historical animosity often not present within textbooks: "So if the bill about gay history passes, we can expect another round of heroes—this time, of course, gay heroes—to enter the books. But that won't help us address the really tough questions about American history, writ large. Why have gays suffered so much discrimination, during the McCarthy era and into the present? What does that say about our nation—about its conceptions of love, of family, and of "freedom" itself?"[94] While Zimmerman makes this charge in the spirit of promoting greater interrogation and critical thinking about American culture, his thought is marred by some flippant statements about contemporary gay culture post-AIDS. Nonetheless, his attention to (what he calls) making our kids "feel good" as the central motivation behind these efforts (what he also labels "history as therapy") can be understood another way: a rhetoric in support of American nationalism that willfully forgets anti-GLBTQ harms.

Such a public memory seems difficult to imagine given the shape of similar current textbook representations. Could we envisage a contemporary social-studies text that ignored the Holocaust, slavery, or the mistreatment of women? What if the genocidal destruction of the Native Americans was presented only as a footnote? How would we understand the place of Asian Americans in this century if we did not learn as students that our own government had interred them during the last century? The point here is that the language of "contribution" in the textbook debate—though serving a vitally important function in affirming the contemporary and historical value of GLBTQ people for a diverse audience—minimizes an equally important discussion of the individual and systemic harms perpetrated against GLBTQ people within a heteronormative culture. Combined with impassioned support for American nationalism, the significant silence surrounding GLBTQ existence in the current curriculum would be replaced with significant representation—but only of the "positive" news.[95] Such a positive narrative not only misrepresents history but also undercuts historical claims of injustice or discrimination or violence that might make today's average student (and citizen) open to social change. The forgetting of harms on the part of advocates was a rhetorical choice, likely one made with varying degrees of risk and comfort. However, by making the choice to ignore heterosexual responsibility for GLBTQ violence and marginalization, the progressive changes to which GLBTQ advocates aspired in the first place were put in jeopardy.

Forgetting Politics

Another forgetting of the GLBTQ past necessitated by the rhetoric of American nationalism was the political history of gay and lesbian rights. Though GLBTQ people and others with same-sex desire and/or gender nonconformity have existed for centuries, the politics of gay and lesbian rights within the United States has often been the most visible aspect of that history. As Scott Bravmann has suggested, despite the profound political contributions of GLBTQ leaders such as Harry Hay, Bayard Rustin, Del Martin, Phyllis Lyon, and others documented in widely read GLBTQ historical monographs, the contemporary gay and lesbian rights movement that has emerged in the cultural imagination is almost exclusively perceived through the lens of the 1969 Stonewall Riots. This political memory of the GLBTQ community—particularly around Stonewall remembrances and, increasingly, HIV/AIDS activism—has become so prevalent that it often draws focus from other aspects of GLBTQ history.[96] However, the politics of the GLBTQ rights movement is an especially problematic part of queer public memory that had to be forgotten to insert the GLBTQ community into the American national canon. This is primarily because the contemporary gay and lesbian rights movement emerged from a line of radical and moderate but still antiestablishment thought which was at its heart contrary to the norms of American nationalism. As the historian Lisa Duggan has suggested, despite "internal conflicts over assimilationist versus confrontational tactics . . . the overall goals and directions of change [within the movement's politics] have been relatively consistent: the expansion of a right to sexual privacy against the intrusive, investigatory labeling powers of the state, and the simultaneous expansion of gay public life through institution building and publicity." However, Duggan demonstrates that, increasingly, these political consistencies from both the radical leftist and moderate center essential to GLBTQ historical politics have often been forgotten by the discourses proffered by contemporary gay and lesbian rights activists in support of neoliberalism.[97] In addition, as we have seen, GLBTQ people had regularly been cast as antinationals based in part on their political beliefs and style, particularly surrounding HIV/AIDS. Representing GLBTQ people both as they might wish to be remembered and as a part of the memory narrative of American nationalism would require challenging these existent political histories or rather erasing them from public consciousness, a dubious task considering how pervasive and widely held they have been and continue to be within American culture. Because of this situation, contemporary advocates made the difficult but targeted decision to minimize discussions of GLBTQ politics in hopes of winning some recognition from an already hostile heteronormative audience. Sadly, this choice necessitated minimizing GLBTQ politics to such an extent that it was made essentially invisible within public memory. What remained with regard to politics, as was the case with antigay harms, was significant silence.

To navigate these difficult constraints, contemporary advocates utilized several rhetorical practices to deemphasize GLBTQ politics. First, reformers took to heart the claim of activists in the 1970s and 1980s that "we are everywhere," distributing GLBTQ people throughout the memory discourse. Despite tendencies by media outlets covering the bill to label its focus on teaching GLBTQ people in "history" specifically, in reality the legislation mandated that GLBTQ people be discussed in every aspect of public education. As a result, activists imagined that GLBTQ contributions to literature, science, math, sports, and the social sciences (among other areas) would all be discussed. At first glance, this is a positive trend, reversing the isolation of GLBTQ people in the curriculum as solely a late-twentieth-century civil rights movement. However, the degree to which GLBTQ people were distributed throughout the imagined curriculum encouraged the other extreme. Individual GLBTQ people would be discussed in so many places in the curriculum that the politics of gay and lesbian rights becomes minimized. By making GLBTQ people visible everywhere, the community and its politics would potentially fade into the background of wider culture, making them unremarkable and unworthy of specific attention. In short, the contributions of GLBTQ people to the political history of the United States were so diluted by additional contributory rhetoric that they lost focus within the wider curriculum. Thus, ironically, the issue most pertinent to understanding the public forgetting of GLBTQ politics became not too little information but too much. In conjunction with other rhetorical moves, advocates unwittingly diminished the prevalent gay and lesbian politics.

A second rhetorical choice that contributed to the minimization of GLBTQ political history was an almost exclusive emphasis on GLBTQ people as individuals in history and not as both individuals and collectivities. The focus on individuals, despite its drawbacks, was a powerful rhetorical choice for advocates. Building upon the inherited ideology of American individualism that permeates our culture, advocates situated GLBTQ "heroes" and "heroines" in a way that was familiar to most readers and could be easily incorporated into existing historical narratives. However, the effect of this savvy focus was a diminished capacity to recognize GLBTQ persons as communities of people—communities that had been and continue to be highly political. This was primarily the result of identifying representative anecdotes in history to highlight GLBTQ identity in the past. Throughout discussion of the legislation in the public sphere, the emphasis was placed on who would represent GLBTQ people from the past rather than on the fact that groups of diverse people known as GLBTQ communities existed and acted in the past. This individual focus is present in several discursive contexts. As the lead spokesperson on the bill, Senator Kuehl was the one most likely to make these individuating moves. In an article in the *Advocate* magazine, Kuehl highlighted Harvey Milk and Bayard Rustin as two prominent gay men who might be figures included in the curriculum change.[98] Elsewhere she suggested that James Baldwin would be another great example of someone she would like to see in the reformed California curriculum.[99] Others within the discourse participated in isolating individuals to make their claims. In a *Los Angeles Times* interview the leader of Equality California identified Langston Hughes as a possible subject of discussion.[100] In her remarks in favor of the legislation, Democratic state senator Jackie Speier identified Oscar Wilde (despite his British citizenship) as an important figure.[101] In an editorial in the *San Francisco Chronicle* Debra J. Saunders suggested Abraham Lincoln, Eleanor Roosevelt, and J. Edgar Hoover would all be likely prospects.[102] Walt Whitman and, again, James Baldwin were highlighted in another editorial.[103] So rhetorically threatening was this individuating discourse that conservative critics of the legislation also chose to engage arguments about representation surrounding the individual. Taken together, they contribute to emphasizing individuals over collectives in historical analysis, making discussion of highly political groups, social movements, and communities absent. However, it was not just the isolation of individuals as representational figures in queer public memory but rather the ways in which these representations were made that impacted this political mnemonicide.

In a third dimension of this effort, the kind of individuals selected as representative anecdotes had two primary qualities that made possible the forgetting of GLBTQ politics: they were figures with cultural contributions and figures who exhibited favoritism toward historical GLBTQ individuals involved in politics generally (not GLBTQ politics specifically). When individuals were highlighted in the memory discourse, those remembered were primarily understood as cultural figures. Without question GLBTQ individuals have been vital contributors to American (and world) culture—and this culture has an important part to play in American nationalism. However, it is the degree to which cultural contribution—sports, entertainment, media, and the arts—was emphasized that served to further minimize GLBTQ political history. Based on the references isolated within the debate, cultural contribution was the most prominent form of GLBTQ contribution to the American project while politics was selectively forgotten.

Indeed, some voices in the debate about the bill embraced cultural contributions explicitly. In a letter to the editor of the *San Francisco Chronicle,* Gustavo Serina praised the bill specifically because it did not focus only on political figures but rightfully acknowledged the "cultural history" of gays and lesbians as well. Citing Thornton Wilder, Tennessee Williams, Walt Whitman, James Baldwin, Willa Cather, and Lorraine Hansberry as examples, Serina suggested that "silence about their sexual orientation denied them a crucial part of their identity as people and artists," and he was grateful that, "thanks to State Sen. Sheila Kuehl's legislation, that [silence] won't be possible in California. The writers cited above, of course, are a very small *sample of gays and lesbians who have transformed American culture.* Many

others—from William Inge to Edward Albee to Tony Kushner—deserve to
be studied."[104] While there is certainly value in the cultural contributions of
GLBTQ persons, a focus on culture at the expense of political representation is an affront to actually existing GLBTQ history and holds powerful,
unstated political consequences.

This is not to suggest that the figures highlighted by the movement had
no political acumen at all. Given the contributory nature of these representations, it would seem unlikely that political figures could be totally removed from any representational display. Certainly, figures explicitly named
in the discourse including Lincoln, Roosevelt, Rustin, and Milk are primarily
known as political actors. However, none of these individuals (save Milk, and
he only recently in popular culture) is remembered primarily for gay and
lesbian politics. It is important to emphasize what I mean by *primarily*. While
the language and intent of S.B. 1437 was to ensure that prominent leaders
such as Lincoln could be identified as having an anachronistic gay identity,
it does not suggest that Lincoln's actions and presidency would be explicitly connected to the gay and lesbian rights movement. Rather a figure like
Lincoln would be regarded as a political and national leader primarily who
happened to be gay (as a secondary or tertiary claim). This in and of itself
is certainly a valuable addition to Lincoln's complex representation and a
positive for GLBTQ visibility. However, it does little or nothing to draw attention to the facts, arguments, tactics, goals, and desires of the decades-
long GLBTQ rights movement and its politics. Thus these figures' political work, while a vital contribution to the nation, is likely to have little
representational effect or to make any direct comment on gay and lesbian
rights (whether or not they should have). By emphasizing these nationalists
GLBTQ figures—over even fairly traditional gay and lesbian politicians and
statesmen like Harvey Milk—the history of political activism that more radical (that is, un-American) queers represent is repressed.

By articulating a rhetorical memory of GLBTQ people as individuals,
aligning those individuals with conservative politics and cultural contributions, and dispersing these figurative anecdotes throughout the curriculum,
reformers sought to remember GLBTQ people as vital to American history
by eviscerating and forgetting their political motivations, goals, and clout.

Forgetting Sex

Finally, contemporary textbook reformers made a considered choice to sacrifice discussions about sex, sexual culture, and queer intimacy as a part of
history in an effort to align GLBTQ people with American nationalism. This
claim may seem erroneous at first. Indeed, given the cultural battles waged
over sex education in public schools over the last twenty years, it would seem

more likely than not that explicit discussions of sexuality are not prevalent in most U.S school textbooks or curriculums. However, when we turn our attention beyond the explicit to the often invisible ideologies in school curriculums, another story emerges. As Michel Foucault has shown, it is often in periods when sex is stigmatized that it is actually the most powerfully disciplined and discussed.[105] When we begin to consider school curriculums in this light, it becomes clear that sexuality (and specifically heterosexuality) has a pervasive presence in public school curriculums—a presence in support of nationalism generally and American nationalism in particular.

Sex and sexuality are highly important aspects of nationalist imaginings. Historically, in the realm of sexuality, "abnormal" behavior (such as masturbation and homosexual acts) came to be understood as detrimental to nationalist projects. Drawing from (and misreading) Darwinist theories of natural selection, nineteenth-century nationalists in Europe and America believed that natural selection "would reward a healthy national organism free of hereditary disease and moral weakness. On the simplest level, this meant dedication to reproduction." In short, "abnormal" masturbators and homosexuals "were a danger to the national community."[106] Nationalism thus has come to rely heavily on rhetorics of population and reproduction. As Foucault suggests in his *History of Sexuality*, sovereign power in the contemporary world has become "a power bent on generating forces, making them grow, and ordering them, rather than one dedicated to impeding them, making them submit, or destroying them." Procreation and reproduction are organized under a "bio-politics of the population" in order to ensure the strength (and power) of the nation.[107] Thus, encouraging "healthy" and "normal" sexuality became conceived of as an essential part to any nation's success and was therefore invested in the ideological apparatuses of the nation. These insights can be traced directly to the development of twentieth-century nationalism in Europe and America; parallel claims and understandings are reflected in the contemporary textbook discourse.

Given the nationalist imperative to promote reproduction and population growth, GLBTQ sexual (and reproductive) culture has been regularly forgotten—despite the fact that many GLBTQ people through history have, for example, been excellent parents in an assortment of family patterns—in order to secure representational clarity. To some degree, the absence of sex as the locus of queer memory practices might be understandable. While sexuality is a topic of conversation for older students, younger students—raised in a culture with a high level of discomfort discussing sexuality and products of an educational system actively against instruction in sexual health—might be unprepared for such material. This likelihood is reflected in both critics' and advocates' perpetual refrain that those discussions be "age appropriate."[108] Also, advocates might not raise issues of sexual culture because, in some substantive ways, that fight had already been fought and won. During the 1990s advocates had been highly successful in including gay and lesbian issues regarding sex into the health curriculum, opening that space up (in the face of extreme challenges) to a greater degree of GLBTQ imaginings of sexuality. In addition, a focus on sex would provide political problems. If sex could be ignored, the old pro-gay/antigay discourse about the proper place of discussions about sex might be avoided, making the legislation's chance of passage more likely. So resolute were contemporary reformers in avoiding this issue that they explicitly disavowed sex as an aspect of their curricular goals. In a widely circulated press release from Senator Kuehl's office, she states that "S.B. 1437 would not mandate discussions of any historical figures' sex lives. A person's sexual orientation and gender identity are identity characteristics, not sexual behaviors. The sex lives of historical lesbian, gay, bisexual and transgender people would not be taught, any more than the curriculum currently discusses the sexual lives of heterosexual historical figures."[109] To gain political advantage Kuehl and other reformers were willing to rule out the validity of sex or sexual culture in any representation of GLBTQ people in textbook reform. However, given the strong correlation between heterosexuality and nationalism, how reformers attempted to forget sex in their representations of GLBTQ people in the past is of primary importance, with powerful consequences for remembering GLBTQ Americans. Several rhetorical practices enforce this forgetting within the discourse.

First, GLBTQ textbook discourse echoed and was complicit in replicating a wider forgetting of gay sexual culture prior to HIV/AIDS. In the decade after the Stonewall Riots, GLBTQ (particularly gay male) sexual culture blossomed in a newly public way. Many gay men participated in sexual practices that radically reconsidered the collective wisdom on sexuality, pushing the limits of sexual propriety and experimenting with themselves and others with regard to the body, pleasure, monogamy, and procreation. These experiments had in mind social, cultural, and political consequences. As Patrick Moore suggests, "these men were using flesh and spirit and sexual energy as their artistic tools. The sex of the 1970s was creative; it was art. . . . Gay men in the 1970s took the radical step of removing the line between life and art, insisting that the performance not wait for the audience to arrive."[110] However, with the advent of the HIV/AIDS crisis in the 1980s and 1990s, the experimentation so cherished in the 1970s became, for some, a political problem. For these persons this sexual experimentation was childish and unethical and brought with it the scourge of HIV/AIDS. In response, a portion of the GLBTQ community actively sought to disavow that period of history and memory, resigning it to a "memory void."[111] According to Christopher Castiglia, these gay men participated in a powerful and consequential act of forgetting, "part and parcel of a larger strategy to vilify queer memory; more

than simply calling for a crackdown by the city, gay 'neocons' enact a form
of enforced amnesia, cutting off gay men from sexual memories that provide
alternative models of public intimacy and political union."[112] Castiglia highlights several power brokers of the new gay center as being key promoters of
this forgetting, including the author and documentarian Gabriel Rotello, the
journalist and commentator Michelangelo Signorile, and the political and
cultural critic Andrew Sullivan.[113] To some degree these claims amount to
lateral hostility within the gay male community that easily draws focus away
from other covert and overt activities by the culture at large in favor of the
toll and trauma of HIV/AIDS and its resultant atrocities. However, given recent attempts in separate books by Moore and by Castiglia and Christopher
Reed and films such as *Gay Sex in 70s* to renew the memory of 1970s gay
sexual culture, it seems some substantive degrees of forgetting about sex has
certainly taken place in American memory.[114]

While debates still rage about the characterization of this time and the
response to it, the textbook debate of the 2000s clearly sought to replicate the
forgetting of some gay male contemporaries by eviscerating both the 1970s
sexual culture and the response to HIV/AIDS from textbook discussions.
This is particularly noticeable not only in the absence of sex as a part of the
discourse but also in the chronological hole that appears in the narrative told
about the GLBTQ past. Noticeably, the historical figures described in the
discourse end with Harvey Milk's assassination in 1978. No other GLBTQ
figure of historical merit after 1978 is mentioned in any discourse. This may
be a simple aberration, but, if so, it is a convenient aberration with two
powerful effects. First, and not inconsequentially, positioning Milk as the
last GLBTQ figure in the narrative perpetuates the stereotype of gay men as
victims—a stereotype already pervasive in the dominant culture. Second, it
obscures the need to discuss or describe any historical figures aligned with
or "tainted by" the memory of HIV/AIDS. By replicating the forgetting already under way in some parts of the gay community, contemporary textbook
reformers effectively removed HIV/AIDS and 1970 gay sexual culture from
memory, thereby neutralizing one of the most dangerous threats GLBTQ
people posed to American national virtues.

Second, and similar, the emphasis on GLBTQ individuals in the past
contributed to desexualizing queer memory. As before, when individual gay
and lesbian figures are the primary representational choices suggested by advocates, the highlighting of individuals removes from the discussion aspects
of GLBTQ identity that are communal—including sex. Whereas I earlier
highlighted the politics and social movements of the GLBTQ community
as causalities of this representational refuge in the individual, in this case
the communal act eliminated from public memory is sex and its attendant
institutions such as same-sex marriage, bathhouses, cruising, and public sex.

Though this absence does not suggest that student readers might not infer that a gay or lesbian figure in the past would have had sex with someone else, it diminishes that inference as likely. It is entirely possible in this representational form that a student might infer historical queers to be individuals with same-sex affinities who never acted on them. Positioned as homosexual virgins within American public memory, these GLBTQ figures—individuals—posed no threat to the nationalist sexual order.

This forgetting is even more troubling given that American history as currently told heavily marks heterosexual couples and sex in numerous ways. Famous couples (presidents and first ladies) and love affairs (Romeo and Juliet), prominent husbands and wives (Franklin D. and Eleanor Roosevelt), exaltations of political sons, daughters, and dynasties (the Adamses, Roosevelts, Kennedys, Clintons, and Bushes)—all of these validated forms are implicitly honored by textbook representations. Through this honoring the heterosexual relationship and sexual act (resulting in children) is deftly reinforced. Indeed, as state senator Debra Bowen reiterated in her remarks directed at conservative critics of the California bill, American history is very concerned with considering people with whom heterosexual individuals in history slept. In particular, she highlighted Thomas Jefferson's "relationship" with Sally Hemings as a "fairly significant section of any Jeffersonian Library." She also cited President Bill Clinton's affair with Monica Lewinsky as further evidence that history frequently records heterosexual sex as important.[115] So prominent are these heterosexual impulses, that reform critics strongly assailed previous gestures to recognize historical homosexuality in American historical figures.[116] Unfortunately, Senator Bowen failed to recognize that simply labeling someone as gay is not synonymous with representing their sexual experiences, values, or practices. Given the pervasive presence of heterosexual sex within American history and the forgetting of any GLBTQ people in a communal sense, students might easily assume historical queers were lifelong bachelors, lonely spinsters, or isolated outsiders.

Ironically, in the face of these efforts to forget the sexual aspects of GLBTQ life it was the conservative critics of the reformers who remained fixed upon the homosexual sexual act as an essential piece of GLBTQ historical imagining. Cindy Moles of the Concerned Women for America stated in the *New York Times* that "we don't need to list all the behavior of historical figures . . . certainly not their sexual behavior."[117] Moles's organization later lambasted the bill as "silencing any objection to homosexual behavior."[118] Gary Bauer, writing in *Human Events*, suggested that in the wake of same-sex marriage movements across the country "references in school textbooks to 'mom' and 'dad' and 'wife' and 'husband' would have to be removed."[119] California state senator Bill Murrow claimed that a historical figure's "contribution to history has nothing to do with their sexual proclivities."[120] While these critics in no way represent a more affirmative imagining of historical GLBTQ lives appropriate for a public school curriculum than that of the GLBTQ advocates, their critiques highlight the fact that sex matters in debates about history. Indeed, unarticulated in this conservative focus upon sex is the fear that moving beyond discussion about sex might destabilize the presumptive place of heterosexuality in American culture while also removing an easily accessible argument that conservatives have used to bludgeon GLBTQ people within discourse broadly. Ironically then, detaching sex from historical imaginings of GLBTQ people posed a significant risk both for those represented as well as for those who sought to maintain their hegemonic grip on the status quo.

By ignoring GLBTQ couples and institutions in which the physical and sexual aspects of same-sex relationships might be discussed, and participating in forgetting the gay male sexual culture of the 1970s, the reformers severely limited the way GLBTQ pasts could be understood by heterosexual and homosexual audiences. This forgetting makes GLBTQ reformers complicit in affirming heteronormativity as one of the complementary rhetorics of nationalism.

Conclusion

■

As a result of the national controversy and facing possible political consequences in an upcoming election year, California governor Arnold Schwarzenegger vetoed S.B. 1437 in late 2006. However, this defeat for representing GLBTQ persons in public school curriculums was not the end of the debate. In 2007 Senator Kuehl and her allies resurrected the bill in a new form, S.B. 777: The Student Civil Rights Act. The less brazen bill removed much of the controversial "rhetorics of contribution" language by political necessity, instead laying out an aggressive nondiscrimination and antiharassment policy applicable to all aspects of the state curriculum, including textbooks. While this new bill made valuable changes to the rights of GLBTQ students in California classrooms, it essentially jettisoned all mandates to recognize GLBTQ people in curricular materials and greatly diminished the bill's value for imagining GLBTQ pasts. With little media attention and the governor safely into his second term, the bill passed both houses of the legislature, was signed into law, and went into effect in 2008.[121] However, in 2010 state senator Mark Leno, who took up Senator Kuehl's mantle after she was term-limited in 2008, introduced a new instantiation of the "contributions" bill, S.B. 48: Fair, Accurate, Inclusive, and Respectful Education Act, better known as FAIR. FAIR again called for "ensur[ing] that the historical contributions of lesbian, gay, bisexual and transgender (LGBT) people . . . are accurately and fairly portrayed" in instructional materials in California's public schools.[122] This time the bill passed the legislature and was signed by Democratic governor Jerry Brown. Brown suggested at the time of his signature that changes to textbooks and other instructional materials would likely not be seen until January 2015.[123]

Given a combination of compelling factors—the toxic amalgamation of forces acting on GLBTQ youth and adults, the persistence of anti-GLBTQ representations and invisibility, and the unique situation presented in California (in particular) in the midst of the same-sex marriage debate—S.B. 1437, S.B. 777, and S.B. 48 have proven worthy rhetorical undertakings. The laws (at least as proposed) made significant and sustained progress in preventing the ideological apparatus of education from acting in an overt way to discriminate against, deter, or discipline GLBTQ youth. Meanwhile, the sheer introduction of the discussion of GLBTQ pasts into the wider public sphere (through controversy or otherwise) was a compelling rhetorical triumph, urging audiences of both heterosexual and homosexual persuasion to imagine their heroes, their icons, and themselves as part of a bit-more-queer nation.

More compelling still is that advocates managed to do so much in the face of a pervasive, coordinated, and systemic effort by the hegemonic center of American culture to resist such imaginings. Advocates faced legislative maneuvers, conservative politics, media campaigns, public smears, skewed debates, grossly unhistorical counterexamples, counter protests, and threats at different times and in different venues, yet all derived from a normative fear that more robust tellings of the past might dislodge the bulwark of heterosexual privilege from its moorings. Through a series of concerted efforts (only one of the most visible herein described) GLBTQ advocates pressed their case and emerged with some tangible results, hopefully to be followed quickly by real material effects in the lives of GLBTQ people.

However, it is important to remember that no choice made by GLBTQ rhetors positioned between the double binds of circumscribed visibility and representational oblivion is free of repercussions. For Kuehl, Leno, and their allies, the choice to minimize criticism of the heteronormative center and adopt a rhetoric of contribution in support of American nationalism led to substantial representational gains at the cost of significant forgettings of the historical GLBTQ experience. In a very clear way advocates were positioned in a lose-lose situation. Such repercussions bring to the fore an ongoing concern within the turn to queer monumentality: the limitations of repetition with a difference. As we have seen over and over again, the monumental turn in queer public memory rhetoric has benefitted particularly from its ability to reproduce the monumental forms of heterosexual memory (commemorative sites, mediated public, textbooks) inflected with a homosexual difference, with substantial results. The textbook case forces us to recognize that—even

with difference—repetition does not and cannot entirely remove all the en-
twined and imbedded forces of the original model. Difference is power, yes,
but its ability to alter the norms in which it is ensconced is limited. This was
very much the case faced by the California advocates—reformers who accepted the already damaged proposition that inclusion is best. They achieved
their goal of a more robust, durable, and visible difference in the ideological
rhetorics of the classroom. However, until the specifics of this victory are
sorted out, we will not know whether the costs of this repetition outweigh
its successes. The lesson learned from the textbook debates is not the failure
of queer monumentality, but its limitations: some abundantly clear from the
beginning and others, visible only in our attempts at rearticulation.

Given the weighty stakes that adopting a queer turn to monumentality
entails, coming to terms with these risks and identifying means by which
these risks can be minimized in the future thus becomes essential to ensuring a productive ongoing effort. Some may suggest that monumentality's
benefits outweigh its noted drawbacks so clearly that the best course lies in
more fiercely adopting the places, forms, and rhetorics of the monumental
and hoping there may be opportunities at a later time to compensate for the
compromises GLBTQ people must make in the here and now. To me, such
an approach feels like a slippery slope into full-blown homonormativity that
must be avoided at all costs. Nor does the answer lie in rejecting monumentality out of hand; doing so would only again raise the specter of a queer
past perpetually at risk of erasure, forgetting, and oblivion. Rather, as we will
see in the remainder of this book, doing queer monumentality better going
forward means making the queer monumentality of the future more respon-
sive to our present paradigm and not just a replication of what heterosexual
history has done before. Doing so will require adopting a both/and approach
to memory and monumentality that is simultaneously fleeting, enduring, and
very much queer.

CHAPTER 5

Preserving a Queer (After) Life

STROLLING DOWN THE SYLVAN COBBLED pathways of the Père Lachaise Cemetery in central Paris, viewers eventually come to the northernmost part of the cemetery and the grave of Gertrude Stein. Stein was a famous American writer, art collector, and intellectual who spent most of her life in France during the early twentieth century. To look at the gravestone—a simple tablet inscribed with Stein's name, date of birth, and date of death—reveals little information about her life. It is only by the chatter of visitors, literary mementos, and pebbles left on her stone that most causal viewers might deduce the reasons for her fame. Depending upon the cultural knowledge with which the viewer is equipped, he or she might bring to mind another important part of her life not represented on the face of the headstone: the fact that Stein was a lesbian who lived her life openly when such choices were even more dangerous than they are today. For many visitors this aspect of Stein's life is easily missed, forgotten by passed decades, erased by knowledge systems that do not value sexuality as a meritable aspect of the *vita activa,* and lost by the often imperceptible forces of heteronormativity. However, even for the less-informed visitor to the grave, the public memory of Stein's lesbianism can still be found, remembered, and celebrated—for those who know where to look. Placed discretely, on the backside of Stein's headstone, is engraved in gold the name Alice B. Toklas, Stein's partner and lesbian lover for more than thirty years. Though hidden from easy public view, the inclusion of Toklas' name on the pair's shared gravestone in Père Lachaise serves as a powerful rhetorical gesture, immortalizing lesbian love and securing for the couple a queer afterlife.

Toklas and Stein's intervention in death-display rhetoric is an exciting instance of queer visual style, not just because it exists but also because it represents something we have not seen in previous chapters: an instance of queer monumentality featuring a simultaneously small but meaningful tactical memory rhetoric. Previous chapters have emphasized the existence of both tactical/ephemeral and monumental memory rhetorics; however, in nearly all instances these have been represented as separate and distinct approaches to the past, either one preceding the other or as memory rhetorics pitted against each other for criticism and critique. But in a cemetery in France a grave installed in 1946 offers a glimpse of something profoundly contemporary in queer monumentality: a both/and orientation to doing queer public memory, suggesting a clever innovation on queer monumentality necessary for its future development.

Unfortunately, in immortalizing the couple as lesbians, the Stein-Toklas grave is the exception rather than the rule. Even today, more than fifty years after Stein's death, dying is perhaps the most efficient way in which an out and proud gay man or lesbian may find him or herself normalized—queerly forgotten—by a heteronormative culture. While this forgetting has destroyed legacies of homosexual identity and same-sex desire for millennia, the HIV/AIDS crisis vividly demonstrated just how cruel and systemic this queer forgetting could be. The British author Simon Watney describes one of the most powerful examples of this heteronormative erasure. In the opening to his book *Policing Desire: Pornography, AIDS, and the Media,* Watney details his motivation for writing, citing the passing of his friend "Bruno": "[Bruno's] funeral took place in an ancient Norman church on the outskirts of London. No mention was made of AIDS. Bruno had died, bravely, of an unspecified disease. In the congregation of some forty people there were two other gay men besides myself, both of whom had been his lover. They had been far closer to Bruno than anyone else present, except his parents. Yet their grief had to be contained within the confines of manly acceptability. The irony of the difference between the suffocating life of the suburbs where we found ourselves, and our knowledge of the world in which Bruno had actually lived, as a magnificently affirmative and life-enhancing gay man, was all but unbearable. . . . My friend was not called Bruno. His father asked me not to use his real name. And so the anonymity is complete. The garrulous babble of commentary on AIDS constructs yet another 'victim.'"[1] For "Bruno" and his family and friends the ritual rhetorics of death provide little in the way of mourning. The often unacknowledged privileges that death and dying rituals provide to heterosexuals—presence at the deathbed, legal decision making, participation in funeral arrangements, decisions concerning religious services and the place where the deceased is buried, and even the right to be buried with one's partner—have often been unavailable to GLBTQ persons.[2] Rather, death magnifies the pain and violence GLBTQ people (particularly those suffering from HIV/AIDS) commonly experience in life. Within that violence is lost much more than a missed loved one; gone also, as Cathy J. Cohen suggests, is "the totality of his life which included lovers and gay friends who also grieve for that loss."[3]

In the face of such destructive regimes of active silencing, revision, mis-representation, and willed forgetting, some queers have made efforts to en-sure that they create for themselves a public legacy that matches their queer identities. However, much like the rhetorical interventions described in case studies above, the ones employed here have long been, by necessity, exclu-sively tactical and ephemeral. Facing persecution in life and regulation in death, queers have found it difficult to make their queer legacies plain and perduring. Resigned to that fact, fleeting speeches, private tributes, and left tokens have all been used by queers to mark in death, in some meaningful way, not only their queer relationships but their GLBTQ identities as well.

While these efforts are certainly powerful, their tactical and/or ephem-eral qualities continue to make them insecure and objectionable. Many of these acts are so hidden that a great many people ignore them. In other cases the gestures are so personal or obscure that they go unnoticed. Others are powerful but fleeting acts that cannot help but fall prey to the test of time, often failing in the end to prevent queer memories from being reclaimed by heteronormative assumptions. Finally, even when these tactical and ephem-eral memory rhetorics are able to endure for a time, there is nothing to prevent them from being contested to the point that their queer meaning becomes, at best, questionable and, at worst, disregarded.[4]

For these reasons and others, some queers have attempted to move beyond improvisational tactical and ephemeral rhetorics to more enduring monumental rhetorics that might outlast even the most vociferous attempts at heteronormative erasure, occupation, and reterritorialization. Yet, as we saw in chapter 4, monumentality is not a surefire means for representing GLBTQ life well. Indeed, in the face of the heteronormative privileges as-sociated with death and dying, GLBTQ people who might actively select a more monumental form of queer expression in death can be easily stymied by funeral directors, church doctrines, cemetery regulations, next-of-kin laws, and homophobic families, to name a few. Facing obstacles to both tactical/ephemeral and monumental means of securing a queer afterlife, far too many GLBTQ lives are completely snuffed out well after their physical passing.

Given the complex, simultaneous, and fluid array of heteronormative forces impeding GLBTQ afterlives, memory makers like Stein and Toklas have turned to both/and approaches to death display to secure their eternal rests with their sexuality intact. These both/and approaches, on one level, mean embracing monumentality's capabilities in simultaneous and some-times contradictory ways that keep it nimble and effective in differing con-texts. At another level, both/and approaches allude to Huyssen's call for a contemporary monumentality that fuses grandeur, greatness, and durabil-ity with a tactical and ephemeral gamesmanship to create a monumental-ity with a "modernist spirit."[5] As such, these contemporary approaches are less evidently instances of queer monumentality proper than they are of the *queering* of monumentality. Undertaking such an innovative revision to queer monumentality is a relatively new concept; despite Stein and Toklas's historical example, such approaches have only begun to gestate in queer public memory. Nonetheless, by beginning the process of queering monumentality in these ways, the GLBTQ people described below illustrate an effective means for securing queer hereafters still largely reliant upon monumentality but with small inflections of something different. In doing so, they give us a glimpse into what, I argue, will be a necessary evolution in how we do queer monumentality.

Graves and Cemeteries as Rhetorical Texts
■

As material and visual manifestations of public memory, death displays can function as important rhetorical texts. However, what makes these texts particularly rhetorical is not always clear and, in fact, varies depending on how the rhetor, audience, and critic of these death displays use those texts. For the purposes of this chapter, two primary rhetorical elements of death displays are important: the individual graves of those interred and the collective meaning of these graves as a whole.

At first glance, symbolic markers of the individual dead, associated generally with personal grieving, might be categorized as part of the private sphere of human life rather than as important public displays. Yet individual death displays—headstones, footstones, mausoleums, and other grave markers—can have highly rhetorical dimensions that impact and shape public beliefs. By virtue of being located outside of the domestic sphere, in an area reserved specifically for those who are deceased, graves acquire some degree of public character. This character is enhanced when circulated within public discourse. As Kendall R. Phillips reminds us, public memory consists not only of the "memory of publics" but also of the "publicness of memory."[6] To the degree that an individual gravestone contributes to remembering an individual in the public sphere, it is highly rhetorical. Though this is often the case with famous gravesites, the more local characteristic of vernacular memory suggests that it could apply equally to the less famous as well.[7] When individual graves take on formal qualities that situate them to address the public at large intentionally (with express inscriptions, for example), this publicness is enhanced. In these ways individual graves can have rhetorical characteristics that influence the perceptions and beliefs of those who view them.

However, while individual death displays have merit in public persuasion, cemeteries and graveyards have more pronounced, everyday rhetorical dimensions. As a collective expression of death within a community, ceme-teries and graveyards speak not of what an individual might wish to say, but rather they render community sentiments about death (and life) visible. In this way cemeteries and graveyards can be pedagogical; in their design, style, arrangement, and invention, they instruct visitors and passersby about death and how one should live in relation to it. This instruction is largely accom-plished through visual rhetorics—the "images, artifacts, and performances of looking" in the public sphere that "function to persuade"—primarily those that conceive of cemeteries as landscapes.[8] The visual consumption of land-scapes is a popular American practice that transforms individual others into participants of a community identity. According to Gregory Clark, "for Ameri-cans the most intense aesthetic experience of a landscape includes images of themselves enacting a new identity there."[9] When these landscapes are publicized for individual consumption—through discourse or material and visual interactions—they do vital rhetorical work "symbolizing a common home and, thus, a common identity."[10] Viewing a landscape induces "a rhe-torical power" between viewer and scene that "prompts people to adopt a public identity they read symbolized in the landscapes they share."[11]

Cemeteries represent a particular kind of landscape, what the rhetori-cian Richard Morris has termed a gravescape. As a visual scene that consists of "memorials and the landscapes containing them," a gravescape works to gather viewers into a community of shared believers about life and death.[12] By erecting particular kinds of death displays as "sacred symbols," commu-nities represent to each other and viewers their shared values, community ethos, and "world view."[13] This epideictic lesson instructs viewers in how to live life so as to fit into the community value of death and, thereby, be inter-polated into the shared identity these cemeteries presuppose.

Critically, the individual and the community as expressed in cemetery representation are always interrelated. While an isolated grave or memorial might be considered in and of itself, within the cemetery setting no single grave can be understood alone. Its possible meanings are always a negotia-tion, in agreement or in contestation, with the other graves that flank it (in some cases, with very little space in between). Equally, a cemetery's possible meanings are reliant upon the chorus of individual voices that constitute the cemetary. Each individual grave contributes to, shapes, and alters the mean-ings of the whole.[14] Therefore, the meanings of a death display are always contextual and contingent (that is, rhetorical).

An important part of that context is the particular meaning of death held by the community and its antecedent judgments about life as they are derived from individual graves within their gravescapes. Because this is so, it is inaccurate to speak of *the* way death is represented, as if all communi-ties and cemeteries were the same. Gravescapes' stylistic displays vary by community, the interred, location, and time. To understand the rhetorical effect of any individual grave or gravescape thus requires an understanding of the particular gravescape style it practices. Several scholars across disciplinary divides have taken to analyzing and categorizing these styles, as well as to indicating the rhetorical values that they claim to represent.[15] For the purposes of this chapter, two particular gravescape styles are of relevance: the memento mori gravescape and the garden cemetery gravescape.

Memento mori gravescapes—also referred to as "plain style" or the "Death's Head" style—feature a fairly simple collection of headstones. The headstones in memento mori gravescapes are almost exclusively modest single or double arches and, sometimes, low horizontal tables (fig. 5). While the original plain style often left no marking on a grave other than the placement of the stone itself, as the style developed, simple inscriptions were placed on the headstones as well. According to James A. Hijiya, such plainness was valued as cost effective and humble before God, while it also "asserted that people's physical remains were of little importance, unworthy of conspicuous commemoration."[16] Later many of these stones were etched with iconic figures such as the "Death's Head"—a winged skull—not to scare viewers but to warn them to prepare themselves for death. Many of these stones also featured the simple inscription "memento mori": remember death.[17]

According to Morris's analysis, the rhetorical message advocated by this style was summed up in those two simple words. He argues that instructing viewers always to remember death was the central task of the landscape style. Placed near major metropolitan areas where they were frequently visible (though less likely to be visited because of their degraded conditions), these cemeteries reiterated, in minute everyday fashion, that sinners must change their behavior and prepare for death if they had hope of reaching a better hereafter.[18] Simultaneously, the sheer numbers of those interred in similar fashion in memento mori gravescapes assured passersby that that they too could join this community of believers who, in death, escaped the tortures of hell and now bask in the glow of an eternal afterlife.[19]

Another popular gravescape style to take root in the United States is what Morris calls the garden cemetery style. Consisting of features from the rural cemetery, lawn and garden cemetery, and the "late Victorian period Monumental" style, the garden cemetery disposed of the memento mori landscape style's propensity to represent death as a haunting warning and replaced it with a natural ethos in which communion with the dead was not only possible but encouraged.[20] Whereas previous landscape styles highlighted simplistic and humble design, the garden style celebrated art and accomplishment as virtues of a well-lived and eternal life. In combination with an emphasis on the natural world, demonstrated by both the artistic subject matter and the omnipresent plant life that adorned the area, these cemeteries

FIG. 5
■

Congressional Cemetery in Washington, D.C., in the
memento mori landscape style. Photograph by the author.

welcomed the living to stroll, enjoy the surroundings, and commune with the
dead. It was hoped that the living would not only be instructed on how to
live a good natural life, but also that they would let loose their burdens for a
rejuvenated return to the world of the living.[21]

Natural is the key to Morris's assessment of the garden cemetery's rhetorical motives. The design of these cemeteries took as their central aesthetic
the promotion of natural plants, the natural orientations of stones, and the
expression of natural imagery across the gravescape. With strict limits set by
cemetery administrators on aesthetics that supported this vision, the artistic
designs of the death displays created "a gallery of art embraced by nature
bejeweled."[22] With this demand made on the visual field, the creation of
memorials was always an effort to "actualize their potential to achieve a
harmonious relationship with nature." In this style, not only was individual
memory more highly regarded; the community of the cemetery as a whole
was strengthened as well to prevent "'unnatural' acts and actions" from in-
truding and being represented within this sanctuary.[23]

While both the memento mori and the garden styles were strongly ad-
hered to by individual persons and their communities, it should be noted
that pure examples of these landscape styles are hard to come by for the contemporary viewer. Certainly, as time passed and community values changed,
cemetery styles were altered or supplemented by more-fitting forms.

Thus it is likely that many cemeteries one might visit today will contain elements out of the ordinary from its original style. However, within certain well-maintained or famous cemeteries, it is still possible to recognize predominant landscape styles—styles that reflect, in form and function, the rhetorical sentiments of their communities.

The Heteronormative Regimes of Gravescapes

■

While each gravescape style overtly represents a particular cultural ethos through its visual frame, in less overt ways these gravescapes also simultaneously represent other rhetorical meanings in their death displays. Among these alternative meanings, most gravescape styles also embed within their visual frames the view that life and death should be understood from a hegemonic heterosexual perspective. Thus gravescapes function as heteronormative apparatuses for obscuring and disciplining queer representations of life and death.

As we have seen, heteronormativity is understood as the unquestionable presumption, both at the level of the individual and of the culture, that all of society's members are heterosexual until proven otherwise.[24] While this presumption can be marked in public ways—such as the debates over same-sex marriage—more frequently heteronormativity operates under the radar, eschewing blatant forms of discrimination by creating a false visage of reality. Because of their marginalized positions, queers are often disadvantaged if not erased from public concern if these presumptions are not brought to light and challenged. Queer theory has emerged, in part, as a response to heteronormativity, seeking to identify and disrupt those relations of power that constitute a "regime of the normal" so as to make space for the expression of queer alternatives.[25]

While it is common to employ a discourse of invisibility to describe the ways in which heteronormativity acts against queer lives, such descriptions are superficial to the multiple, simultaneous ways that heteronormativity really works. Indeed, as Lauren Berlant and Michael Warner have detailed, heteronormativity can take on a diverse set of forms. They argue that heteronormativity's "coherence is always provisional, and its privilege can take several (sometimes contradictory) forms: unmarked, as the basic idiom of the personal and the social; or marked as a natural state; or projected as an ideal or moral accomplishment. It consists less of norms that could be summarized as a body of doctrine than of a sense of rightness produced in contradictory manifestations—often unconscious, immanent to practice or to institutions."[26]

Given this conceptualization, GLBTQ persons do not face merely a single one-dimensional act of repression but a convoluted array of opposing assumptions that challenge often misplaced faith in a single form of resistance. These manifestations are interspersed throughout the wider culture, making resisting these forces even more complicated. As cultural institutions, cemeteries utilize these different forms of heteronormative privilege to produce their own effects that constrain queer alternatives, though the prevalence of each form is different depending upon the gravescape. Thus, as we will see, to resist heteronormativity within a gravescape requires GLBTQ rhetors not to undertake a single rhetorical response but to employ a constellation of rhetorics intervening at different points within the matrix of heterosexual power. In our case studies the aligned use of tactical/ephemeral and monumental memory rhetorics will serve this purpose in differing ways. However, central to this task is explicating the dynamics by which each form of heteronormativity functions within specific gravescapes.

Taking the last of Berlant and Warner's three forms of heteronormative privilege first, there are explicit heteronormative policies that are pervasive in making gravescapes antiqueer in their orientation through the projection of heterosexuality as a cultural ideal or moral accomplishment. Many of these policies are inscribed both into the laws of the nation and individual states and into the rules that regulate cemeteries as spaces of what Foucault would label biopolitical action.[27] At the most basic level these laws police the form and style of gravestones and other death displays. While these vary in degree and effect across the nation, perhaps the worst historical offenders have been the policies of Arlington National Cemetery and the U.S. military. As a result of the recently overturned Don't Ask, Don't Tell (DADT) policy, military veterans eligible for burial in the revered national cemetery have long been held to a tightly heteronormative regime in order to gain entrance. As a matter of policy, while the U.S. military authorizes "personalized words of endearment" for veteran headstone inscriptions, the Department of Veterans Affairs reserves the right to review and approve all such text. Historically, Veterans Affairs has rejected GLBTQ-affirmative words such as *gay, lesbian,* or *queer* from appearing on gravestones, as well as any other descriptive text that indicates a same-sex relationship.[28] Similarly, less-explicit gestures to such relationships have also been rejected by Veterans Affairs in the context of same-sex relationships. For instance, while the U.S. military offers such inscriptions as "My Beloved" for any opposite-sex spouse, family member, or significant other, such gestures have been rejected for use between same-sex partners.[29] However, without these explicit (or even veiled) inscriptions, service members interred in the cemetery are assumed to be heterosexual. Even though "Don't Ask, Don't Tell" has been overturned and the Department of Defense has signaled a willingness to allow GLBTQ veterans to be buried in these cemeteries, it seems unlikely the standards regulating acceptable inscriptions will be radically altered in the near term.[30] These policies extend beyond

Arlington to all military cemeteries that, incidentally, often set a cultural standard for how other cemeteries are imagined and policed.

In conjunction with these explicit regulations is a superstructure of heteronormative state and national laws and religious exemptions that prevent queer subjects from acting to ensure their identities beyond death. Among the plethora of such laws regulating marriage, inheritance, and property rights are explicit laws in reference to funerary rights and planning. While the U.S. Supreme Court has recently recognized same-sex marriage as both a valuable and legal social relationship, many states still have laws on the books that prevent one same-sex partner from making funeral arrangements for their significant other. For instance, liberal-leaning Minnesota has on a number of occasions denied same-sex partners funerary rights, even in cases where same-sex couples have completed their paperwork giving power of attorney to each other.[31] In these instances funeral plans—including the design and selection of headstones and any rituals performed at the burial—revert to the next of kin, many of whom who might be downright hostile to same-sex relationships or might make more-conservative representational choices that contribute to the erasure of their kin's queer identity in public memory. This risk was dramatized in early 2015 when it was revealed that the parents of transgender teenager Leelah Alcorn, who contributed to their child's suicide by forcing her into a Christian-based "transgender conversion therapy," refused to have her "true name" and gender engraved on her tombstone.[32] Currently, only the state of Rhode Island has passed legislation to attend to similar discrepancies affecting GLBTQ deaths while other states have not even recognized this issue—intentionally or not—as a problem.[33] Meanwhile, in the wake of the federal government's recognition of same-sex marriage, antigay actors have turned to other government protections to limit queer afterlives. Most commonly, religious institutions and vendors in the funeral industry have invoked faith-based objections to refuse funeral services for GLBTQ people, a form of discrimination now legally affirmed and likely to spread after the media attention surrounding Kentucky clerk Kim Davis and the Supreme Court's ruling in *Burwell v. Hobby Lobby*.[34]

These are just a few examples—not to mention the difficulties faced by GLBTQ persons in relation to their HIV/AIDS status—of the most explicit ways gravescapes take on and enforce a heteronormative posture. Drawing on Berlant and Warner's definition, these regulative regimes "project . . . as an ideal or moral accomplishment" heterosexuality in a way that privileges that relationship and discriminates against alternatives, to the point that those alternatives cease to be represented easily within the public eye. In doing so, gravescapes participate in solidifying the larger culture's assumption that heterosexuality is the only viable form of human desire and (re)secure for viewers the privileges of heterosexuality in every facet of human life, including death.

However, as Berlant and Warner's definition demonstrates, queer-affirmative spaces within gravescapes can also be undermined by two other forms of privilege. Each of these forms of heteronormative privilege can be seen in the two particular gravescapes described above: the memento mori style and the garden style.

In the memento mori style heterosexuality is privileged because it is "unmarked." To be heterosexual becomes compulsory "as the basic idiom of the personal and the social."[35] By this, Berlant and Warner suggest that to be heterosexual is, essentially, to be described as a person or part of a community. As we have seen already, cemeteries and their gravescapes can be thought of productively as social or community spaces. Thus in the context of a cemetery gravescape, heterosexuality is privileged by virtue of one's inclusion, both as an individual and as a part of the wider community. By being buried in the community cemetery among others, not only is the deceased individual incorporated into the ethos of that community; at the same time, by this simple act of inclusion, the deceased is presumed to be heterosexual. Certainly, heterosexuality can be marked visibly in these spaces: opposite-sex couples' names are regularly inscribed on common graves, for instance. However, the heteronormative quality of gravescapes is so pervasive and so invisible that this kind of explicit display is not necessary to suggest heterosexuality. To be buried in a memento mori cemetery is to be presumed heterosexual—and no marker is needed to make this explicit.

Despite the fact that markings are not needed (or, in fact, desired) to characterize those buried in this gravescape as heterosexual, it is worth considering several aspects of the memento mori aesthetic that contribute to making this unmarked presumption possible. The unstated nature of this heterosexuality is enhanced by the style and form of the gravescape itself. The plain style usually associated with memento mori aesthetics functions both to limit markings that might distinguish one grave easily from another and to emphasize community (that is, heterosexual) unity among all the graves and those buried there. However, when stylistic flourishes do appear on the graves, what is often inscribed also contributes to the heterosexual imperative.

Perhaps the most obvious of these stylistic claims to heteronormativity can be seen in the name of the style itself. "Memento mori"—Remember death—is the name of this style not only because it summarizes the rhetoric of the gravescape, but also because the words were frequently inscribed upon the headstones of the dead. By inscribing this motto on the headstones, the deceased and the community continually gestured to the living to forget life and to remember the coming judgment they would face in the afterlife. Such a discursive claim is enhanced by the use of shared iconography. Winged skulls and crosses in particular become visual markers that speak both to the literate and the illiterate passerby, reproducing in a different form the same message that the inscription puts forth. Both this inscription and the iconography are highly unifying moves that sweep away the individuality of particular lives in favor of remembering the individuals' souls through the perspective of religious morality. Yet when lived experiences are homogenized and forgotten, queer identities and desires fall by the wayside.

In addition, the few inscriptions placed on memento mori graves, while functioning to limit the reflection upon life and to focus it upon the common march toward death, prevent elaborations that might mark a grave's owner as queer. Besides displaying phrases such as *memento mori*, the majority of these headstones allow only for a brief inscription, including the name of the deceased, date of birth, and date of death. Even when the extraordinary step of including other details was taken in the memento mori style (family status or religious affiliation, for example), these details left little room for marking a nonheterosexual aesthetic. Thus the inability of those placed in memento mori cemeteries to include discourse that might mark them as queer is just another example of how queers who might speak become unable to express themselves in death displays intelligibly.

Finally, the denial of the body is largely productive of heteronormativity within the memento mori gravescape. For Morris, the most "salient memorial expression" for producing the worldview of the memento mori gravescape is the reliance upon the body-soul dichotomy.[36] The body is minimized in its representational form so that the soul might be remembered. However, the denial of body as an ephemeral object is in many ways a denial of homosexuality itself. Despite the fact that queer identities (since the beginning of queer theory) have largely focused upon the discursive construction of the body, making the body mainly a product of language and symbolism rather than something that exists a priori, the body remains a primary means for developing queer epistemologies.[37] Indeed, much of assuming the position of a queer subject derives from experimenting with the body (one's own and others) or having one's bodily interactions disciplined and policed by others. However, it is because queer bodies are often not constituted by society as "bodies that matter" that the body becomes a key part of queer existence: a tool for interrogating heterosexuality. It is through queer work to resignify the body that queers might "expand the very meaning of what counts as a valued and valuable body in the world."[38] Indeed, as Berlant and Elizabeth Freeman have argued, queer bodies can often be used in visibility politics to express heteronormativity's pervasive effects. As in the rhetorical acts of the queer activist organization Queer Nation, it is the "bodies of Queer Nationals to act as visibly queer flash cards, in an ongoing project of cultural pedagogy aimed at exposing the range and variety of bounded spaces upon which heterosexual supremacy depends."[39] As such, denial of the body is a rhetorical resource central to the traditional memento mori style.

Similarly, the garden style cemetery is permeated by normative heterosexuality. However, unlike the memento mori style, the garden style proceeds to make its claim not by presumption but by explicitly marking heterosexuality. In this way the garden cemetery takes on the characteristic quality of heteronormativity (described by Berlant and Warner) by being "marked" as part of a "natural state."[40] Indeed, as we have seen, the rhetoric of the natural is fundamental to understanding the work done in a garden cemetery. Thus, the death displays and their heteronormative rhetorics presented within the garden cemetery gravescape highlight what are presumed to be natural qualities of community life and death.

Several representative forms are present within the death displays of garden cemeteries that mark heterosexuality as not only normative but natural as well. First, the garden cemetery is designed visually to represent desire and romance. As spaces that combined art and nature in hopes of creating a beautiful landscape, garden cemeteries largely had as their telos the production of romantic emotions. As Blanche Linden-Ward suggests, these displays of death "intended to elicit specific emotions, especially the so-called pleasures of melancholy that particularly appealed to contemporary romantic sensibilities."[41] Indeed, romance was often the goal not only of the displays themselves but also of those who visited these places. In the height of the garden style's popularity suitors and young couples frequently visited these rural picturesque cemeteries as part of their wooing activities. More than a few couples were so overcome with the romantic nature of the graves that they used the sometimes secluded spaces of the cemeteries for more-torrid physical expressions of romance.[42] Because of this circumstance the gravescapes were romantic not only in the sense of the natural beauty of the grounds and the pathetic designs of the markers but also in the sense that those who visited the cemetery observed other couples romantically enjoying it. Thus the garden cemetery gravescape (in ways never possible for the memento mori space) became a venue where romance was put on display, performed, and then redisplayed in performances before others. It goes without saying that these performances and representations of romance and desire were overwhelmingly heterosexual. For the visitor to the garden gravescape then, heterosexual desire was endlessly on display in ways that encouraged its cultural value and performative reproduction.

Where the garden gravescape succeeded in representing heterosexual romance and desire, it also relied upon grave markers that expressed highly heteronormative imagery. Heteronormative imagery does not mean markers that contained male and female figures in romantic embraces (though they exist) but symbolic markers that instructed viewers in the importance of this cultural value. One way this was achieved was by prominently featuring two figures within the art of garden cemetery gravescapes: women and children.[43] The inclusion of women and children, of course, tellingly leaves out the other figure requisite to the heterosexual norm: the male and/or father figure. However, his absence in this gravescape makes sense in two ways. First, the male figure is often used to represent rationality, a cultural value antithetical to the pathos-driven goals of the garden style. Second, the male figure is never needed to be present in these representations for the sheer fact that he is always there a priori. In Peggy Phelan's characterization, it is because the male is considered normative that he is unmarked: "Within this psycho-philosophical frame, cultural reproduction takes she who is unmarked, and re-marks her, rhetorically and imagistically, while he who is marked with value is left unremarked, in discursive paradigms and visual fields."[44] Thus it is because of the very cultural necessity of man as a valued part of representative life that he need not appear. It is, of course, ironic that masculinity is assured in this case because it is unmarked, while homosexuality is made precarious through a similar, though different, unmarked valence. However, it is because masculinity is normatively assumed in Western culture (unlike homosexuality which is normatively not assumed) that the man's presence may be made clear without explicit acknowledgment. Without the representational appeal to a man, however, how do these forms represent heterosexuality as the preferred mode of living (and dying)? The images of women and children do so in their own way, each contributing to shaping a public view that ensures heteronormativity.

The form of the woman in funerary art—while serving other representational purposes including pathetic appeal—supports heterosexuality by providing the male gaze with an object of pleasurable looking. Women have frequently served this role within visual culture in many diverse gazing settings, and cemeteries are no exception. While women in gravescapes and monuments generally serve allegorical purposes,[45] the aesthetic that they embody is always favorable to the male gaze, a gaze that Laura Mulvey reminds us is highly "erotic" in its choice of object.[46] By visualizing highly desirable yet allegorical women in funerary art, garden gravescapes serve much the same function that classical male statuary did for some homosexual men during the Victorian era: as galleries of desire.[47] While such a desirable gaze can be imagined by women viewers in the cemetery as well, it seems likely that those stares would be policed, leaving the beautiful female forms of the garden gravescape the purview of (and instructor in) heterosexual desire.

Perhaps more important than depictions of women, the image of children is a prominent signifier of the heterosexual imperative. During the nineteenth century, when the garden cemetery came into popularity, the symbolic use of children in funerary art became a prevalent refrain in American culture. In the pathos-driven environment of these gravescapes, the loss of the child was perhaps the most difficult and frequently necessitated an elaborate display.[48] While angels or cherub figures often represented the graves of children, sculptures of children themselves were also sometimes used to adorn garden cemetery gravescapes. According to Viviana A. Rotman Zelizer, during the nineteenth century in large cemeteries in France, Italy, and the United States, "small children quickly became the favorite subject of funerary art."[49] Even when children were not themselves represented in a physical form in the cemetery sculpture, children were highly visible in the garden gravescape. Scholars have noted how, at least since the early eighteenth century, cemeteries began the trend of placing smaller headstones to mark visually the deceased as having died in childhood.[50] In this landscape children are a prominent visual feature.

The highly visual marking of children in representational funerary displays had important meanings. First, representations of children suggested the cyclical nature of life and death made possible through reproduction.[51] In the nineteenth century the only possible means of bringing a child into the world was through heterosexual intercourse. Thus heterosexuality was demanded to maintain this cyclical logic. Second, these representations showed the exceptional cultural value of children. Within this visual frame, children are perpetually cherished. Their deaths are mourned extraordinarily and marked with highly elaborate displays. Thus the loss or absence of a child signified not only a personal but also a cultural tragedy. This significance may not appear to be necessarily antiqueer. However, Lee Edelman has suggested that representationally children are symbolically opposed to queer existence, because they signify and demonstrate the value of the future-oriented drive for reproduction.[52] Hence, Edelman argues, the common rhetorical appeal to "save the children" exceeds the politics of the Left or Right, often to the detriment of those who cannot biologically reproduce. Though many queers challenge Edelman's read, at the very least the elaborate visual and material culture organized around children in the garden funerary gravescape signals to any viewer that children (as the product of heterosexual intercourse) are of high epideictic value.

In conjunction with the prominence of images of children, other representational logics were used to instruct viewers in the value of compulsory heterosexuality. Prominent among these are how grave organization instilled a cyclical sense of time within the gravescape, representing heteronormative reproduction as the measure of order, success, and identity. As opposed to the memento mori style that focused upon the fleeting quality of earthbound life, the garden gravescape "consistently and continually recapitulates a view of time as cyclical."[53] Key to securing this conception was the notion of generations. In short, if the gravescape promoted cyclical time, reproduction became a primary means of representing that notion. Thus it should not be surprising that "family" is an exaggerated representational element in garden death displays. Indeed, the landscapes of garden cemeteries are highly communal. Mausoleums and family crypts are promoted as ideal representational forms for those who could make such a monetary investment. For others the plans of cemeteries "encouraged families to have a centerpiece memorial surrounded by matching footstones."[54] No matter the design choice, the gravescape operated by the logic that family was a key means for assessing a life's worth. In this way the garden cemetery's logic participates fully in what Warner might call a repro-narrativity rhetoric—a visual message that reproduction is everything, a rhetoric that by its very nature can be antithetical to many queer lives.[55] And, as Edelman reminds us, "that rhetoric is intended precisely to assert that this issue *has* only one side."[56] For the lone queer this representational form was largely unavailable. This is not to say that a queer might not find a place within a family plot. But outside of the confines of marriage and family, the single deceased person, either within or outside of the family-plot system, becomes positioned as the queer "old spinster" or "bachelor." Thus biological families became not just the organizing logic of these gravescapes but also the visual reflection of a well-lived life, surrounded by waves of generational heirs.

Projected, marked, and unmarked: each form of heteronormative (non-) representation within rhetorics of death contributes to the marginalization of queer alternatives. The contradictory natures of these three forms of heteronormativity suggest the complex relations of power that make the heterosexual presumption difficult to overcome. For a queer activist, attacking any one form on its own would be inherently useless, because the other forms of heteronormativity would compensate for the activist's challenge until the singular queer effort to resist would presumably be reterritorialized or enveloped back into the fold.[57] A queer project of resistance to the heteronormative death-and-dying apparatus requires a combination of simultaneous disruptive monumental and tactical and ephemeral memory acts focused on the highly contextual (that is, rhetorical) needs of each form. Of these, the heteronormative form that projects heterosexuality as an ideal has already come under sustained interrogation by queer-affirmative forces. Traditional and unconventional repudiations of DADT, DOMA, funerary-rights laws, and discrimination have been and continue to be undertaken regularly. They have also been written about extensively. Because this is so, our emphasis here is on the two other forms of heteronormativity—its unmarked and marked (but natural) forms—within the confines of gravescapes as the locus of queer rhetorical action.

The Queering of Congressional Cemetery
■

Along the banks of the Anacostia River, a few miles before it empties into the Potomac basin that surrounds Washington, D.C., sits the famed and forgotten Congressional Cemetery. Founded in 1807 as a burial site for an Episcopal church, the cemetery quickly became the favored burial ground for Washington and the nation's most revered souls. Interred in its grounds are American luminaries, congressmen, vice presidents, Supreme Court justices, soldiers, and others including John Phillip Sousa and J. Edgar Hoover, giving the cemetery an important place at the very heart of our cultural epideictic. The prestige of the cemetery lasted decades until after the Civil War when Arlington National Cemetery, largely based upon the design of Congressional Cemetery, was constructed a few miles to the west.[58] In the decades that followed, the popularity of Congressional Cemetery for displaying the national dead waned, and the burial ground fell into disrepair by the end of the twentieth century and was almost forgotten by the nation that once so prized its pristine ethos.

Within this needed but neglected national space has emerged a compelling rhetorical recuperation by a group of gay men and lesbians seeking to build their own lasting space of queer memory amid the national ethos. The queering of Congressional Cemetery, by an assortment of queer individuals, has been under way for several decades, and it is only recently that these efforts' full potential has come into public view. Drawing upon the turn to queer monumentality, this project has been highly successful not only at creating enduring queer spaces of meaning but also at disrupting the heteronormative apparatus that is present in the cemetery's rhetorical gravescape.

However, while monumental in form and aim, this rhetorical endeavor simultaneously relied upon tactical and ephemeral opportunities rarely seen earlier. Perhaps most important, this act of queer monumentality was not a monolithic coordinated effort of queer memory making. This queer project is better understood as the work of a series of singular and fragmentary acts perpetrated by individuals and groups at different times and in uncoordinated ways, but united by a shared perspective and with the common queer aim of resistance. Reading and analyzing the rhetoric of all these acts together is an effort at synthesizing a viable text from fragmentary rhetorics dispersed over several decades.[59] The contributors to these acts can best be understood as three different waves of queer subjects.

The first is the original known queer inhabitant of the cemetery: Peter Doyle. Doyle is widely regarded as Walt Whitman's most enduring and cherished lover.[60] He is buried in one of the older parts of the cemetery, in a shared grave with his brother Edward. His headstone is appropriate to the stylistic constraints of a memento mori gravescape: a simple marble arch with his name, date of death, and age at the time of death (fifty-nine years). Though there is little in Doyle's death display to mark him as queer, his notoriety has made his grave a popular tourist site for queer visitors. Thus Doyle's grave can be read as a queer representation only for an audience already in the know.

The second wave of queer death display is the most prominent: the Gay Vietnam Veterans Memorial, also known as the grave of Sergeant Leonard Matlovich (fig. 6). Matlovich was a gay Vietnam veteran who challenged his dishonorable discharge from the United States Air Force in 1975. With the support of the National Gay Task Force (now the National LGBTQ Taskforce) and his military-appointed attorney, Matlovich waged a cautious public battle to remain in the military and continue his service as a decorated airman (Matlovich earned the Purple Heart when he received extensive injuries while removing a minefield in Vietnam in 1971). Matlovich would become the heavily promoted public face of the modern gay and lesbian rights movement, appearing on such popular television shows as *Donahue* and becoming the first openly gay person to make the cover of *TIME* magazine in 1975. His conservative politics, military heroism, and patriotic beliefs made him an appealing representative for many within the GLBT community and made him a noted public figure. Nonetheless, the Air Force succeeded in removing Matlovich from the service after the civilian courts upheld his initial dismissal in 1976. However, Matlovich was able to appeal his "general" discharge, receiving an honorable discharge soon thereafter, a feat rarely repeated until recently. While Matlovich will perhaps always be best known for his challenge of military policy, his work extended far beyond that issue alone. He would become a prominent advocate for gay and lesbian rights and a highly visible figure within the movement. Matlovich also founded the short-lived Never Forget Project, which focused on creating memorials for GLBTQ people.[61] However, like those of many men of his generation, Matlovich's contributions were cut short by an early death. Within a few months of his diagnosis, Matlovich would die of "AIDS-related illnesses" in June 1988 at the age of forty-four.

Prior to his death Matlovich designed and installed the Gay Vietnam Veterans Memorial at the future site of his own grave in Congressional Cemetery. Confronted by a grim prognosis and having faced death earlier in his life, Matlovich, perhaps more than most, was aware of the ease with which an individual's sexuality could be wiped away in the process of death and dying: "Had I died in Vietnam when I hit the mine, I would have been just another dead Vietnam vet, you see. I would not have been a specifically *gay* Vietnam veteran who died for his country."[62] Having lived near Congressional Cemetery and once asked by a passerby where the grave of Peter Doyle was located, Matlovich was intrigued by the possibilities of creating a memorial

FIG. 6

Gay Vietnam Veterans Memorial, also known as the grave
of Sergeant Leonard Matlovich, in Congressional Cemetery,
Washington, D.C. Photograph by the author.

site where gay men and women could gather and where gay veterans in particular could be remembered "not only for their sacrifice but also for their
sense of self-worth as gay people."[63] This feeling was only strengthened after visiting the grave of Stein and Toklas on a trip to Paris. Two years after
conceiving the idea, he completed and installed the memorial.[64] More than
most other early leaders of the gay and lesbian rights movement, Matlovich
understood the potential of queer public memory projects to do rhetorical
work, setting the standard by which many others would soon follow.

The third and most recent wave of queer memorialists is a collection of
gay and lesbian veterans, artists, and activists who have followed Matlovich's
lead and sought to mark intentionally their graves as queer within the public
space of Congressional Cemetery. This group consists of about ten to fifteen
gay and lesbian people[65] who have either been interred or have placed their
markers in the cemetery, including pioneering gay and lesbian rights leaders
Franklin Kameny, Kay Tobin Lahusen, and Barbara Gittings.[66] While separated by years and with backgrounds and politics often different from those
of Matlovich himself, the third wave of memorialists has largely adopted his

approach toward marking homosexuality within the gravescape. Collectively, these three waves of death displays work to disrupt the heteronormative gravescape of Congressional Cemetery while simultaneously making space for enduring images of queer alternatives.

The key to understanding these queer legacy makers' strategies lies in identifying the cemetery's preexisting public messaging.[67] Like most cemeteries in existence over several centuries, the style of Congressional Cemetery has evolved to include more contemporary forms. However, by and large Congressional Cemetery can be understood as a memento mori gravescape. The vast majority of the graves in the cemetery are simple headstones with modest inscriptions that participate in a visual argument to passersby to remember that death is always present and to make haste in preparing for its coming. Within Congressional Cemetery, life is seen as fleeting, bodies become unimportant to the soul, and all participants join the chorus in echoing the call to prepare for eternity now.

Amid this meaningful imagery queer subjects and viewers have intervened to challenge this heteronormative rhetoric and make space for queer alternatives. This rhetorical intervention has been successful largely because it suits the forms of heteronormativity that function within the memento mori landscape that leave sexuality an unmarked expression within death display. Thus in a gravescape in which homosexuality is made invisible, gay and lesbian graves have been designed to make homosexuality visible for others to see.

However, before these activists could undertake these mostly monumental works, a tactical undertaking was first required. In this case, building explicit GLBTQ-affirmative monuments would be meaningless without having an appropriate place for them to reside. As the first of the activists to face this reality, Matlovich confronted the troublesome task of finding a cemetery to accept his monument. As a veteran, Matlovich would perhaps have ideally erected his monument in Arlington National Cemetery; however, as a gay veteran dismissed with great fanfare, efforts to that effect appeared unlikely to succeed. Likewise, military restrictions at the time would have never permitted him to make explicit references to his sexuality on his marker, thereby erasing his identity in exactly the ways he sought to avoid. Facing these obstacles, Matlovich selected Congressional Cemetery with great tactical acumen. Though not Arlington, Congressional Cemetery had the prestige of its interred and its use as a model for official military cemeteries, which gave it the allure of importance and respectability without the constraints of military administration. Similarly, because Congressional Cemetery was increasingly deteriorating as a popular burial site, its administrators seemed willing to accept Matlovich's elaborate and unusual burial plans, even despite the cemetery's historical connections to the Episcopal Church. Therefore, the various efforts to mark GLBTQ lives monumentally in Congressional Cemetery owe much of their success to the shrewd tactical memory choices made by Matlovich at the outset.

For the graves themselves the memorialists utilized a number of different monumental strategies—in this case material and enduring forms—to mark their identities as queer within the memento mori gravescape: drawing attention and scrutiny through design, marking through inscriptions, highlighting with iconography, signifying with bodies, juxtaposing with other monuments, and circulating reproductions of the graves to a wider audience.

The memorialists' first strategy was to draw attention and scrutiny to their graves through the monument's design. An important aspect of the heteronormative quality of memento mori style graves is their normative, universal appeal. In traditional viewing practice memento mori gravescapes were not inspected deeply or lingered upon. Rather they were viewed from afar, requiring a repetitive, highly visible series of images and icons to make their rhetorical case. This practice was encouraged often by the disrepair into which memento mori cemeteries were allowed to fall. Containing only the remains of the deceased, little attention was given to maintaining these graves, which served only as empty vessels.[68] Viewers have looked at Congressional Cemetery in a similar manner, particularly during the several recent decades when it was in a high state of disrepair. By virtue of this limited viewing practice, few graves received individual scrutiny and community outliers were rendered mute to the community worldview. Because of this situation the memorialists marked homosexuality within the cemetery to obtain the attention of passersby and invite their scrutiny. This act of rhetorical summoning, if done successfully, would provide the rhetorical situation for other interventions to be made that might more fully speak to queer identity.[69]

The memorialists managed to hail their audiences in several ways. One way is by color. Almost every traditional grave in Congressional Cemetery is white or gray in color. However, Matlovich's grave and the graves of F. Warren O'Reilly and Emmanuel "Butch" Zeigler all stand out for their dark black granite color, a gesture toward the postmodern Vietnam Veterans Memorial a few miles to the west on the National Mall. The joint grave of Charles Fowler and Kenneth Dresser is a similar dark color. In addition, the stones of Michael Hildebrand and Clyde Tolson are of a pinkish hue that stands out especially on brighter days. Recently, a gay donor placed bright red benches near the gay graves to invite further attention to the cemetery from outside its gates.[70] Even from afar, many of these graves are quite noticeable as distinct from the others.

Similarly, form is another way in which queers play with attention in the visual field. While some of the headstones utilize the traditional arch pattern, Hildebrand's stone, for instance, is triangular, featuring a squat pyramid

FIG. 7
■
A death display using form to queer the gravescape.
Photograph by the author.

design that would be more common in newer cemeteries. Most powerful, however, is Fowler and Dresser's joint marker. It features a polished cube, about two feet long on each side, in a three-dimensional form. The distinction of form is accentuated because the cube is raised above the ground and turned on its axis so that it is tilted into the air (fig. 7). In a gravescape where flat vertical stones reach for heaven and one's ability to erect a taller stone ensures a grander place in the hierarchy of souls, Fowler and Dresser's cube speaks not of hierarchy but of both a cosmic equality and an equality shared by these two same-sex lovers. Of all the stones it is unique in the gravescape, particularly as it is featured near the main gate at the center of the cemetery.

Finally, location is another way in which the gay and lesbian graves garner attention. While each of these graves is distinctive in some way that marks it as queer, in a cemetery where more than fifty-five thousand bodies are buried it would be extremely difficult to locate one, even for the highly perceptive viewer. Because of this circumstance queers have attempted to utilize a shared location to magnify the graves' visual impact. Though many of the graves are scattered across the cemetery because of cost and space needs, nine graves are clustered near one another in a spot that has become unofficially known as the "gay corner" or "gay ghetto."[71] This unique commemorative zone is a highly trafficked area within the cemetery, positioned at the intersection of two of the major prescribed pathways within the space.[72] At least one gay or lesbian grave is situated on each side of the intersection, making it all but impossible for a passing visitor's eye to miss. This location is also powerful from a distance: not only is it visible on a low slope from the center of the cemetery, but, by placing all these markers together, their visual impact in color and form is heightened further. This position is enhanced by material elements that gesture to viewers to pause for greater inspection. In particular, the corner features both a bench—which is an addendum to the Matlovich memorial—and a shade tree. Both of these elements appeal to the material needs of the viewing body, inviting relief from weary feet and intense sun while simultaneously raising audience attention. By utilizing color, form, and location to hail viewing audiences from both inside and outside the cemetery gates, these graves encourage attention to the unique set of rhetorical headstones, both marking them as outsiders (that is, queer) vis-à-vis the normative appearance of the other interred and positioning viewers for an array of other rhetorical efforts from close range. Having garnered the viewer's attention, these gravescape put to work an assortment of other rhetorical interventions to mark them as queer and disrupt the heteronormative presumption of the gravescape.

The second monumental strategy employed by the memorialists is the use of complex rhetorical inscriptions to mark themselves as queer. As Morris has suggested, the marker inscriptions in memento mori gravescapes "characteristically provide only the deceased's name, age, date of death, and, less frequently, date of birth, cause of death, and family or community status, with by far the largest number providing nothing more than a very brief inscription."[73] This is the norm in Congressional Cemetery, even on the larger markers. Indeed, even on the famous cenotaphs of Congressional leaders, only the name, dates of birth and death, and state and/or district they represented are engraved.

However, queer memorialists defy this stylistic expectation, utilizing their headstone inscriptions to make powerful and explicit coming-out statements in the context of a heteronormative afterlife. Matlovich's grave is perhaps the most notable in defying this convention. His headstone is inscribed with text above and beyond name and birth and death dates. Most important is the main text: "A Gay Vietnam Veteran." Two aspects of this text have powerful rhetorical effect: the anonymity of the phrase and the use of the word *gay*. By using the anonymous inscription "Vietnam Veteran," Matlovich manages both to disrupt the convention of memento mori graves that requires a proper name and to create a (monumental) space for not just himself but for all gay and lesbian veterans who have gone forgotten in cemeteries around the world. By using the word *gay* explicitly on the headstone, Matlovich makes a statement of identification. Etched into the stone, the text here serves as a vehicle for a commemorative coming out. While countless other gay and lesbian veterans have given their lives in support of country, many of them continue to go unacknowledged because their identity is so easily forgotten in its ephemeral state. By engraving *gay* on the tombstone itself, Matlovich rhetorically attempts to prevent any effort to minimize or forget his intersectional position. More important than even his name (which would be added to his footstone later), the title "Gay Vietnam Veteran" defines Matlovich's identity so as to persist through time in monumental fashion.

Beneath this main text another secondary inscription appears on the gravestone: "When I was in the military, they gave me a medal for killing two men and a discharge for loving one." This inscription is powerful in that it again makes explicit the fact that Matlovich and other veterans had same-sex attractions while simultaneously serving their nation honorably. The statement contradicts the logic of DADT, which attempted to bifurcate homosexuality and service as incompatible. In addition, this line of inscription is powerful because it is a quotation that Matlovich frequently used in his speeches, interviews, and protests. By reproducing this ephemeral form of public address in stone, Matlovich ensures that not only will he be remembered as queer but also that persuasive intent will live beyond him.

While Matlovich's headstone offers perhaps the best-known and most-often viewed uses of inscriptions in the cemetery, several other gay and lesbian memorialists' graves use inscriptions to make their queer identities visible. Like Matlovich, F. Warren O'Reilly's grave marks his military service with the phrase "A Gay W.W. II Veteran." He also uses a favored line of public address to make a perpetual political statement: "During my eventful lifetime, the only honest and truthful ending of the Pledge of Allegiance was '. . . with Liberty and Justice for SOME.'" Tom "Gator" Swann mimics this act, marking his military service as a "Proud Gay Veteran" while reminding his grave's viewers to "Never give up hope or give in to discrimination." William Boyce Mueller's headstone also relies on inscriptions, though not to mark his military service. Instead Mueller highlights that he was the "Founder of Forgotten Scouts," an organization committed to opening the Boy Scouts of America to gay scouts and scoutmasters. More recently interred gay liberation leaders have continued this rhetorical strategy. Lahusen and Gitting's memorial bench proclaims them "gay pioneers who spoke truth to power" and "Partners in life, Married in our hearts," while plans for Kameny's stone will include his iconic phrase "Gay is Good." While inscriptions vary, the use of inscription to mark queer identity in a way to prevent the forgetting power of heteronormativity is a powerful means of disrupting the heterosexual gaze and perpetuating queer activism after death.

In conjunction with the textual inscriptions, a third monumental strategy uses iconography on headstones to challenge the conventions of memento mori death display and mark queer identity visibly. Again Matlovich's marker sets the standard. Whereas memento mori displays generally rely heavily upon a group of deathly images—winged skulls, skeletons, crosses—to remind even the illiterate of the message of impending death, Matlovich's display embraces two important icons with powerful significance in the gay and lesbian community: both the upright and inverted pink triangle. The first triangle (worn by homosexuals in concentration camps) is a ghostly reminder of the persecution homosexuals faced during the Nazi regime—a persecution that continued after the war because homosexuality was considered illegal by liberating Allied forces. Therefore, while Allied liberators freed Jewish prisoners, homosexual individuals remained imprisoned.[74] The second is a symbol of the gay liberation movement, an inverted symbol of persecution reclaimed by a people in search of political and cultural recognition. Enhancing the iconography of the triangles are two phrases, one just below each icon: beneath the pink triangle the phrase "Never Again" and below the inverted pink triangle the phrase "Never Forget."

While the effect of these gay and lesbian icons is similar to that of any icons in that they translate the rhetoric of the headstones' words into visual form (in this case, marking a queer identity), the icons also simultaneously return the viewer to a reflection upon life, not death. As Morris suggests, the limited use of icons on memento mori graves was intended to emphasize only the eternal soul and not the empty vessel of the human body. By privileging an alternative set of icons for the viewer, Matlovich is able to question the superficiality of life on earth. In particular, by utilizing both triangles in linear fashion Matlovich's iconographic rhetoric suggests not only that life matters but also that life can produce important works—in this case, progress from the persecution of gay and lesbian victims to the liberation of gay and lesbian activists. Similar iconography of victory and liberation through life's vital work is represented in other gay and lesbian graves in the cemetery.[75] Thus, in addition to reinforcing the fact that this grave marks the remains of a queer person, the use of these alternative icons signals that we should remember life—particularly as it is within life that many gay and lesbian people can most easily mark their sexuality.

Fourth, another monumental strategy in marking homosexuality visibly within the gravescape is reliance upon making queer bodies visible. While the majority of the monuments that populate the Congressional Cemetery gravescape are vertical and contribute to the heavenward imperative to forget the ephemeral existence of life, many of the queer death displays seek to draw attention to their queer bodies to provide an alternative rhetoric. For instance, the Matlovich memorial, despite its vertical elements, is largely horizontal in its dimensions. This visual form is created in part by a squat headstone, but, more important, by the large black memorial tomb that marks the location of Matlovich's body in the grave. While Matlovich's grave is not the only one to contain a memorial tomb in the cemetery, it is one of only a few. Equally, it features several visual elements that make it more powerful than others. The visual weight of this tomb is enhanced by its color—a black granite to match the headstone itself. The tomb is adorned with a small decorative plaque from the United States government and engraved with the signature of President George H. W. Bush, signaling Matlovich's status as a veteran and thanking him for his military service to the nation (an important, albeit, hard-won recognition that would require minimal effort on the part of heterosexual veterans to secure).

The highly visible presence of the body at Matlovich's memorial is a key way in which heteronormativity is disrupted. Amid the other graves, the bodies of the deceased disappear into the headstones. We witness the stones but do not linger upon what they mark. This, in itself, speaks to the success of the memento mori displays: their desire to push the corporeal body away as inconsequential to the soul. But by foregrounding the body in its posthumous physical container, Matlovich's grave prevents such work from happening. The body here is ever present; it retains epistemological value, and, as such, is able to instruct the viewer in a rhetoric that is queer-friendly and contrary to that espoused by the cemetery as a whole. Though Matlovich's body is not something upon which a greater queer message is written, its presence, its embodiment, serves to argue for the serious contemplation not just of the dead's pious soul (a notable antigay standard by most interpretations) but also of the embodied lives we lead here on earth. By privileging instead of fearing the body, the rhetoric of the Matlovich memorial expands the availability for queer existence within a heteronormative landscape.

For other queers the body becomes present in another way: a shared-burial plot for same-sex lovers. While Matlovich's early death on account of HIV/AIDS prevented him from ever finding the life partner he had so desired, several gay men are buried in shared plots in Congressional Cemetery after long lives together. Shared plots, while cost effective, are also highly rhetorical in what they say about the two persons buried together. They indicate, at the very least, a powerful relationship between the two. Importantly, this relationship is rendered corporeal in a gravescape, not just spiritual. According to Alan Bray, "the hope that gesture makes concrete . . . is not a hope of distant life in heaven, but a corporeal hope on this earth: that on the Last Day, at the general resurrection of the dead, the first figure his awakened eyes will see will be him."[76]

Two people of the same gender sharing a grave is not necessarily a radical statement in a cemetery. For centuries the practice occurred frequently involving two male friends who participated in a certain liturgical rite that made them "sworn brothers."[77] David Wallace, in a review of Bray's important book *The Friend,* characterizes the relationship of sworn brothers as "the particularly embodied, same-sex person to whom an individual elects to be ceremonially bound for life, to love unto death, and to be buried within a common grave."[78] While this rite in many ways seems comparable to similar early forms of same-sex union, there is much disagreement about its meaning.[79] However, perhaps more important to its visual meaning is that this practice largely became unintelligible among same-sex friends after the nineteenth century, when married couples and other family members were almost exclusively buried together.[80] In contemporary times placing two men in a common grave that is marked and visible to passing visitors signals the meaning affiliated with a spousal relationship between gay or lesbian lovers.

To further prevent the possibility that such graves might be attributed to a friendly or, in some cases, brotherly relationship, some of the couples include inscriptions on the stone qualifying how their shared corporeal marking should be understood. For instance, the memorial bench for Gittings and Lanhusen explicitly describes their relationship as partners and their wish to be married, plainly renouncing reading the monument as meant for two close friends. Likewise, the tomb of John Frey and Peter Morris recounts unambiguously the nature of their relationship with a romantic poem. The representations of these shared plots are prominent ways in which heteronormativity is disrupted within the cemetery. The memorialists question the standard assumption of same-sex interaction by removing the interred from the context of individual graves where they might more easily be discerned by the passing viewer as a presumed heterosexual man or woman and placing them within a mutual grave commonly shared by heterosexual spouses.

Fifth, juxtaposition of graves is a highly effective means of disrupting the heteronormativity of Congressional Cemetery. While we have already seen how the proximity of the gay and lesbian graves to one another frequently enhances their rhetorical value—despite the ghettoization and tokenism that might be read by some viewers—the way in which these graves are differentiated from others is also a powerful visual rhetorical act. Putting into dialogue the various gay and lesbian graves with another prominent grave within Congressional Cemetery—that of J. Edgar Hoover—most effectively demonstrates this dynamic.

Most visible of all the graves in generating a queer dialogue within the cemetery gravescape is Matlovich's visual interaction with the grave of J. Edgar Hoover. The juxtaposition is perhaps most satisfying not only because of the proximity of the two graves but also because both men are held in esteem for their service to their country. The fact that Matlovich chose to be buried only a few plots away in the same row as the (in)famous Hoover sets up a telling rhetorical frame, though it is not entirely clear that Matlovich selected the location with a specific intent.[81] Indeed, whereas Matlovich established his gravestone to contrast with the other stones in the cemetery, he also seems to have established a stark point of comparison between himself and the deeply closeted FBI director, who actively persecuted gay men through the FBI in what some might psychoanalyze as a consequence of his self-loathing.[82]

Juxtaposed within a single frame of vision, Hoover's and Matlovich's graves are a story in contrasts: Matlovich in black granite, Hoover in pure white granite; Matlovich with a highly eloquent statement of pride and defiance, Hoover with only his name, birth and death dates; Matlovich buried as the single gay man he was, Hoover buried in a shared grave with his mother and sister. These contrasts alone speak to a certain queer ethos. Making the comparison even starker, in the more dilapidated days of the cemetery the FBI erected a high black iron gate around Hoover's grave. Ostensibly to keep out troublemakers, today the fence seems to lock Hoover away behind the secretive veil he so guarded while he was alive. Reflected in the large colored seal of the Federal Bureau of Investigation that fronts the fence, the heteronormative state apparatus seems to swallow Hoover and his sexuality whole. Interestingly, employees at Congressional Cemetery have noted that this closeted, normative rhetoric at Hoover's grave is not always respected: apparently, on a yearly basis a solitary women's high-heel shoe is left hanging on the gate fronting Hoover's final resting place. Who leaves this token is unclear; nonetheless, it can certainly be read as another instance of tactical and ephemeral memory rhetoric pointedly undermining heteronormativity alongside and in conjunction with the gay and lesbian memorialists more-monumental efforts.[83]

Perhaps most poignantly in considering the dialogue between Hoover's and Matlovich's graves is the fact that situated between them lies another small grave of a man named Clyde Tolson. Tolson was an associate director of the FBI and a protégé of Hoover. Many believe that Tolson and Hoover were also lovers. For decades they worked together, ate all their meals together, vacationed together, and socialized together at various nightclubs. After Hoover's death, he left almost everything to Tolson. While biographers squabble over how to label their relationship, the fact that Tolson took immeasurable effort to be buried as near as possible to Hoover suggests at the least a deeply powerful homosocial attraction, if not a full-blown love affair.[84] While Tolson's body lies in limbo, hidden forever a few feet away from his likely lover, Matlovich's body lies alone in his tomb made for two, in perpetual hope that the love of his life, who never materialized, could be buried next to him openly and proudly. Simply stated, from these conflicting representational forms emerges a powerful argument for living a queer life and the consequences of having one's life decimated by paying fake tribute to the heteronormative powers that be.

The final and most recent of these monumental strategies is the reproduction of the gay and lesbian graves of those buried in Congressional Cemetery in museum displays, other monuments, and GLBTQ media—including magazines, blogs, travel guides, and books—to enhance their circulation. The reproduction of memorials, as Blair has suggested, has a number of positive benefits, chief of which is the democratization of access to these rhetorical and commemorative acts.[85] Thus efforts to reproduce these gay and lesbian graves in other settings have the potential to shape memory practices beyond the gravescape.

The most prominent reproduction is, not surprisingly, of Matlovich's grave. It has been reproduced in two formats with high visibility and, thus, the opportunity to enhance public persuasion. The first of these is a photograph of the grave reproduced for display during the groundbreaking 1994 exhibition *Becoming Visible: The Legacy of Stonewall* at the New York Public Library. According to the authoritative text, the exhibition "was the largest and most extensive exhibit on lesbian and gay history ever mounted in a mainstream American museum or gallery space."[86] Not only was the exhibition itself large; it was also well attended. In Lisa Duggan's account: "It is hard to overstate the importance of this exhibition which broke attendance records at the library, drawing 17,258 visitors in its first week and an average of 1,000 per day thereafter."[87] It is estimated more than one hundred thousand people visited the exhibit during its run. Images of Matlovich's grave featured prominently in the exhibit, circulating his rhetorical appeal beyond visitors to the cemetery itself.[88]

The second of these reproductions is a life-size replica of Matlovich's gravestone as a plaque on display on a sidewalk-facing wall near the Castro Theatre in San Francisco. The plaque is a modified replica of the original, changed in substance and colors, height, and text to include Matlovich's name. The Service Members Legal Defense Network (now known as OutServe-SLDN), a nonprofit organization that represented gays and lesbians dismissed or closeted in the U.S. military before the repeal of "Don't Ask, Don't Tell," installed the plaque. Appropriately, the plaque was unveiled on November 14, 2008, during ongoing queer activism for same-sex marriage and against DADT. The goal of the plaque, according to the official OutServe-SLDN website, is to honor Matlovich's life and activism and to "inspire" us all with "his courage, his commitment and his love."[89]

In many ways these two reproductions of the Matlovich grave are powerful rhetorical acts that further mark the public memory of Matlovich as queer. Through them, Matlovich's initial effort to create a queer afterlife is enhanced for heterosexual and homosexual viewers on the San Francisco streets or visitors to the New York Public Library. In some ways this monumental strategy also has an impact on Matlovich's memory in his original gravescape as well, to the extent that viewers learn that there is an actual gravestone in the cemetery in Washington, D.C. The monumental strategies of Matlovich and his gay and lesbian brothers and sisters at Congressional Cemetery used to mark themselves as queer in the medium of death displays are circulated, potentially providing others with techniques for queering their own afterlife.[90]

While the monumental rhetorics of the gay and lesbian veterans, artists, and activists to claim within Congressional Cemetery the space and time for an enduring queer afterlife are powerful, it would be inappropriate to suggest that they have completely overcome the heteronormative demands of death and dying. Indeed, despite the persuasive and apparently propagating rhetoric at work that seems to ensure a monumental memory of queer existence within the gravescape, heteronormativity is a powerful force. Visitors to the cemetery have already witnessed the luckily temporary forgetting of Matlovich's grave during the deterioration of the cemetery in the 1980s and 1990s. It is possible his acts to queer this space would have been entirely forgotten if not for the symbolic circulation of his gravescape in the queer public sphere in photographic form in 1994. Though renewed in public attention, Matlovich's queer grave and his admirers are a powerful intervention with regard to public views of sexuality. But heteronormativity still persists. The fact that few of the queer gravesites were mentioned in a public tour or map of the cemetery until recently is a haunting reminder of just how insidious efforts to forget the queer past can become. However, though perhaps more fleeting than we might wish, collectively these six monumental strategies function effectively together to mark for the casual viewer the pervasive heteronormative stylings of Congressional Cemetery. Simultaneously, they argue, through powerful visual markings, that these spaces need not be heterosexual alone—that those interred here might be remembered otherwise.

Naturalizing Lesbian Love in the Garden
■

Sixteen years after Matlovich's gravestone was placed in Congressional Cemetery, New York sculptor Patricia Cronin installed her own grave marker in a distinguished public cemetery to sanction her and her partner's legacy as same-sex lovers in marriage. The statue is entitled *Memorial to a Marriage* and features the sculpted bodies of Cronin and her real-life partner (artist Deborah Kass; Kass and Cronin legally married in 2011) naked and embracing one another beneath the covers of their heavenly bed in eternal rest (fig. 8). In design the statue is influenced by several sources. In part its subject matter and title are a homage to the famous *Adams Memorial* designed by Augustus Saint-Gaudens which Henry Adams commissioned in memory of his wife Clover Hooper Adams, both to mediate upon her traumatic suicide

FIG. 8
■
Patricia Cronin's
*Memorial to a
Marriage* (2002).
Courtesy of
Patricia Cronin.

and to celebrate their marriage after her death.[91] The design of the piece itself also relies heavily upon the work of lesbian artist Harriet Hosmer, a prominent nineteenth-century female artist of whom Cronin is both an admirer and a student. Some ascribe much of the influence on the design to Gustave Courbet's painting *The Sleepers* or *The Sleep* (1866).[92]

However, despite the influences on the sculpture, *Memorial to a Marriage* is distinctly its own and a prominent example of the turn to queer monumentality in the last twenty years. The original installation is one piece of white Carrara marble, carved by the artist herself using advanced twenty-first century technology. At eighty-four by forty-two by twenty-seven inches, the installation is larger than life-size, giving the memorial presence to compete within the cemetery's visual smorgasbord but not so much as to exaggerate the figures and their realistic qualities. In addition to the memorial itself, the grave markers that surround the installation are of extraordinary importance. The installation is located in a small valley at the base of a slowly slopping hill, dotted with diverse kinds of markers. While there are several small headstones directly in the vicinity of *Memorial to a Marriage,* the grave-scape is dominated by a series of mausoleums and epic statuary, along with a large number of trees and shrubs.

Like Matlovich's gravestone, *Memorial to a Marriage* derives a great deal of its rhetorical effect from its circulation as an iconic image. The piece itself has been featured prominently in several gallery shows (both national and international), circulated on the Internet, and reproduced on the cover of artistic periodicals such as *Sculpture* and popular queer publications such as the *Gay & Lesbian Review.* The piece has also been prominently discussed and displayed in more "mainstream" forums, including the *New Yorker,* the *New York Times,* the *Village Voice,* and the *Houston Chronicle.*[93] While it is doubtless that this circulation has reached and affected numerous individuals in the heterosexual public, it is likely that the vast majority of viewers of these reproduced images would consider themselves to be homosexual or their allies; therefore, photography of the memorial alone cannot explain its wider rhetorical impact among nonhomosexual audiences.

However, unlike Matlovich's grave, *Memorial to a Marriage* resides in an entirely different kind of gravescape, thus relying upon a completely differ-ent rhetoric to produce a powerful queer public memory (fig. 9). *Memorial to a Marriage* was originally installed in Woodlawn Cemetery in the Bronx, what is known as one of the United States' premier examples of the garden cemetery movement. The Woodlawn and Congressional gravescapes share much in common: their purpose, their renown, their proximity to major ur-ban centers, and their age. However, in contrast to the gay and lesbian graves in Congressional Cemetery, the successful disruption of heteronormativity within the garden gravescape does not rely upon heavily marking or mak-ing visible same-sex desire. In Congressional Cemetery heteronormativity is ensured by exclusion, by leaving all other alternatives unmarked. Hence, a rhetoric of visibility was appropriate and effective.

Yet in the case of the Woodlawn Cemetery, it is not visibility that is at issue but rather the rhetorical performance of that visibility. Because Wood-lawn is a gravescape that provides greater creativity to the individual, ex-clusion is not the preferred or sometimes the possible option. Rather, it is by visually marking a grave within the gravescape as valuable in its social hierarchy that heteronormativity is ensured. In this gravescape "valuable" is equated with the rhetoric of the natural. As Morris reminds us, it is by cre-ating highly natural graves that the deceased demonstrated their value and in the process warded off unnatural expressions within this sacred space.[94] In this vein it is by marking the grave as both queer *and* natural that hetero-normativity can be disrupted.

FIG. 9

∎

Memorial to a Marriage in Woodlawn Cemetery's
garden gravescape. Courtesy of Patricia Cronin.

To achieve this both/and effect *Memorial to a Marriage* relies upon monumentality to grant its message meaning and durability; however, a significant degree of its success lies in turning to tactical and ephemeral rhetorics
as well. In this case a tactical appropriation of the visual rhetoric of the
gravescape, married with a monumental form, becomes the key rhetorical
approach of the Cronin memorial.[95] At the core of this approach lies the
postmodern technique described by Gilles Deleuze, Félix Guattari, Jeffrey T.
Nealon, and others as "repetition with a difference." Utilizing a rhetorical
"repetition with a difference," *Memorial to a Marriage* turns the rhetoric of
the hierarchical and exclusionary forms of heteronormativity against itself to
embrace a queer potential and to create a space for queer public memory.[96]
Through appropriation of the cemetery's style, the memorial also appropri-
ates its visual rhetoric, rendering the queer condition of its figures within the
security of the natural landscape. To put it another way, while *Memorial to
a Marriage* is a "monument," it is also a tactical act in line with de Certeau's
usage of the term.[97] Just as Wilde used heterosexual history to excuse his own
queer behavior, Cronin uses heteronormative grave designs to shroud her
queer incursion. *Memorial to a Marriage,* therefore, uses visual trickery and
guile to invade the traditional space of heteronormativity. By entering this

queer form into the cemetery landscape in stealth, the memorial seeks simultaneously to make space for queer alternatives and disrupt heteronormativity.

To succeed in this undertaking, the death display must first represent the queerness of the grave. The most obvious and visually striking choice Cronin makes to represent the homosexual relationship between her and her lover is to embody them within the memorial. However, it is not just the existence of the bodies that do this work. History has demonstrated effectively that the mere presence of two women's bodies in proximity can easily be reasoned away as platonic if such an interpretation is not within the interest of the desiring (supposedly male) viewing subject. Rather it is the fact these bodies are engaged in a form of visual, same-sex affection that leaves little room to question their queer propensity. This queer visibility is especially keen in acquiring rapt, if not favorable, attention and infusing that attention with rhetorical consequence. As Charles E. Morris III and John M. Sloop have argued in relation to queer public kissing, putting representations of queer affection of display in the public sphere can have a radical political effect because such displays "constitute a 'marked' and threatening act, a performance instantly understood as contrary to hegemonic assumptions about public behavior, and the public good, because it invites judgments about . . . *deviant sexual behavior* and its imagined encroachments, violations and contagions, judgments that inevitably exceed the mere fact of their having a mutually affirming encounter."[98] While Morris and Sloop suggest that these displays are especially powerful when they include kissing, men, and media, I would suggest that the highly charged sexual connotations of the memorial beyond kissing, in conjunction with the touristic qualities of the cemetery, make the fact that this display features lesbians equally, if not more, significant in furthering a queer political act.[99] Certainly, the blissful and intimate embrace shared by these two naked women's bodies in the memorial can easily be read as sexual, serving (in a visually compelling way) not only to hail the attention of the passerby but also to mark the object of their gazing as intensely queer. Thus the memorial functions, within another visual frame, as a *"queer juggernaut."*[100]

Simultaneously, the memorial identifies its participants as queer by failing to take part in the heteronormative logic of space within the visual field. Spatially, the memorial is isolated in the middle of a lush green bed of grass. Though there are other more traditional grave markers near it, contrast in colors, the orientation of the grave, and a few intentionally placed plants clearly mark *Memorial to a Marriage* as separate from these others. This isolation is unusual in that the excessively elaborate styling of the grave is not a central marker around which familial others are organized. This effect is visually heightened by the assortment of family mausoleums that flank the grave on all sides. Their presence makes it abundantly clear that a more familial orientation is an option within the gravescape; just not the option selected by those to be buried here. The memorial also suggests this nonreproductive rhetoric by not having a connection to ritual upkeep by the living family. As Doris Francis, Leonie Kellaher, and Georgina Neophytou outline, garden gravescapes, with their exotic plant life, ornate designs, and welcoming atmosphere, created a cult of visitation to cemeteries by the deceased's family to keep up the grave and commune with their loved one.[101] However, Cronin's design breaks this bond. Indeed, this design requires little upkeep. No plantings adorn the plot. No flags need to be placed or gates secured. The memorial is very much monumental—self-contained and perpetual, preventing at the material level the need for a lineage to maintain it. In lieu of participation in the material structuring of graves to duplicate biological kinship patterns, the grave of the two lovers is alone. Visually isolated, unencumbered by the organization of familial plots, the memorial positions Cronin and Kass as persons outside the logic of reproduction and, therefore, outside the compulsion to heteronormativity.

While the absence of reproductive imagery and organization in *Memorial to a Marriage* serves to rupture heteronormative gazing, the way in which the memorial visualizes the queer alternative, particularly what Edelman calls the queer "death drive," is also a powerful rebuke. The death drive refers to the Freudian compulsion to start anew (or to die), a product of an excess of signification.[102] Drawing from Freud, Edelman situates the death drive not within individual psychologies but within the social at the level of culture. For Edelman, the queer represents the death drive within the social world: a manifestation not focused upon the perpetual reproduction of itself into an endless future (as represented by the "child") but rather focused upon the present moment, the maximization of the existent, the reliance upon the past and the now rather than always looking toward the future.[103] To feature this highly controversial form of queer ethics within her work was likely not Cronin's desire. However, Edelman might suggest that any representation of the truly queer signals the death drive over the child. If this is true, then, representationally the rhetorical work done by the memorial is intended to answer the question posed by T.S. Eliot in "The Waste Land" and reanimated by Edelman: "What you get married for if you don't want children?"[104]

Memorial to a Marriage suggests that there is much to desire within a (queer) marriage minus children. This is highlighted first by the highly sexual yet totally nonreproductive quality of the subjects its represents. Clearly, the sculpture can be read as two lovers in the aftermath of a sexual encounter. This reading is reinforced if the viewer takes into account Cronin's characterization of the sculpture depicting her and her lover in a moment of "post-coital bliss" (rather than as two slumbering women).[105] In this case the sexual nature of the scene is clear; but so is the fact that this sexual quality is not reproductive (by virtue of it involving two women exclusively). Thus sex here is represented, rhetorically, not as something with an end goal of reproduction (future) but a present goal of pleasure (present).

In addition, not only is this scene nonreproductive (in terms of procreation); it is also frozen in time. It is out of chronological time, a moment taken from an (at the time) unrecognized marriage and left suspended in animation to be cherished by those who view it. While describing a grave display as frozen may sound ridiculous—aren't all graves frozen?—the key here is not that the figures do not move but that the viewer believes that they could have and now are not. Rather than representing a face in a static state reflecting death, Cronin's *Memorial to a Marriage* reflects live bodies frozen in a moment of time. Such a distinction does not encourage the viewer to ask what might happen next but rather to linger in the queer moment. In all these ways the rhetoric of the piece shifts from the deliberative to the epideictic genre. The monument is no longer proscriptive as to how the viewer should choose to live life—that is, heterosexually with the intent of reproducing biologically—but descriptive, praising an alternative cultural value that should be enacted in the present. Thus by combining a presence of queer sexuality while intentionally effacing more traditional markers of compulsory heterosexuality, *Memorial to a Marriage* leaves the viewer in a new mode of viewing.

Finally, the death display positions the two lovers as queer in a unique way: by literally not placing their bodies within their shared grave. This is no radical act of queer deception: it is simply the case that Cronin and her now legally recognized spouse are not dead yet. Indeed, not only are they alive but they are both young (Cronin created the piece at age thirty-nine) and might expect to live for many more decades together before either one's remains would be interred where their marker exists. Such a situation is not highly unusual. Many thoughtful individuals make arrangements for death well in advance of their actual passing. In the case of shared graves or family plots, it is common that gravestones are simply reinscribed with the names of new members as they pass away. Indeed, Matlovich and several of the gay and lesbian graves that populate Congressional Cemetery were created and installed well before any bodies were placed there. Simultaneously, this approach is beneficial in preempting any efforts less-GLBTQ-affirmative next of kin might make to normalize or minimize the deceased's identities.

However, the effect of the absence of physical bodies in a highly publicized grave serves to position Cronin and her lover as queer figures in the broadest sense of the term. They are outsiders—literally outside of their graves—able to question their deaths and their representations in death with a perspective that can only be considered "ghostly." While this reality is likely often lost on viewers of the memorial in the gravescape, for those in the know the death display becomes an even more powerfully queer device, a place, a "positionality vis-à-vis the normative" from which a queerer way of life and death might be envisioned.[106]

Yet making the queer memory of the Cronin-Kass marriage visible is not the end of this rhetorical endeavor. To disrupt the visual rhetoric of the gravescape effectively without being written off as a failed death display, *Memorial to a Marriage* had to maintain its lesbian representations while aesthetically participating in the natural style revered in garden design. To do this Cronin adopted a number of different approaches to appropriate and configure *Memorial to a Marriage* within the rhetoric of the natural.

Several aspects of the design contribute to giving *Memorial to a Marriage* a garden-style imprimatur. First, the color and kind of stone used in the memorial are highly traditional to garden gravescapes generally and to Woodlawn Cemetery in particular. White marble was a traditional stone used in nineteenth-century monument making. Cronin uses a similar marble to reflect this style, despite the fact that marble is today largely not approved for monument making because of its soft texture and ability to be worn down.[107] Yet by going to extra lengths to use a stone that visually matches the gravescape, the memorial becomes a seamless part of the cemetery's visual frame. (It is worth noting the new iteration installed in 2011 is much darker in color and no longer made of same substance).

Not only the substance of the memorial but the style of the design as well are what one would expect within a garden gravescape. The memorial features a number of qualities that harken to the representational field of a natural rhetoric. Most of these are represented in the bodily aesthetic on display. Despite the fact that these two bodies are traditionally viewed as unnatural by their default existence in two feminine forms, each body individually displays attributes in tune with a communion with nature. The flowing hair of each woman is a prominent flourish on the grave, mimicking both living forms as well as designs often seen in Art Nouveau that focus upon nature and the natural as sources of inspiration.[108] The almost complete nakedness of the two women's bodies highlights their natural state while also serving to draw attention and incite queer visibility. The postcoital imagery of the scene represents the very natural act of human sexuality, despite the fact that it may not necessarily represent a reproductive act. This stylistic imagery aided in conferring naturalness upon the otherwise "unnatural" figures, securing for *Memorial to a Marriage* a comfortable place within the logic of the garden gravescape.

In addition to the aesthetic and imagery, by featuring women *Memorial to a Marriage* emphasizes a theme found in other garden gravescapes. Women were a common representative form within these cemeteries. By choosing the imagery of women to make a commentary on queer desire—as opposed to two male forms, a transgendered form, or three or more forms that would exceed a traditional monogamous couple—Cronin makes a rhetorical selection that, while meeting her representational threshold, also raises the fewest visual hackles possible.[109]

Finally, the memorial also exudes pathetic appeals at the core of garden commemoration. As opposed to memento mori gravescapes that focus upon the mind, the garden gravescape's gesture to the emotions—specifically romance, grief, mourning, and melancholy—can be seen in *Memorial to a Marriage*. The embodied figures exude intimacy, nestled together and clearly representing a substantial emotional bond. Their faces revel in emotion, somewhere between desire and happiness, as they lie in each other's arms. In a pose reminiscent of a long line of nineteenth-century art, the figures represent sleep, a state powerful not only for its metaphoric resonance with death but also for the emotional trust required for two people to share that state together. By embracing pathos *Memorial to a Marriage* replicates the natural emotional bonds between the deceased and their loved ones visible within numerous death displays on the Woodlawn Cemetery grounds.

By hewing closely to the conventions of the rhetoric of the garden gravescape, *Memorial to a Marriage*, at least to some degree, manages to insert itself into the rhetoric of the cemetery as a whole. The seamlessness of this insertion within such a renowned cemetery is compelling, as described by the art critic Jerry Saltz: "Here, among the tombs and temples, amid the urns, broken columns, inverted torches, medieval Celtic castles, carved weeping women, forlorn angels and heartbroken figures, *Memorial to a Marriage* doesn't stand out, it blends in. So much so that it's almost invisible—just another monument to death, love and loss in this amazing garden of graves. Only when you think about why *Memorial* blends in does it stop being conventional and start being insurrectionary."[110] It is the combined use of monumental rhetorics of materiality and tactical rhetorics of appropriation that makes this insertion so seamless.

The effect of this powerful combination can be seen in *Memorial to a Marriage*'s reception among heterosexual audiences. Upon its initial reveal the heterosexual public expressed sentiments that were both worried and condemnatory. Yet despite these outbursts, the Cronin-Kass memorial has become the third-most-visited statue in the cemetery grounds behind the memorials to Duke Ellington and Miles Davis.[111] However, the reception that it receives when it is visited is not always so clear, as demonstrated by an anecdote from the *Village Voice*: "When I asked a clean-cut, twenty-something couple who they thought the carved women in Cronin's sculpture were, the young man said, 'mythical people or saints'; the woman, 'angels.' I said, 'I think they're lesbians, and that they've just had sex.' The couple peered down, widened their eyes, tottered slightly, then began shaking their heads back and forth. I don't know what, only that *Memorial* did something to them."[112] Such responses are to be expected and, indeed, hoped for, by this powerful act of queer public memory. In a garden cemetery, with the rhetoric of the natural as the locus of attention, Cronin's display speaks with two voices, each heard differently by different audiences. The first is a disruptive rhetoric that challenges the unequivocal prayer to unity through nature by revisualizing and materializing a heretofore unconsidered characterization of the natural. For the visitor to the cemetery closed-minded to the possibilities of alternative conceptions of joy, love, and happiness imagined in *Memorial to a Marriage,* the memorial serves as a visual flashpoint to destabilize the idea of the heterosexual individual as the sole bearer of the natural, both as culturally performed by the other memorials in the gravescape and those repeated within the performance of heteronormativity in the individual constructs of everyday life. In all conceivable ways this memorial performs a very militant queer rhetorical vision.

In contrast, for a more inclusive viewer who looks upon the gravescape, the memorial does not signal a challenge to the rhetoric of nature but a life-affirming recharacterization of what is natural. Within the loving, emotional embrace of the two women's bodies is manifested a rhetorical hurrah previously only articulated in speech—that the love between people of the same sex is not unnatural but something of humanity, granted by God, or a part of nature.

Conclusion

While earlier acts of queer resistance relied solely on tactical and ephemeral efforts to ensure the viability of queer legacies, both the gay and lesbian graves currently spreading through Congressional Cemetery and the contribution by Cronin in Woodlawn Cemetery have shifted attention to acts of queer memory making with more enduring features. The people responsible for these monumental memory rhetorics have much to hope for if current receptions among heterosexual audiences are any evidence. While the number of graves already marked visibly queer in Congressional Cemetery is already substantial, new graves are purchased every day. Indeed, in 2012 the nonprofit organization the National Veterans LGBT Memorial purchased ten plots abutting Matlovich's grave to install a memorial as "a place of honor for LGBT veterans and their families." This new memorial, expected to be dedicated in a few years, will further enhance the existing public memories' already prominent message.[113] Indeed, after years of neglect the gay and lesbian graves of Congressional Cemetery are now regularly visited, particularly by GLBTQ military veterans, their allies, and supporters.[114] At the same time other cemeteries in the United States have become marked by similar funerary projects. Both Palm Springs, California, and Phoenix, Arizona, have created their own visibly queer markers to honor gay and lesbian veterans in public cemeteries.[115] With the reproductions of the graves in media and material form in recent years, the likelihood of preserving Matlovich and his compatriots' queer afterlives seems even more assured.

While one should perhaps not expect the same level of reproduction for such a unique work of art as *Memorial to a Marriage,* here too the rhetoric of queer public memory has been largely successful. In line with the gravescape in which it occurs, Cronin's memorial's success stems mostly from its acceptance as appropriate and desirable within the existent cemetery space rather than from its replication or visibility. At the time of this writing, it seems that the initial grumblings of some visitors to the memorial have largely passed without incident. With the exception of one year during which the original marble piece was absent before it could be replaced with a more durable duplicate, *Memorial to a Marriage* is now one of the most-visited sites within Woodlawn Cemetery.[116] It is important to note that most of its visitors are of a more diverse heterosexual nature rather than an audience limited to homosexual admirers. And much of this success can probably be attributed to the continued interest in the piece as it has been displayed in several more exhibits since its release in 2002. Yet perhaps the best measure of Cronin's rhetorical success is how favorably *Memorial to a Marriage* has been incorporated into the regular tours offered by Woodlawn's professional staff, particularly the "Beautiful Women of Woodlawn" tour.[117] Clearly, despite the important difference *Memorial to a Marriage* brings to its representation of queer death and memory, its repetition has been viewed favorably enough not only to include it with its ilk, but to reappraise what the cemetery's viewers conceive of as "natural."

Beyond the measure of effects, both Matlovich's and Cronin's efforts to construct a queer afterlife raise important theoretical concerns for doing queer public memory and queer monumentality and for the larger concerns of the present study. First, if queer memory projects—particularly those that adopt monumental form—are successfully to affect the judgments of the heterosexual public, a more sophisticated view of heterosexual power and its deployments is needed. While earlier efforts to remember queer lives have focused on the language of remembering/forgetting to justify and plan their rhetorical preservations, such a view of the heteronormativity that plagues queer memory is simplistic at best. Like other intersecting forms of power, queers require a postmodern view of heteronormativity if they are to find actually existing modes of resistance. This suggestion calls into doubt the already dubious claims to success advocated by more traditional forms of queer visibility. In this argument visibility in and of itself is the key to queer empowerment. Yet, as work cited earlier by both Phelan and Berlant and

Warner demonstrates, visibility is only one means of affecting resistance. In facing the threats of postmodern heteronormativity, queers must employ a series of simultaneous and potentially contrary approaches to memory making in order to generate longer moments of resistance, safety, and security. Thus the visibility politics that have been successful in Congressional Cemetery must be joined with the pseudo-invisibility politics of *Memorial to a Marriage* and to a collection of other such approaches if heteronormativity's "manifold relations of power" are to be deftly resisted. Analyzing these postmodern forms of heteronormativity and theorizing and producing these additional methods of resistance thus becomes a familiar focus for scholars, newly amended to represent the shifting realities of contemporary queer politics.[118]

Second, and related to this point: if a postmodern heteronormativity requires an array of attendant postmodern queer methods for generating acts of resistance, the iron-clad distinction between tactical/ephemeral memory rhetorics practiced during much of the last century and more recent monumental queer rhetorics cannot stand. Indeed, while there are real distinctions between the two which can be productive for describing previous eras of queer public memory and their shifts over the last three decades, the case studies above illustrate significant opportunities may be lost if we see them only as contradictory approaches to the past. While Matlovich succeeded in creating an enduring space for a visible queer memory within Congressional Cemetery that might be best labeled an act of queer monumentality, his success was largely made possible by tactically recognizing both the strange official/unofficial status of Congressional Cemetery in representing the nation and its persuadable leadership during the time he purchased the lot as opportunities to make advances that would normally be forbidden. Similarly, while *Memorial to a Marriage* excels at claiming and remaking the rhetoric of the "natural" in Woodlawn Cemetery to include same-sex desire by inserting a (now) durable monument in this heteronormative space, it is not by an imperialistic crusade but rather by a shrewd tactical appropriation of form and style that such an accomplishment was achieved. If we draw from these examples and take them as serious starting points, we may begin to conceive of more ways in which monumentality and tactical/ephemeral memory rhetorics can be used in coalition. The coalition described here resulted in obvious rewards: securing several queer legacies meaningfully in the public sphere. But if we take these prospects further to begin to conceive of a new kind of queer monumentality, we may find our way to even more effective means for combatting heteronormativity's multifaceted and entrenched tools of oppression.

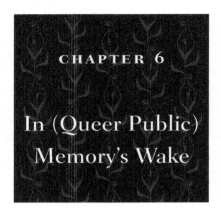

CHAPTER 6

In (Queer Public) Memory's Wake

ON MAY 30, 2014, U.S. SECRETARY of the interior Sally Jewell stood at a podium before an audience gathered in front of the Stonewall Inn in New York City, the infamous site of the 1969 riots commonly characterized as inaugurating the contemporary gay and lesbian rights movement.[1] Before the assembled group and watchful media, Jewell—joined by the director of the National Park Service Jonathan B. Jarvis and Tim Gill of the Gill Foundation—announced the creation of the National Park Service theme study focused on LGBT Americans.[2] Part of the National Park Service Heritage Initiative, theme studies are conceived as "multi-faceted projects exploring ways in which the legacy of underrepresented groups can be recognized, preserved, and interpreted for future generations."[3] While similar theme studies already existed for Asian American Pacific Islanders, the Latino communities, and women, the only comparable undertaking for the GLBTQ community was a 2010 National Park Service effort actively seeking out GLBTQ historical sites that might be listed on the National Register of Historic Places or as National Historic Landmarks.[4] Jewell's announcement hoped to remedy that inequity. In her speech Jewell argued that the new theme study recognized that "members of the LGBT community have been historically underrepresented in the National Park Service." Inaugurating the study, Jewell continued, would "help ensure that we understand, commemorate and share these key chapters in our nation's complex and diverse history."[5] This new enterprise represented queer public memory's transition from a passionate and exclusively community-driven project to a sacred promise sanctioned and supported by a part of the United States government. The LGBT theme study also represents an opportunity once again to ruminate on the merits of remembering the GLBTQ past, the obstacles that these memories can present, and the unique capacity of more-monumental forms of queer public memory to bridge the gap between cultural amnesia and social and political exigency.

Jewell's hopes for the theme study pinpoint several ways in which telling queer public memories can function as valuable public and rhetorical acts. From fragmentary accounts publicized in scientific texts to prominent monuments gracing public squares, these efforts demonstrate over and over again GLBTQ people's capacity to invent and innovate upon compelling historical narratives to defend themselves and secure their goals in the public sphere. As such, they qualify as significant rhetorical undertakings. When the efforts described above in the present study are magnified by the reach of the National Park Service, these often local, quirky, and contentious rhetorical acts can be transmuted into thundering calls for progress and change. Overseeing, protecting, and promoting more than eighty-four million acres of land in four hundred sites nationwide, the National Park Service has the opportunity to bring the queer past into the lives of countless Americans who never considered such a past previously.[6] While members of the theme-study team will debate among themselves and with the community over the coming months and years as to what qualifies as a queer place worthy of commemoration and how the stories of the queers who inhabited it will be told, initial discussions of the National Park Service's goals reflect just how influential a successful national queer memory project might be. Initial sites generated by the committee and the public suggest a future in which dozens, if not hundreds, of GLBTQ memory sites will be operated from coast to coast by the National Park Service. Conceivably, every American would be within only a few hours' drive of a historical location that could speak to the role of GLBTQ Americans in our national story. Preserved through cooperation by various interests in the federal government, these queer sites might finally be secured from inattention, disrepair, vandalism, gentrification, or decimation. Better yet, many of these queer sites might someday soon be staffed by park rangers who can help relay queer memories to new generations of Americans for whom GLBTQ people have always been a part of our imagined community. This image of the theme study's ultimate outcomes might be justly rejected as a fantasy at this stage; much effort and persistence will be needed to bring this vision to reality. Yet if even some of the sites and a few of the stories from this theme study finally come to sustained public attention, their potential to radically reposition the scope and meaning of the queer past in public memory will be assured. Through these imperfect but hopeful aims, the ultimate ambitions of the GLBTQ rights movements so often glimpsed in the telling and retelling of the queer past may finally come into full and lasting view.

At the same time the National Park Service's initiative reminds us of familiar and new challenges that GLBTQ people in particular face when they turn to memory. Other case studies in this book have enumerated powerful motivations not to remember that will certainly haunt the National Park

Service's project, including painful childhoods, a history of violence, missing documentation, questioned evidence, and heteronormative reterritorialization, among others. The theme study announcement points to two additional obstacles to queer public memory: the everyday features of the GLBTQ pasts and distrust of the state apparatus to remember the GLBTQ past over the long haul.

In his remarks following Secretary Jewell, the gay philanthropist and activist Tim Gill took a few minutes to raise one of the ironies often found in commemorating the GLBTQ pasts: so many of the great strides in social acceptance for GLBTQ people have occurred outside the grand public purview of monumentality. According to Gill: "LGBT history is not littered with historic, larger than life figures; rather it is a history made by each and every individual who works for equality."[7] Much of this sentiment rings true. Despite the grand deeds highlighted in the case studies above, significant strides in GLBTQ equality also sprang from individual coming outs, particular transitions, private conversations, small victories, and internal struggles—events that do not fit easily into our traditional tellings of civil rights struggles and social change. These meaningful moments of the GLBTQ past are fleeting and ephemeral, not necessarily because they are risky to undertake (though they are) but because, when they succeed, they rarely win worldwide acclaim. As a result, finding the balance between historic sites of queer memory can be as much about where we look as it is about what we preserve.

Likewise, the pomp and circumstance of the day's announcement raises another potential obstacle for remembering the GLBTQ past: what becomes of the queer past when it enters the domain of a national heteronormative apparatus such as the National Park Service? For centuries the survival of the queer past has relied expressly upon avoiding or co-opting heteronormative society's historical management structures. Such an impulse reflects significant evidence that national institutions cannot be trusted to take GLBTQ memories seriously. Indeed, national governments around the world have multiple times infiltrated, confiscated, and burned gay and lesbian archives, leading some GLBTQ advocates to trust only a community-based collection that can "go underground with its people to be cherished in hidden places" if necessary.[8] While there are at present pockets of progress that should embolden queers in general against this history of hatred, giving control of our past to an institution still talking out of both sides of its mouth about GLBTQ issues may ultimately be the single greatest threat facing queer public memory today. Several anxieties spring to mind: Why, for instance, if the National Park Service is so invested in remembering the GLBTQ past, was this initiative only agreed to when the Gill Foundation offered to fund such an undertaking?[9] How important is GLBTQ history to federal, possibly heterosexual actors in the real world of tightened budgets, political pressure, and fire, floods, and natural disasters? Also, how much faith can GLBTQ people really place in an executive branch whose control can easily swing from a proud ally to a hateful enemy or, worse yet, to a bureaucratic underling without supervision or accountability? Perhaps most important, what becomes of these memory sites when their meaningfulness and mutability are removed from the passionate control of their people? These concerns for queer memory are of a different order and magnitude than those faced by the community over the last one hundred and fifty years. How they will be navigated at this early stage is also unclear. Only time will tell whether this new fashioning of queer public memory ultimately achieves its promise or puts the queer past at greater risk than ever before.

Despite these legitimate fears, the LGBT theme study, if given the benefit of the doubt, also illustrates that it is not just wider attention to queer public memory that will be key for mitigating the erasure of GLBTQ pasts; casting those memories through queer monumentality is essential as well. The National Park Service is not typically the steward of archives or ephemera; it does not educate the public through paper trails and cloistered conversations. The National Park Service is, in many ways, an institution founded on monumentality. From the grandiose and sublime views at Rocky Mountain National Park to the hallowed reverence of the Martin Luther King, Jr., Memorial, the National Park Service excels at connecting more than 11.7 billion visitors annually to their collective past, emphasizing virtues we must renew and places we must preserve with an appreciation for grandeur that rightly earned the park service and its charges the title of "America's best idea."[10] That the National Park Service, therefore, would take up the GLBTQ past in equally monumental terms should be no surprise. The initial vision for the queer past as told by the National Park Service is not merely one of recognition; it is also a monumental task to which GLBTQ memories are rarely accustomed. Its focus on meaningful places and consequential spaces bodes well for giving the queer past an eternal security rarely imagined. Its willingness to entrust scholars and the public in finding and telling these stories may ultimately point to a queer past aligned with the nation but perhaps not wholly derived from it. Indeed, the decision to include GLBTQ people in these programs at all reveals that, for perhaps the first sustained time in our nation's history, queer Americans will be viewed as worthy, important, and virtuous. Finally, by directing federal power into preserving and sharing the queer past with those who will listen, the study may offer GLBTQ people in the past the opportunity to exist without the ever-present threat of erasure. Queer monumentality, practiced on a scale never before seen, may be the next step in making the greater gay world long desired and regularly denied.

The Value of Queer Public Memory
■

Queer public memories offer powerful rhetorical possibilities to contemporary rhetors, and these possibilities are deeply constrained by a variety of forces aligned in urging that this past be forgotten. A turn toward more monumental forms of queer public memories may provide recourse against heteronormative impulses to forget in ways that offer hope for a more inclusive and secure GLBTQ future.

The case studies in the preceding chapters highlight the ability of queer public memory to do valuable rhetorical work to shape public audiences and affect social change. In each case study a diverse array of GLBTQ rhetors used monumental queer public memories for distinct rhetorical goals. For instance, the Alexander Wood statue served a vital public purpose: creating both a triumphant historical image and a durable gay democratic space in which new forms of GLBTQ citizenship might be practiced while ensuring that, despite the trend toward gentrification within the Church-Wellesley area (and similar former gay ghettos), the presence of the queer past will always persist. Wood's memory also serves as a vital symbol over which community members debated their identification with one another and with Wood himself. In the example of Matthew Shepard, both gay and lesbian and queer counterpublics used reiterative memories, affective affiliations, and malleable meanings circulated within and between publics to prevent Shepard from being forgotten and to help persuade heterosexual audiences that bias crime legislation was necessary to protect GLBTQ people from harm. Simultaneously, remembering Shepard offered these differing counterpublics an opportunity to argue over the stakes of anti-GLBTQ violence, the state of GLBTQ people as a whole, and whether Shepard was capable of representing a community much wider and more diverse than himself. The California curricular reformers also used an array of GLBTQ historical imaginings to argue for legislative changes that could produce powerful effects for GLBTQ and heterosexual youth and urge heterosexual citizens to reimagine how they constitute their sense of community to include or exclude GLBTQ people. Meanwhile, Patricia Cronin, Leonard Matlovich, and other gay and lesbian veterans, artists, and activists used their diverse monumental and ephemeral/tactical memory rhetorics to make expressly epideictic claims about who they are and how they should be remembered in the future. By their examples Matlovich and Cronin also helped steel GLBTQ people for ongoing debates surrounding same-sex marriage and GLBTQ military service. Each case testifies to the diverse ways in which queer memory rhetorics can be used to shape public life. If one way we might choose to determine an act's rhetoricity is by the effects it has on public beliefs, perceptions, values, identities, and laws, then these projects demonstrate the potent rhetorical potential within the ongoing queer *"turn toward* memory."[11]

The case studies in this book also illustrate the enormous challenges GLBTQ individuals and institutions face in their attempts to remember the queer past. In its own way each case corroborates scholarship that identifies an array of obstacles—both within heterosexual history and GLBTQ historical imaginings—for doing productive queer memory work, including heteronormativity, homonormativity, mnemonicide, willful erasure, HIV/AIDS and survivor's guilt, the subjugation of GLBTQ knowledges, and the questioning of GLBTQ evidence.[12] However, the present study also raises challenges particular to public memories in the era of queer monumentality. As camp viewers of the Wood statue have demonstrated, the Church-Wellesley Business Improvement Area's embrace of monumentality in order to remember Wood both limited and calcified his identity and the identity of the community. Because this is so, the statue makes static what, if more queerly understood, should be a highly fluid, intersectional continuum of being. The decision to rally around Shepard was calculated to make inroads into wider heterosexual culture but illustrated the propensity of monumental rhetorics to select "safe" figures from the GLBTQ past who can confine much of the community to the closet. The debate over California textbook reform illuminates that, despite the promise in adopting textbooks and curriculums as sites for queer memory, entering monumental forms and spaces already occupied by heteronormative forces commonly requires making difficult choices. In this case reforms resulted in troublesome forgettings that made GLBTQ politics unimportant, antigay violence unremarkable, and same-sex desires and acts inconspicuous. The examination of death displays also poignantly demonstrates how easily the heteronormative apparatuses of death can reterritorialize out and proud GLBTQ persons after death when they are no longer able to speak for themselves. Thus we must recognize with open eyes that, while queer public memories may be a valuable rhetorical tool, deploying these memory rhetorics is never without risk, cost, or restriction.

Despite these risks, the present study validates the turn to monumentality within queer public memory. While most thinkers and advocates rejected monumentality as too prone to exploitation in the wake of the horrors of World War II and the twentieth century's many fascist regimes, beginning about 1980 GLBTQ people and institutions saw latent potential in the concept for overcoming their erasures from memory. Among these virtues, monumentality's durability, epideictic energy, power, and opportunities for expansion are critically important.

Durability has been perhaps the most firmly asserted value in the case studies above. Within monumentality, queers have capitalized on durability over and over again, cognizant that a GLBTQ past long unable to endure the slings and arrows of heteronormativity might find significant and sustained advantage by giving their subject matter the ability to persist. Perhaps not surprisingly, durability has often been achieved in the queer turn to monumentality through the creation of enduring material monuments. The Wood statue perhaps most directly illustrates that a queer public memory encased in stone might have the best chance of outlasting hostile criticism from heterosexual culture, playful detractors armed with graffiti and ill-intent, and even socioeconomic trends that are increasingly pushing GLBTQ people out of the neighborhoods they long claimed as their own. The ongoing erection of queer monuments across the globe, the gravescapes depicted in chapter 5, and the LGBT theme study described above only further confirm that materiality is a compelling feature of monumentality that is well equipped to fix a queer problem.

While materiality is a vital means for achieving durability, durability can also be accomplished through nonmaterial, but still monumental, forms of public memory. In the Shepard case, by continually reiterating alternative, affective, and malleable memories of Shepard within queer counterpublics and ultimately communicating those memories to the wider heteronormative public sphere, GLBTQ rememberers sought to give Shepard's memory a durable position within society. Given that Shepard's image today continues to grace legislation, hate-crime discourse, and political debates in the wider public sphere in ways closely aligned with those articulated by various gay and lesbian counterpublics, it seems that materiality need not be the exclusive means for imbuing GLBTQ pasts with a durability that can withstand the annihilating impulses of heteronormativity.

Another great advantage that monumental memory rhetorics hold over their tactical and ephemeral counterparts is their ability to more fully empower GLBTQ people themselves as tellers of their own pasts. This newly empowered GLBTQ relationship to the past provided by queer monumentality is confirmed through the monuments profiled in this book and their relative independence from heterosexual history. The independence of our monumental case studies is particularly distinct from the queer bricolage of earlier decades. For many years the queer past was able to emerge within the public sphere only when it could be made from the detritus of heterosexual history. Oscar Wilde claimed Michelangelo, Shakespeare, and Plato as like himself not because they were known homosexuals, but because they were already represented in history and, if read queerly, could be turned to his advantage. This "making do" offered Wilde a powerful, yet temporary, counterargument against heteronormativity. But because these figures were derived from heteronormativity—because dominant culture was deeply invested in reading these men as heterosexual—Wilde could make no lasting claim on them. It would only be a matter of time before each of Wilde's representative anecdotes would be returned to the heterosexual fold. Thus tactical and ephemeral memory rhetorics such as bricolage are limited in their independence and, as a result, their power.

However, the many rhetors we have seen adopt queer monumentality were able to act differently. They selected and built public memories around figures that were not already heavily tied to heterosexual history. In doing so they identified valuable and important GLBTQ people in the past and built public discourses around them. This independent nomination process in queer monumentality obviously posed its own problems: Matthew Shepard was not representative enough, Alexander Wood's morals were questionable, and many figures in the textbook debate distracted from important parts of the community. However, these figures each also granted queer public memory a greater degree of independence in their articulation. In selecting their subjects, rhetors inclined toward monumentality foregrounded queerness as a value in itself, not a fortuitous and secondary "making do." Equally, because these subjects were notably queer, heterosexual history had less incentive to patrol their sexuality. The memories erected around these monumental figures could be articulated, controlled, and shaped almost exclusively by the GLBTQ community itself, relatively free of the fear of reterritorialization. By conceiving, creating, and generating queer memories from our own raw materials, not the scraps of heterosexual history, GLBTQ people can further enhance their own powerful positions in a still-heteronormative world.

Highly intertwined with independence and power is the epidictic value inherent in queer monumentality. As we know, monumentality is not just about sending a lasting message through time but a meaningful message that transmits a profound statement about what communities of the past valued. This is largely achieved through identifying great heroes and heroines of a given age and marking their value through grand, ornate, and elaborate display. To be fair, the examples of queer monumentality herein do not readily match the most noted instances of monumental epideictic we see elsewhere in our society. This is particularly true in the grandeur of queer displays: no case study in this book is as opulent and visually poetic as the Palace of Versailles or the Lincoln Memorial. This is for good reason: these grandest examples of monumentality in heteronormative culture have significantly more resources and assurances behind them that GLBTQ people may only have begun to access with the National Park Service initiatives discussed above.

Nonetheless, every case study we have examined exceeds a threshold for monumentality established in the introduction: lifting exemplary instances out of the realm of everyday life. In doing so, each case demonstrates attention to epideictic's dual interest in virtue and high style. Leonard Matlovich's patriotism, bravery, struggle, and inspiration are deeply foregrounded in his marker while Patricia Cronin has rejected the burial norms of our contemporary age to produce a grave marker to match the grandeur of a garden cemetery. California curricular reformers secured for their GLBTQ subjects a place alongside the poster children of American nationalism within such a hagiographical genre as the public school textbook. Reiterated characterizations of Shepard as a martyr for the cause and secular saint celebrated not just through everyday talk but also in vigils and speeches that echoed through the streets of New York City and in the walls of the U. S. Capitol building expressly pushed him beyond the typical, even when they lauded his common qualities. Perhaps most conventionally of all, by labeling him a warrior, community leader, and "gay pioneer" in the very conventional form of a statue in a public square (with a "gay flair," no less), Wood sets a new bar for how a historical queer figure can be proudly commemorated. By embracing both dimensions of the epideictic inherent within queer monumentality, GLBTQ advocates firmly established their own heroes as celebrated inspirations worthy of eternal remembrance.

Last, this inspirational quality apparent in queer monumentality helps us begin to understand the final value witnessed in this recent trend: the capacity for monumental queer memory rhetorics to be replicated and repeated in an expansive undertaking. The Wilde case shows that there is important value in the retelling of tactical and ephemeral memory rhetorics; they give everyday GLBTQ persons important resources for defending themselves and others against the heteronormative oppression in which they reside. Yet these ephemeral rhetorics by their very nature do not provide a firm foundation on which to build. For centuries a momentary retelling of a queer tale from the past has been followed up quickly with haughty laughter, confessional interrogations, corporal punishments, and, understandably, instantaneous retractions. To put it another way, as José Esteban Muñoz reminds us, the virtue of an ephemeral past is that it can evaporate at a moment's notice; but a self-destructive past always prepared to disappear can never advance beyond itself.

By contrast, when memories enriched with queer monumentality are repeated, both the new memory and the original memory continue to persist. Because they are independent and durable, a fitting and inspirational example from the queer past can continue to arouse energetic interest while its new derivatives can themselves encourage greater repetition. In other words, by virtue of an initial instance of queer monumentality's ability to gain and hold territory in the public imagination, it acquires ground with an eye toward expansion. We have seen this repetition lead to self-perpetuating advances for the GLBTQ past throughout this book: the Wood memorial was inspired by the model of the *Gay Liberation* statue; the success of the FAIR Act relied on critical insights from debates over S.B. 1437; advocates for other victims of bias crime have used and critiqued Shepard's memory to raise attention and broaden the public understanding of antigay/trans violence; Matlovich drew inspiration from the grave of Alice B. Toklas and Gertrude Stein, just as other gay and lesbian memorialists drew inspiration from his Vietnam Veterans Memorial. In each case the capacity of these monumental memories to endure, be remembered, and be deployed in second-generation rhetorical innovations are a key resource for the GLBTQ community to expand the queer past. Chaining out in multiple lines from central rhetorical acts, monumental queer memory rhetorics generate powerful effects, which in turn inspire greater action beyond themselves. Thus queer monumentality allows for substantial gains in power that tactical approaches to the past alone cannot.

These four values of queer monumentality are not an exhaustive list of this trend's potential. I am certain that with a wider scope of analyses, more monumental values will be revealed in time. However, these four values emerge as primary benefits from the case studies discussed above. Collectively, by making GLBTQ memories durable, powerful, epideictic, and expansive, queer monumentality offers important advantages in counteracting anti-GLBTQ forces that may offer some of the best paths forward to social change.

While the recent initiatives by the National Park Service provide an interesting and useful occasion for summarizing the complex possibilities and pitfalls of queer monumentality at this present moment, the current effort does not address every issue needing attention. Also important is the future of queer public memory research and how queer monumentality in particular might be further improved.

The Future of Queer Public Memory

If all acts of public memory are as much about the present and future as they are about the past, it is important to highlight what these collected examples suggests about the future study and practice of queer public memory. In my view key dimensions of this future include the continued turn by GLBTQ people and institutions to memory, vital and ongoing roles for tactical and ephemeral forms of queer memory, and the need to do monumental forms of queer public memory better.

Perhaps the easiest prognostication about the future of queer public memory is that the *"turn toward memory"*—or what I have termed a (re)turn to memory—as a rhetorical resource for GLBTQ people, communities, and institutions will only continue.[13] The persistent "memory mania" of the last three-plus decades currently shows little sign of abating and interest in the GLBTQ past has intensified. Evidence for this ongoing interest even now exceeds the GLBTQ community itself. President Barack Obama's inclusion of the Stonewall Riots in his second inaugural address, the queer past's notable emergence in popular media (for example, *Milk*, *Dallas Buyers Club*, *The Imitation Game*, and HBO's *Liberace* and *The Normal Heart*) and the National Park Service's initiatives all suggest that curiosity about the queer past is growing.[14] Therefore it seems clear that as long as the past continues to be a palatable place to find persuasion, GLBTQ rhetors will continue to mine its resources. Yet it is also likely that, within the "*turn toward* memory," efforts to embrace monumental forms of queer public memory will persist and, indeed, accelerate. Consider, for instance, that during the first two decades of the memory boom (approximately 1980–2000), only a handful of material GLBTQ monuments were created and installed, many of them requiring years of planning, fundraising, and public engagement. By contrast, more than a dozen prominent, permanent GLBTQ memorials or commemorative sites have been erected or begun in the last fifteen years, the vast majority during the last five years.[15] In line with the case studies in this book, most of these emerging monuments have pointed to earlier GLBTQ monuments as inspiration. Considering GLBTQ culture's penchant for bricolage, repetition with a difference, thoughtful borrowing, and queer monumentality's valuing of expansion, I suspect that GLBTQ people in other communities will continue to borrow from earlier monumental projects to undertake similar work. Because this is so, these monumental queer memories will spawn greater effects, admirers, and imitators in the years to come.

Another (somewhat counterintuitive) claim about the future of queer public memory is that, while the turn toward queer monumentality will likely accelerate, tactical and ephemeral GLBTQ memory rhetorics will continue to play a vital role in remembering the queer past. At the outset of this project, I did not expect tactical and ephemeral memories to play a significant part in the powerful GLBTQ memory displays that were emerging on the public scene. Rather I anticipated that the turn to monumentality would be an undeniably positive contribution to GLBTQ rhetorical action that would make earlier tactical and ephemeral acts of queer public memory outmoded and unnecessary. This presumption is not completely incorrect: I maintain that queer monumentality represents a net positive for queer public memory practice, that it will become increasingly prevalent, and that it holds valuable lessons for those in similarly situated subject positions. However, it has also become progressively clear that tactical and ephemeral acts of remembrance will remain an essential resource for faithfully representing the GLBTQ past for several reasons.

The first reason stems from an abundance of caution. Far too often GLBTQ people have acceded to the idea that progress is both inevitable and irreversible. We put our faith in notable accomplishments, content that milestones have been met, change has occurred, and things only "get better."[16] Yet experiences of GLBTQ people around the world tell another story. Few of the early homophiles in 1920s Germany predicted that their progressive lifestyles would soon be swept away by state-sponsored persecution, imprisonment, and war. Likewise, many urban and coastal gays and lesbians were shocked to see news of Shepard's death in 1998 as a victim of violence reminiscent of a time they thought had past. Egregious, harmful setbacks continue today. How many GLBTQ couples have celebrated their nuptials since 2004 only to have those same unions intermittently nullified by court action, legislation, or referendum? Why should GLBTQ people believe they are secure when, as recently as 2010, Pride events in Pennsylvania were surveilled under direct orders from the state's chief homeland security official?[17] How can the world speak of progress on GLBTQ rights when Russia and Uganda have only recently added harsh penalties for queer speech, acts, and existence where few existed before? Both historical and contemporary incidents illustrate that progress is not irrevocable and repression can come with little warning. Because this is true, the GLBTQ community should be wary of equating monumentality with victory. Though they might be important and durable, memorials can be torn down and textbooks rewritten far easier than we might suspect. GLBTQ tactics generally, and GLBTQ tactical and ephemeral memories specifically, are essential stopgaps against these hopefully overzealous concerns. Disposing of them would be imprudent and potentially complicit in future GLBTQ marginalization.

Tactical and ephemeral queer memories are also needed still because they provide access to historical knowledge not yet readily incorporated into monumental forms of queer public memory. As local, fleeting, and *metistic* forms of action, tactical and ephemeral memories are essential for preserving the diverse, everyday pasts of GLBTQ life. For the moment at least monumental memory rhetorics are (by and large) far too biased toward "great" men and women, normative forms of accomplishment, and accepted spaces of recognition. Indeed, activism and scholarship in queer historiography, homonormativity, and "gay shame" has explicitly expressed similar concerns.[18] Gladly, GLBTQ life, in the past and present, is not found exclusively among people and places amenable to narrow rhetorics of gay pride and monumentality. Everyday GLBTQ people, self-described freaks, gender benders and gender fucks, leather daddies, queens, exhibitionists, outsiders, nonconformists, political radicals, and others continue to permeate the GLBTQ experience. Indeed, it is often through the still-marginalized aspects of GLBTQ life that we renew our queer orientation to the world around us. On the borders of our identities, where diversity and difference are most pronounced, challenges are most felt, and representation costs so dearly, GLBTQ people have innovated to create forms, styles, and epistemologies that by necessity feed their existence. These experiences, acts, people, and

events need to be remembered not because someday they will be incorporated into a more monumental form but rather because that day is still highly
unlikely to come. Many of these tactical and ephemeral memories cannot be
contained in these more traditional monumental forms; others may wither
and die under such constraints. Tactical and ephemeral ways of remembering keep alive the vibrancy of queer life and should be preserved at all cost.

Also, tactical and ephemeral memory rhetorics are crucial for holding
monumental forms of queer public memory accountable for its choices. This
book is replete with examples of queers questioning the public memories
which supposedly represent all GLBTQ people. Using innovative rhetorical
acts—graffiti-ing and dragging the Wood statue and foregrounding victims of
violence beyond Shepard are just two examples—tactically oriented queers
can highlight deficiencies in more-monumental displays of the past. While
many rhetors constructing monumental GLBTQ memories might view these
critiques as a nuisance, contestations in the era of queer monumentality
are essential for serving the greater good of the queer counterpublic. These
critiques demand that our visions represent real diversity as present and important; they challenge notions of stable identity when many are highly fluid;
they counteract powerful voices that drive blindly toward inclusion; and they
recall events that some may find uncomfortable or objectionable but that
are central to understanding the GLBTQ past. When these parts of our
shared past go unheard or unrecognized, the campy queer potential to raise
a ruckus and act out in disruptive ways vibrantly restores the contestation
essential to a strong public memory. By keeping these monumental forms of
queer memory honest, tactical and ephemeral memories do an invaluable
service to the entire GLBTQ community.

A final dimension of the future of queer public memory is that queer
monumentality must be done better. This book, along with the work of several scholars and critics of the GLBTQ past, has made explicit the many challenges and costs that have emerged as a result of how queer public memory
practice has been conducted in recent years. These challenges include issues
of diversity, equity, homonormativity, heteronormativity, forgetting, shame,
and static notions of identity, among others. These flaws within queer public memory discourse are serious and should be identified. However, in my
experience some critics are too quick to condemn certain practices as problematic and ill-advised without offering prospects for resolving those problems. While I have devoted much attention to highlighting the valuable ways
monumental memory rhetorics can promote social, cultural, and political
change, I have also pointed to issues that raise concerns. At the same time I
have sought to introduce new ideas that address these concerns as well. In
imagining the future of queer public memory, those suggestions bear reiteration and expansion.

There are several steps that can be taken to do queer monumentality better. First, in line with Bravmann's characterization of the "queer cultural studies of history," GLBTQ scholars and activists need to be critically aware that our own tellings of pasts are often as contingent and as flawed as the heterosexual histories against which they react.[19] Showing greater awareness of the representational deficiencies within the GLBTQ past and making an effort to include diverse others essential to our communities may greatly enhance the value of these projects, for both our own community and the wider culture. Such awareness can contribute to doing queer public memory better in many ways, but it may be most transformational if Bravmann's methods are altered from a cultural-studies approach to criticism to a form of self-reflexive practice. Clearly, if GLBTQ rhetors build a critical reflexivity into the process prior to designing commemorative sites and memorials, honoring GLBTQ heroes and heroines, and making other representational choice about the GLBTQ past, they may make a great deal of difference in preventing or at least mitigating the more troublesome erasures endemic to queer memory practice so far. Queer monumental rhetorics that result from a more self-reflexive process will be better positioned to unify the community for collective action and challenge other hegemonic pasts at the center of dominant culture.

Second, queer memory makers may do better by specifically embracing more-diverse forms of evidence for understanding the GLBTQ past. It is important to remember that while there are many similarities between history and memory, they are two distinctly different phenomena: memory represents our lived, everyday experiences in the world while history is a collective means for managing our accelerating loss of memory.[20] Whether because of memory's loss or history's powerful ideological value, history has often been the default means of understanding the past, including for many GLBTQ rhetors. Without a doubt the GLBTQ history done by thoughtful scholars and made publicly accessible has been highly beneficial to the community. However, by too rigidly embracing history, scholars, activists, and everyday people miss the opportunities to highlight memories that have distinctly different and important views on the past to offer. For instance, consider how our understanding of the GLBTQ past changes if we learned about the Stonewall Riots from archived news coverage (history) rather than from a preserved oral history interview with one of its participants (memory). What do we lose in our understanding and appreciation of Alexander Wood if we examine only his entry in the *Dictionary of Canadian Biography* or his documents in official archives? How much more might we gain by visiting his statue, "rubbing the bum" in the presence of others, and watching his form be played with in a communal emergence of meaning? How do we come to see the past contrarily with a visit to the Leather Archives in Chicago or the

Lesbian Herstory Archives in New York rather than limiting ourselves to a traditional museum exhibit such as *Becoming Visible* at the New York Public Library? History can be an important and essential basis by which we judge our actions and ourselves; but it can also be a tool used to shape our perception of the past while hiding its own ideological values. Similarly, reliance exclusively upon memory opens the door to the natural frailties of human and collective memory and even (at times) to the rigor of detailed analyses and debate. However, by bringing them together, by augmenting our history with a *"turn toward* memory" and its rich resources—film, pulp, ephemera, scandal, gossip, posters, performance, among others—we are able, in the very best moments, to bring our histories to life and invest them fully with rhetorical zeal. Perhaps more important, when needed most, memories give us recourse to challenge and disrupt the hegemony inscribed by those who practice history thoughtlessly or with open or veiled malice. In either case, by representing the GLBTQ past as memory rather than as history alone, greater opportunities for rhetorical action are likely to present themselves.

Another means of improving queer public memory is to consider meaningfully less-material instantiations of monumentality. Concerns about the limits of materiality have been a primary factor in the evisceration of monumentality within the wider public sphere. For instance, James E. Young has shown that, rather than preserve memory, some material monuments fail because they "seal memory off from awareness altogether." In doing so, traditional monuments—made of marble, bronze, and iron—become not insurance that the community will remember but rather an authorization that gives viewers permission to forget.[21] Similarly, the historian Lewis Mumford argued decades ago that the excessive use of statuary, memorials, and museums in certain commemorative zones could overwhelm their intended meaning, leaving those meant to be remembered unremembered and those living and working among these monuments constrained in the public square.[22] In addition, the contemporary architectural scholar Kirk Savage argues that in particularly important representative spaces—such as the National Mall in Washington, D.C.—the perpetual addition of new material monuments to represent an ever-growing list of subcultures, ethnicities, and identities may be counterproductive and unsustainable.[23] Given these concerns, the expansion of queer monumentality focused too heavily on building sites and installing shrines may be a rhetorical approach with diminishing returns. Luckily, as the present study asserts firmly, there are other productive ways to make the past durable beyond the use of physical markers, ways that can counteract these worrisome critiques. Queer monumentality's possibilities in the digital realm are only one such possibility. Today the Internet, social media, and other digital technologies offer queers a recourse to the monumental that is not as weighty or physical as other monuments. In digital monuments, mobile apps such as Quist, online archives and encyclopedias devoted to GLBTQ history, and important undertakings such as the ACT UP Oral History Project, advocates have found a powerful means to rethink queer monumentality in meaningful ways. If these and similar reimaginings of monumentality are done cautiously, reflexively, and selectively, such undertakings may productively expand GLBTQ memories while addressing some concerns about materiality.

Similarly, we can do queer monumentality better by embracing opportunities presented by other scholars and activists to make monumentality in all its forms more contemporary. By this I mean expressly to take up Andreas Huyssen's search for a monumentality that is "fundamentally informed by the modernist spirit of a fleeting and transitory epiphany, but that is no less memorable or monumental for it."[24] A monumentality that is both ephemeral and enduring, tactical and strategic can seem impossible for most communities, a contradiction in terms that cannot stand and therefore must be rejected. But GLBTQ people, familiar with doubt, turned on by failure, and enlivened by contradictions, are not most communities. As we have seen, there are possibilities not only in turning to monumentality as queers but in queering monumentality to serve our needs better. This means adopting a both/and approach that takes the best features of monumentality and marries them to the best qualities of the nonmonumental. While few of the case studies in this book have fully addressed this challenge, we can begin to see the possibilities in the contradictory gravescape memories described above. Without a doubt, Matlovich, Cronin, and their admirers adopted monumentality's durable, epidictic, expansionist, and empowered values in giving themselves a queer afterlife. But, as we have seen, there are crucial tactical and ephemeral memory rhetorics at work here as well. Selecting a crumbling cemetery once at the heart of the heteronormative American epideictic and making it a site of queer monumentality requires ephemeral risks and tactical thinking. Adopting the generic expectations of a (heteronormative) garden gravescape only to subvert them to monumental and queer ends is as much in line with Oscar Wilde's tactics as it is with the Alexander Wood statue's materiality. These instances demonstrate what can happen when doing queer public memory brings tactical/ephemeral and monumental memory rhetorics together not as adversaries with competing visions or to keep each other honest but united in complex, multivocal, simultaneous queer acts. Fleshing out this both/and vision of queer monumentality operating alongside and in common cause with tactical and ephemeral memory rhetorics is work still to be done. We see glimpses of its prospects in the NAMES Project AIDS Memorial Quilt's grandeur and softness, the adorning of national monuments with rainbow flags, and the queer kisses in red lipstick on Oscar Wilde's tomb. By taking up these exciting possibilities in the future, we may find in queer monumentality an even more meaningful path to making sure the queer past survives and thrives.

A final way of doing queer public memory better is recognizing that monumental recognition of GLBTQ lives is not the point of arrival but only a further step in leveraging the GLBTQ past for rhetorical purposes. As we more fully enter a postmodern state of politics, rife with complex and intersecting forces of power that have radically reengineered their methods of normalizing and disciplining queer people and cultures, the future of the queer past will require constant vigilance in order to continue both to exist and to resist. Just as tactical and ephemeral memories have their limitations, monumental queer rhetorics do as well. The coming years will demonstrate heteronormativity's efforts to compromise queer monuments and whether or not they will be successful. Yet working in combination, monumental and tactical/ephemeral uses of the past can be an effective series of rhetorical moves for continuing to claim greater queer empowerment.

While these suggestions may seem difficult to implement at a time when the era of queer monumentality is still in its nascent stages, efforts to refine queer monumental memory practices are already under way. One short example should suffice. In October 2009 a new queer monument was erected to Natalie Barney, a lesbian born in 1879. Barney was an heiress, philanthropist, and writer who published her first book of poems, *Quelques Portraits-Sonnets de Femmes,* in 1900. The poems consisted largely of insights into the lesbian experience, a theme she returned to throughout her life, in addition to political writings in support of feminism, paganism, and pacifism. Though Barney lived most of her life as an expatriate in Paris (where open homosexuality was to some degree tolerated), she was born and raised in Dayton, Ohio, where a large state historical marker bearing her name, her biography, and identifying her sexuality was placed in Cooper Park outside of the Dayton Metro Library.[25]

In many ways this memory project is similar to the more traditional monumental rhetorics described above: it is a material marker, endorsed by public authority and difficult to ignore. It has also been subject to attacks and attempts to destroy it as other GLBTQ monuments have.[26] However, for several reasons this marker is an exciting example of doing queer monumentality better. Barney was a lesbian, and her monument is one of the first in the world to inscribe the word *lesbian* on the commemorative plaque. In addition, Barney was a self-described lesbian, and thus the monument avoids issues of false reclamation or transient identity. Also, what Barney is remembered for is important. As an activist and author, Barney is remembered for her contributions to GLBTQ life and heterosexual life. She is no queer masquerading as a heterosexual but rather a protoqueer radical in her age who inspired and taught others within her literary salons. Perhaps most telling of all is where this monument is located: Dayton, Ohio. Unlike almost all the public memories described above that emanate from the liberal coasts or gay meccas or that replicate rural queer voices through the urban centers of New York and California, this monument recognizes Barney in a small city in the middle of Rust Belt America. Her memory disrupts the biases of space and beliefs that might mitigate the rhetorical work of earlier projects, instead being remembered in public before an audience perhaps less accustomed to such interventions and hopefully more affected by them. Though still not a flawless GLBTQ monumental rhetoric, Barney's marker is a refined vision of how GLBTQ rememberers in the future can do better. Encouragingly, as I write, more projects to reclaim and recast the queer past with monumental designs and durable effect begin every day. It is in these projects that we look for a better practice of queer public memory to emerge, and it is these projects that we must continue to watch—ever vigilant of the prospects and pitfalls of remembering and forgetting the GLBTQ past with rhetorical intent.

A Monumental Memory

■

At the end of this book, my own queer memory draws me back to a particular moment in my research on Alexander Wood. I had studied the Wood statue from afar for months, tracing its discourse on the Internet, looking through visitors' photographs online, and preparing to visit Toronto myself to experience the monument personally. On arrival in Toronto, I quickly dropped my bags at the hotel and proceeded a few blocks up the road to see the statue for the first time. It was a powerful moment not just because I had waited so long to see it, but because it was the first time I had witnessed a public monument explicitly marking someone as gay—in stone. The experience was gratifying and reassuring; it confirmed for me that somewhere in the long struggle for GLBTQ rights, some progress had been made.

The next day I arose early to visit a local archive that held Wood's papers. Walking into the sprawling city library, I was not sure what to expect. I had read extensively about the erasure of GLBTQ people from history but this was my first archival experience. I had found Wood's letterbooks in the finding aid, but what, if anything, would they reveal? Submitting the call slip to the archivist, my nervousness deepened. What if there was nothing there? Had this entire trip been in vain? You can imagine my exhilaration when the archivist returned with several good-sized boxes. After gingerly putting on my white gloves, I delved into the letters and notes spanning much of Wood's life. Wood was a complicated man, but it is clear from his archive that he was a meticulous record keeper. His letters were almost all dated, and he kept them for nearly every year of his life. It was thrilling. I didn't expect a rainbow flag or a love letter to another man to be among the contents, but still I felt sure there would be something of value here. As my fingers walked through the files, 1806 . . . 1807 . . . 1808 . . . I had one particular date in mind: 1810, the year of Wood's infamous scandal, persecution, and departure from Canada. However, after 1809 my fingers paused. Where an 1810 folder should have been, there was literally a gap in the records.

Where that void came from, I will never know for sure. It is possible that Wood, mortified by his scandal or fearing his letters might be used against him, did not keep any records for that year or simply destroyed them. It could be that Wood's (few and distant) survivors may have expunged the records for 1810, fearing that his embarrassment might become their own. It is plausible that the collectors who acquired, split up, and sold Wood's letters over the decades may have made careful choices, making sure that just a few of the letters were put away in a drawer, safe from troublemaking or prying eyes. It is even possible that a previous owner, perhaps a prominent Toronto citizen himself, knowing that Wood's name was celebrated in the history of the city, actively removed the 1810 folder, preventing the scandal from tainting the city again. In the end it does not matter. The hole in the records may have resulted from one, none, or a combination of these factors. However, the particular motives behind the gap's existence matter little since each possibility is derived from a common root: a matrix of heteronormativity that for centuries has insisted that GLBTQ people should be hated, waylaid, silenced, ignored, papered over, and erased, even if GLBTQ people themselves had to do the erasing. Until that root cause is excised, until GLBTQ people are recognized for the valuable, loving, creative, thoughtful, and intelligent people they are and always have been, the history of silence, misrepresentation, and eradication will continue. And until that time, it is critical that GLBTQ people and their allies make a past for themselves and their predecessors—a past that can endure this heteronormative impulse for as long as possible.

Later that evening, after my encounter in the archives I returned to the gaybourhood. It was Friday night and the clubs blared rhythmic beats, the aroma of food and wine lingered in the air, and same-sex couples walked down the street hand in hand, not thinking twice about it. The street was loud; queer voices shouted out from every direction, calling for friends, laughing, flirting, and making plans for the rest of the night. The moon was bright, eerily so, reflecting cheerful faces on every street corner. As I rounded the corner to stroll by the Wood statue for the second time, I was caught off guard by an unexpected sight. The statue was there, of course, as was the regular large group of bearish gay men sitting on benches and street corners, cruising each other around the Wood statue. However, directly in front the statue, arm in arm and hand in hand, stood two women smiling at a camera.

They both wore white, and each woman held a bouquet of flowers in her hand. Clearly the women had just been married, and they wanted a photo with the statue. I paused for a moment to consider the scene—the regular clamor of everyday GLBTQ life, a community of bears, the celebration of a special union for two young lesbians, and, towering above, the statue of Alexander Wood in the moonlight. Fifty years ago that image would have been impossible. Today the image persists in my memory in ways that can never be forgotten.

NOTES

1. *Invert* was the prevailing medical term for a homosexual individual in the early twentieth century.

2. In addition to his medical post at Bronx Hospital, Robinson was the editor of several journals, including *Medical Critic and Guide* and the *Journal of Urology.* Robinson, "My Views on Homosexuality," 357–58. The phrase *step-children of nature* has been credited to German neurologist Dr. Richard von Krafft-Ebing in his controversial *Psychopathia Sexualis* (1886). See Rosario, *Homosexuality and Science,* 64.

3. Robinson, "Nature's Sex Stepchildren," 424–25. Hirschfeld was a homosexual Jewish German physician and homophile advocate. His politics were based on his own research which claimed that all people consisted of variable mixes of masculinity and femininity. Thus homosexuality was not unnatural. See "Hirschfeld, Magnus," *GLBTQ: An Encyclopedia of Gay, Lesbian, Bisexual, Transgender, and Queer Culture,* last modified 2004, http://www.glbtq.com/social-sciences/hirschfeld_m.html (accessed February 12, 2015).

4. Minton, *Departing from Deviance,* 20.

5. *Homophile* was a term coined by Hirschfeld, who argued that other terms were degrading. For an example of the letters directed to Robinson, see Rosario, *Homosexuality and Science,* 49.

6. Minton, *Departing from Deviance,* 20.

7. Robinson, "My Views on Homosexuality," 358.

8. Chauncey, *Gay New York,* 282.

9. Robinson, "Nature's Sex Stepchildren," 424. Also cited in Chauncey, *Gay New York,* 285 (emphasis added).

10. For the possible ways of viewing such gay and lesbian rhetorics, see Brookey, "Speak Up!," 195–219.

11. Berlant and Warner, "Sex in Public," 548.

12. *GLBTQ, gay and lesbian,* and *queer* are loaded terms in both academic and cultural discourses. I use these terms in this book in very specific ways to distinguish between their communal, political, and critical natures. I use *GLBTQ* to signal the wide and diverse community of individuals often united by their

exclusion from the "norms" of exclusive heterosexuality, opposite-sex desire, and gender conformity. In particular, I have arranged the initialism's letters to reflect the historical emergence of such terms (*gay and lesbian* predating *bisexual, transgender,* and *queer*). Though such an arrangement reinscribes a problematic gender inequity, as a historically focused work this book aims to utilize the terminology that reflects the popular designation of the day. I use *gay and lesbian* or *gay men and lesbians* to refer to a part of the GLBTQ community identified primarily by their homosexual desire and their strong identity as a discrete community. I use *queer* to signal an additional part of the GLBTQ community that seeks to disrupt static notions of identity. While the distinctions between these terms are often blurred in popular and scholarly usage, I use them precisely to specify distinctions.

13. Vivian, *Public Forgetting,* 59.
14. Morris, "Introduction," 1–19, and "My Old Kentucky Homo," 95–96, 103.
15. Castiglia and Reed, *If Memory Serves,* 39–54.
16. Morris, "My Old Kentucky Homo," 95.
17. Blair, Dickinson, and Ott, "Introduction," 5–6.
18. The focus on the "West" in this book is used to narrow the scope of the project to make it more manageable, to draw attention to a specific set of acts that has emerged in Europe, Canada, and the United States in the last thirty years, and to prevent characterizing all experiences of same-sex desire across the world as interchangeable.
19. For a good introduction to issues of queer temporality, see Freeman, "Queer Temporalities."
20. Nora, "Between Memory and History," 8–9.
21. Huyssen, *Present Pasts,* 4, 2.
22. Huyssen, *Present Pasts,* 2.
23. Althusser, "Ideology and Ideological State Apparatuses," 100–140.
24. Foucault, *Power/Knowledge,* 85.
25. Katz, *Gay/Lesbian Almanac,* 10–11.
26. Bravmann, *Queer Fictions of the Past,* 4.
27. On *rigor,* see Muñoz, "Ephemera as Evidence," 7.
28. Nora, "Between Memory and Forgetting," 8–9.
29. Huyssen, *Present Pasts,* 30; Kammen, *The Mystic Chords of Memory,* 628; Olick, Vinitzky-Seroussi, and Levy, introduction, 3.
30. Halbwachs, *On Collective Memory,* 38.
31. Halbwachs, *On Collective Memory,* 38.
32. Halbwachs, *On Collective Memory,* 38.
33. Casey, "Public Memory in Place and Time," 21.
34. Sturken, *Tangled Memories,* 3.
35. On popular memory, see Foucault, "Film and Popular Memory," 24–29.
36. Blair, Dickinson, and Ott, "Introduction," 4.
37. Phillips, introduction, 2.
38. Casey, "Public Memory in Place and Time," 30.
39. Blair, Dickinson, and Ott, "Introduction," 6.
40. Blair, Dickinson, and Ott, "Introduction," 7.
41. Assmann, "Collective Memory and Cultural Identity," 132.
42. Casey, "Public Memory in Place and Time," 37.
43. Casey, "Public Memory in Place and Time," 25, 37.

44. Nora, "Between Memory and History," 8; Casey, "Public Memory in Place and Time," 37.
45. Huyssen, *Present Pasts*, 2.
46. Blair, Dickinson, and Ott, "Introduction," 6.
47. Halbwachs, *On Collective Memory*, 40, 43.
48. Aristotle, *On Rhetoric*, 36.
49. Morris, "My Old Kentucky Homo," 89–92.
50. See Morris, *Queering Public Address* and *Remembering the AIDS Quilt*; Dunn, "Remembering Matthew Shepard," 611–52, "Remembering 'A Great Fag,'" 435–60, and "The Quare in the Square," 213–40; Enoch and Jordynn, "Remembering Sappho," 518–37; Castiglia and Reed, *If Memory Serves*; Bessette, "An Archive of Anecdotes," 22–45.
51. Berlant and Warner, "Sex in Public," 562, 559.
52. Foucault, *History of Sexuality*.
53. Cvetkovich, "Sexual Trauma/Queer Memory," 356.
54. Halberstam, *In a Queer Time and Place*, 159, 161. Yet Halberstam is also suspicious of memory's institutionalizing tendencies, championing forgetting's capacity to "[unleash] new forms of memorialization" that may keep the past disorderly in the best possible way. See Halberstam, *The Queer Art of Failure*, 15.
55. Chisholm, "City of Collective Memory," 197–98.
56. Castiglia, "Sex Panics," 160, and with Reed, *If Memory Serves*, 11.
57. Warner, "Introduction: Fear of a Queer Planet," 7; Edelman, "The Future Is Kid Stuff," 23; Freccero, "Queer Times," 489.
58. Love, *Feeling Backward*, 7.
59. Zarefsky, "Four Senses of Rhetorical History," 28–29.
60. Cvetkovich, *An Archive of Feelings*, 8; Bravmann, *Queer Fictions of the Past*, 47–96; Moore, *Beyond Shame*, 64, 70–71; Nealon, *Foundlings*, 99, 141.
61. Bérubé, *Coming Out Under Fire*, x–xi; Cvetkovich, *An Archive of Feelings*, 240–44.
62. Muñoz, "Ephemera as Evidence," 5–7
63. Berlant and Warner, "Sex in Public," 559.
64. Muñoz, "Ephemera as Evidence," 5–7, and *Cruising Utopia*, 65–67.
65. Certeau, *The Practice of Everyday Life*, 37.
66. "Rhetoric, the science of the 'ways of speaking,' offers an array of figure-types for the analysis of everyday ways of acting even though such analysis is in theory excluded from scientific discourse." See Certeau, *The Practice of Everyday Life*, xx.
67. Certeau, *The Practice of Everyday Life*, 37.
68. Quoted from Kaufman, *Gross Indecency*, 70. It is important to note that Kaufman and numerous other academic sources acquire this passage from a supposedly verbatim transcription of the trial produced in Hyde, *The Three Trials of Oscar Wilde*. However, critical Wilde scholarship in recent years has cast doubt upon the validity of this transcription. See Moran, "Transcripts and Truth," 236–38. Nonetheless, claims in 2003 to the "real" transcript published by Wilde's grandson, Merlin Holland, still demonstrate allusions to Shakespeare and "the Greeks" by Wilde in his defense of the "love that dare not speak its name," alhough this transcript is certainly less eloquent. Holland, *The Real Trial of Oscar Wilde*.
69. Lévi-Strauss, *The Savage Mind*, 17.

70. Derrida, "Structure, Sign, and Play in the Discourse of the Human Sciences," 285.

71. Derrida, "Structure, Sign, and Play in the Discourse of the Human Sciences," 285, and Hebdige, *Subculture*, 102–4.

72. Certeau, *The Practice of Everyday Life*, xv.

73. Ellman, *Oscar Wilde*, xv.

74. Fraser, "A Visual Field," 554, 564.

75. Davis, "Homoerotic Art Collection from 1750 to 1920," 247–77.

76. Chauncey, *Gay New York*, 284.

77. Bérubé, *Coming Out Under Fire*, 195.

78. "1883, April, Drs. J. C. Shaw and G. N. Ferris," *Gay/Lesbian Almanac*, 190.

79. "1883, March, 1883, March, Dr. William Hammond," *Gay/Lesbian Almanac*, 187.

80. "1895, September, Dr. James Weir, Jr.," *Gay/Lesbian Almanac*, 285–86.

81. "1883, May 27, *Detroit Post and Tribune*," *Gay/Lesbian Almanac*, 191–94.

82. Kinsey, Pomeroy, and Martin, *Sexual Behavior in the Human Male*.

83. Mack Fingal, "Hadrian and Antinous: The Love-Life of an Emperor," *Mattachine Review* (November/December 1955): 21; Lyn Pedersen, "The Importance of Being Honest," *Mattachine Review* (September/October 1955): 28.

84. D'Emilio, *The World Turned*, 214.

85. Certeau, *The Practice of Everyday Life*, xix.

86. *Dictionary.com*, s.v. "monumentality," accessed February 12, 2015, http://dictionary.reference.com/browse/monumentality.

87. Meyers, "The Experience of Monumentality in Etruscan and Early Roman Architecture," 7–14; See Huyssen on Wagner in *Present Pasts*, 45.

88. Alexander Rehding, "Music Theory: Music and Monumentality," YouTube video, 15:10, from the *Harvard Faculti Series* posted on April 23, 2014, http://youtube/x-nm8uoS-g8, and *Music and Monumentality*, 3–4.

89. Lefebvre, *The Production of Space*, 221.

90. Aristotle, *Rhetoric*, 47.

91. Rehding, *Music and Monumentality*, 10.

92. Trigger, "Monumental Architecture," 119.

93. Rehding, *Music and Monumentality*, 27.

94. See Osborne, *Approaching Monumentality in Archaeology*, 53, 58 111–12, 135–36.

95. Trigger, "Monumental Architecture," 119–32.

96. Rehding, *Music and Monumentality*, 9, 5.

97. Mann, *Reflections of a Nonpolitical Man*, 17.

98. Rehding, *Music and Monumentality*, 9.

99. Rehding, *Music and Monumentality*, 8.

100. Giedeon, Léger, and Sert, "Nine Points on Monumentality."

101. Blair, Jeppeson, and Pucci, "Public Memorializing in Postmodernity," 271.

102. Dunn, "Remembering 'A Great Fag,'" 448.

103. Isherwood, "The World in the Evening," 51.

104. Halberstam, *The Queer Art of Failure*, 3.

105. Morris, "My Old Kentucky Homo," 95.

106. Castiglia and Reed, *If Memory Serves*, 3.

107. Sturken, *Tangled Memories*, 16.

108. Olick, Vinitzky-Seroussi, and Levy, introduction, 3–4. See also Tilmans, van Vree, and Winter, *Performing the Past*, 81–83.

109. Rosenfeld, "A Looming Crash or a Soft Landing?," 141.
110. For a good summary of this institutional history, see D'Emilio, *Sexual Politics, Sexual Communities.*
111. Society of American Archivists, Lesbian and Gay Archives Roundtable, "Lavender Legacies Guide: Introduction," 2014, http://www2.archivists.org/groups/lesbian-and-gay-archives-roundtable-lagar/lavender-legacies-guide-introduction (accessed February 12, 2015).
112. Norton, *The Myth of the Modern Homosexual,* 162.
113. Escoffier, Kunzel, and McGarry, "The Queer Issue," 1.
114. Before these publications, few of the early chroniclers of the GLBTQ past were trained historians. See Bérubé, *Coming Out Under Fire,* x–xi.
115. For instance see Escoffier, Kunzel, and McGarry, "The Queer Issue," 1; Padgug, "Sexual Matters," 3–23; Newton, "The Mythic Mannish Lesbian," 557–75; and Vicinus, "Distance and Desire," 600–622.
116. For instance, see Bérubé, *Coming Out Under Fire;* Newton, *Cherry Grove, Fire Island;* Chauncey, *Gay New York;* Kennedy and Davis, *Boots of Leather, Slippers of Gold;* Escoffier, Kunzel, and McGarry, "The Queer Issue," 4.
117. The first casting was commissioned in 1979 and completed soon thereafter; however its installation in New York City was delayed until 1992 by neighborhood homophobia, criticisms from some GLBTQ activists, and government bureaucracy.
118. Rehding, *Music and Monumentality,* 8.
119. Beauvoir, *The Second Sex,* 288–89.
120. For example, see Gillis, introduction to *Commemorations,* 10.
121. Biesecker, "Remembering World War II," 402.
122. For an introduction to gay shame/pride, see Halperin and Traub, *Gay Shame.*
123. Scholars including James W. Chesebro, Sally Miller Gearhart, Joseph J. Hayes, Joseph A. DeVito, Fred Jandt, Karen Foss, James Darsey, Larry Gross, Dorothy Painter, and R. Jeffrey Ringer (among many others) presented for the first time in the communication discipline what they called, at times, queer lives. However, the work of these scholars is less likely to be classified within the same theoretical lineage as what is contemporarily referred to by persons in the academy as "queer." See Chesebro, *Gayspeak,* and Ringer, *Queer Words, Queer Images.*
124. A special edition of the *Journal of Homosexuality* in 2003 and a simultaneously copublished collection, *Queer Theory and Communication,* belong more closely to this lineage. See Yep, Lovaas, and Elia, *Queer Theory and Communication.*
125. Berlant and Warner, "Sex in Public," 562.
126. Foucault, *Power/Knowledge,* 93.
127. Deleuze and Guattari, *A Thousand Plateaus,* xvii, 9–11; Hardt and Negri, *Empire,* xiii.
128. Huyssen, *Present Pasts,* 46.
129. Rehding, *Music and Monumentality,* 11.
130. Huyssen, *Present Pasts,* 46.

CHAPTER 2
A Monument to "A Great Fag"

1. "A great fag" is quoted from Dennis O'Connor, as reported in Camille Roy, "Monument to 'A Great Fag,'" *Toronto Star,* June 26, 2005, A3. No image of

Wood has survived other than a reproduction of a Georgian silhouette. Thus Wood's appearance is largely derived from the research and impressions of the artist Del Newbigging: "I have worked from the silhouette and researched the period for clothing styles and also added a gay flair which I am convinced he would have had." "Statue Honouring Alexander Wood Unveiled in Toronto's Gay Village," *Xtra*, last modified June 1, 2005, http://dailyxtra.com/canada/news/statue-honouring-alexander-wood-unveiled-in-torontos-gay-village-53751.

2. Norton claims *molly* was the word used by most men with same-sex desires to refer to one another in England during the same time period. See Norton, *Mother Clap's Molly House*, 9, and Norton, *Myth of the Modern Homosexual*, 85.

3. Edith G. Firth, "Wood, Alexander," in *Dictionary of Canadian Biography*, vol. 7, University of Toronto/Université Laval, 2003, http://www.biographi.ca/en/bio/wood_alexander_7E.html (accessed February 12, 2015).

4. Archival evidence suggests that Wood never married and had no children. No record of a same-sex romantic relationship exists in his papers. It is interesting that Wood's papers are largely absent for the year 1810. Alexander Wood Papers and Letterbooks, Special Collections, Toronto Reference Library, Toronto, Ontario. After the scandal Wood was reportedly harassed in the street, and his business suffered. Later in Wood's life Chief Justice William Dummer Powell publicly aired the allegations against Wood in refusing his appointment to a civic post. Wood sued Powell for damages and won. See Firth, "Wood, Alexander." In 1838 a "satirical broadsheet" notoriously announced the "wedding" of Wood to a male colleague as a public attack on his character. See Gerald Keith, "Alexander Wood: A Queer Tale of Early Toronto," *Sightlines*, 1993, 24.

5. Firth, "Wood, Alexander."

6. Muñoz, "Ephemera as Evidence," 5–7, and *Cruising Utopia*, 65–67.

7. See Young, *The Texture of Memory*, 2–4; Bodnar, *Remaking America*, 13–14.

8. Blair and Michel, "Commemorating in the Theme Park Zone," 70.

9. Blair, "Contemporary U.S. Memorial Sites as Exemplars of Rhetoric's Materiality," 50.

10. Mulvey, "Visual Pleasure and Narrative Cinema," 11.

11. Blair, "Contemporary U.S. Memorial Sites as Exemplars of Rhetoric's Materiality," 37–45.

12. Finnegan, "Recognizing Lincoln," 62.

13. In addition, the kinds of images featured (whether denotative, connotative, or subjunctive), which allow viewers to freeze meaning in time, signal greater meaning, or reconsider what could be, all contribute to how memory is made visible. Zelizer, "The Voice of the Visual in Memory," 158–60.

14. In using the expression *gay space*, I am deploying John Grube's terminology.

15. Chauncey, *Gay New York*; Bérubé, *Coming Out Under Fire*; Kennedy and Davis, *Boots of Leather, Slippers of Gold*. For examinations of curbing queer space in a variety of cities, see Bailey, *Gay Politics, Urban Politics*, 249–80; Higgs, *Queer Sites*; and Ingram, Bouthillette, and Retter, *Queers in Space*.

16. Grube, "No More Shit," 128–29. Problematically, Grube generally conceptualizes these democratic spaces as primarily male spaces.

17. I use Castiglia and Reed's spelling *countermemory* rather than Foucault's *counter-memory* because of their extended and substantive use of the term. Foucault, by comparison, uses the term sparingly in his work.

18. Ceccarelli, "Polysemy," 409.

19. Muñoz, "Ephemera as Evidence," 5–6.

20. Ceccarelli, "Polysemy," 410.

21. Bodnar, *Remaking America*, 13–14, 16.

22. Grube, "No More Shit," 128–29.

23. "Statue Honouring Alexander Wood Unveiled in Toronto's Gay Village."

24. Councillor Kyle Rae, quoted in "Toronto Unveils Gay Statue," *San Francisco Bay Times*, last modified June 9, 2005, http://www.sfbaytimes.com (site discontinued).

25. CBC News, "Omnibus Bill," http://www.cbc.ca/archives/categories/politics/rights-freedoms/trudeaus-omnibus-bill-challenging-canadian-taboos/theres-no-place-for-the-state-in-the-bedrooms-of-the-nation.html (accessed February 12, 2015).

26. Smith, *Lesbian and Gay Rights in Canada*, 68, 110.

27. Patricia Reaney, "Support for gay marriage high in developed nations: poll," *Reuters*, June 18, 2013, http://www.reuters.com/article/2013/06/18/us-gaymarriage-poll-idUSBRE95H09T20130618 (accessed February 12, 2015).

28. Historically, queers have been defined as anticitizens, largely because rights justify citizenship and queers are often denied those rights. Bell and Binnie, *The Sexual Citizen*, 142. See also Bennett, *Banning Queer Blood*; Berlant and Freeman, "Queer Nationality," 149–80.

29. Del Newbigging, unpublished oral history interview with the author, June 12, 2008.

30. Del Newbigging, "The Alexander Wood Project," http://www.delnewbigging.com/awoodproject.html (accessed February 12, 2015).

31. On postmodern memorial design and memory, see Blair, Jeppeson, and Pucci, "Public Memorializing in Postmodernity," 263–88, and Soukup, "I Love the 80s," 76–93.

32. "Statue Honouring Alexander Wood Unveiled in Toronto's Gay Village."

33. "Statue Honouring Alexander Wood Unveiled in Toronto's Gay Village."

34. Quote by Dennis O'Connor cited in "Toronto Unveils Gay Statue."

35. Zoë Bake-Paterson, "Ye Olde Cocksucker: The Legend of Alexander Wood Rises Again," *Xtra*, September 29, 2004, last modified September 30, 2004, http://dailyxtra.com/toronto/ye-olde-cocksucker-54414.

36. Roy, "Monument to 'A Great Fag,'" A3.

37. Cameron French, "Statue of Gay Hero Draws Monumental Flak," *Reuters*, last modified June 14, 2005 (no longer accessible). Currently accessible via the *Houston Chronicle*, last modified June 15, 2015, http://www.chron.com/news/nation-world/article/Toronto-statue-of-gay-hero-draws-monumental-flak-1948293.php.

38. Dennis O'Connor, unpublished oral history interview with the author, June 16, 2008.

39. Dara Skolnick (Revenante), "Alexander Watches Over the Crowd," Flickr, JPEG Image commentary, https://www.flickr.com/photos/revenante/176732847/ (accessed February 12, 2015).

40. Gross, "What Is Wrong with This Picture?," 143.

41. Dow, "*Ellen*, Television, and the Politics of Gay and Lesbian Visibility," 137.

42. Brookey, "A Community Like *Philadelphia*," 40–56; Shugart, "Reinventing Privilege," 67–91.

43. Newbigging, oral history interview with the author.
44. Savage, *Standing Soldiers, Kneeling Slaves*, 11. See also Savage, "The Politics of Memory," 131.
45. Sender, *Business, Not Politics*, 239.
46. Burke, *Language as Symbolic Action*, 45.
47. "Statue Honoring Alexander Wood Unveiled in Toronto's Gay Village"; "Toronto Unveils Gay Statue"; Roy, "Monument to 'A Great Fag,'" A3; Newbigging, "The Alexander Wood Project."
48. Rachel Marsden, "A Statuesque Disgrace," *National Post*, last modified June 11, 2005, http://www.rachelmarsden.com/columns/woodstatue.htm.
49. Examples include "Alexander Wood is a Stiff," *London Fog* blog, last modified July 13, 2005, http://thelondonfog.blogspot.com/2005/07/alexander-wood-is-stiff.html, and "And a Penchant for Buggery," *Sick Day* blog, last modified June 16, 2005, http://einspahr.blogspot.com/2005_06_12_archive.html.
50. Smith and Windes, *Progay/Antigay*, 35–36.
51. Marsden, "A Statuesque Disgrace."
52. Comstock, *Violence against Lesbians and Gay Men*, 8, 12–13, 17–18.
53. Marsden, "A Statuesque Disgrace."
54. Marsden, "A Statuesque Disgrace."
55. Rachel Marsden, "The Trouble with 'Normal,'" *National Post*, last modified June 25, 2005, http://www.rachelmarsden.com/columns/pubschools.htm.
56. Morris, "My Old Kentucky Homo," 103.
57. Sontag, "Notes on 'Camp,'" 53.
58. This performative dimension is gleaned most easily from comparisons between *camp* and *kitsch*. While camp involves a certain degree of "insight" on the part of the producer or critic who recognizes failure (and thus the ability to derive some pleasure from it), kitsch is often an "attribute" signaling failure of which its producer is unaware. Ross, "Uses of Camp," 316.
59. Hayes, "Gayspeak," 260. While Hayes is addressing "gayspeak" as something distinct from camp in his essay, he also argues that camp can play a meaningful role in how gayspeak is done.
60. For a short summary of the debates and politics of camp as an exclusively gay sensibility, see Flinn, "The Deaths of Camp," 434–35.
61. Shugart and Waggoner, *Making Camp*, 22–26, 165–66.
62. Cleto, introduction, 304; Flinn, "The Deaths of Camp," 435–38; Ross, "Uses of Camp," 320.
63. "Necrophilic tendencies" is a characterization of camp as understood by Ross in "Uses of Camp." Ross, however, does not use the same phrase but rather "necrophilic trappings." See also Flinn, "The Deaths of Camp," 434.
64. Flinn, "The Deaths of Camp," 436.
65. Finch, "Sex and Address in *Dynasty*," 24–43; Román, "'It's My Party and I'll Die if I Want to!,'" 305–27.
66. Flinn attributes this characterization of camp to Fran Leibowitz, among others, in "The Deaths of Camp," 433.
67. For instance, Román suggests that contemporary camp functions by drawing focus to a "pre-AIDS moment." See Román, *Acts of Intervention*, 100.
68. Booth, *Camp*, 143–44.
69. Cleto, introduction, 304; Flinn, "The Deaths of Camp," 435–38; Ross, "Uses of Camp," 320.

70. Cleto, introduction, 28.
71. Isherwood, "The World in the Evening," 51.
72. Shugart and Waggoner, *Making Camp*, 33, 26.
73. Flinn, "The Deaths of Camp," 447–48.
74. Harpham, *On the Grotesque*, 13.
75. Sontag, "Notes on 'Camp,'" 56.
76. Rubbing the bare buttocks of the groped young man on the fondling plaque has evolved as a playful tradition unplanned by the statue committee. It is another way in which queer visitors add meaning to the statue, particularly as a means of transmitting ephemeral memories as "gesture." See Muñoz, *Cruising Utopia*, 65–67.
77. French, "Statue of Gay Hero Draws Monumental Flak."
78. "Statue Honouring Alexander Wood Unveiled in Toronto's Gay Village."
79. *Molly Wood*, written by John Wimbs and Christopher Richards, was performed in the gaybourhood at the Bathurst Street Theatre.
80. Geoff Chapman, "*Molly Wood* Goes the Way of All Flash," *Toronto Star*, October 27, 1994, E6.
81. Gilbert, *Ejaculations from the Charm Factory*, 227.
82. Blair, "Contemporary U.S. Memorial Sites as Exemplars of Rhetoric's Materiality," 47.
83. Blair, "Contemporary U.S. Memorial Sites as Exemplars of Rhetoric's Materiality," 40.
84. Pollock, "Introduction: Making History Go," 27.
85. Hass, *Carried to the Wall*, 1–2.
86. Newton, "Role Models," 98.
87. Babuscio, "The Cinema of Camp (*aka* Camp and the Gay Sensibility)," 124–25.
88. For instance, Christiansen and Hanson have shown how the exaggeration of gender and sexuality in ACT UP protests allowed for productive protest work and debunked common antigay, anti–HIV/AIDS arguments. See "Comedy as Cure for Tragedy," 165.
89. *Monument Treatment Summary: Alexander Wood* (Toronto: David Sowerbutts Art Conservation 2005–2007); Neal Jennings (Sweet One), "DSCN6011," Flickr, JPEG Image, http://www.flickr.com/photos/sweetone/3670404259/ (accessed February 12, 2015); Canadian Pacific, "Parade Watcher," JPEG Image, http://www.flickr.com/photos/18378305@N00/2699548185/ (accessed February 12, 2015); NKRD, "IMG_7634.jpg," JPEG Image, June 30, 2008, http://www.flickr.com/photos/nkrd/2630300367/ (accessed February 12, 2015); Stephanie Fysh (Lú), "Alexander Wood," JPEG Image, https://www.flickr.com/photos/lu_/21785267/ (accessed February 12, 2015); S.S. Poseidon, "Toronto Pride Day 2 007," JPEG Image, http://www.flickr.com/photos/21795768@N05/2628197015/ (accessed February 12, 2015).
90. *Monument Treatment Summary*.
91. *Monument Treatment Summary*.
92. Zelizer, "The Voice of the Visual in Memory," 162–65.
93. Dennis Hensley, "Going My Way: Hensley Live From Toronto's Halloweek!" *OutTraveler*, last modified November 7, 2007, http://www.outtraveler.com/exclusives/2007/11/07/exclusive-going-my-way-hensley-live-torontos-halloweek?page=0,1 (accessed February 12, 2015).
94. Newbigging, oral history interview with the author.

95. Blair and Michel, "Reproducing Civil Rights Tactics," 32–33, 42.
96. Blair, "Contemporary U.S. Memorial Sites as Exemplars of Rhetoric's Materiality," 46.
97. Berlant and Warner, "Sex in Public," 548, 558.
98. Morris and Sloop, "'What Lips These Lips Have Kissed,'" 12–13.
99. Berlant and Warner, "Sex in Public," 561.
100. Buckland, *Impossible Dance,* 17–18.
101. Blair, "Contemporary U.S. Memorial Sites as Exemplars of Rhetoric's Materiality," 48.
102. For instance, see Grube on cruising as "placemaking" in "No More Shit," 130–31.
103. Bright and Rand, "Queer Plymouth," 274.
104. For instance, see Brouwer, "The Precarious Visibility Politics of Self-Stigmatization," 114–36; Bennett, *Banning Queer Blood;* Erni, "Flaunting Identity," 311–26; among many others.
105. In particular, see Blair, "Contemporary U.S. Memorial Sites as Exemplars of Rhetoric's Materiality," 37, 44, 48; Morris, *Remembering the AIDS Quilt.*
106. Foucault, *Power/Knowledge,* 81–83.
107. Castiglia, "Sex Panics, Sex Publics, Sex Memories," 158, and Morris, "My Old Kentucky Homo," 103.
108. Duberman, Bauml, Vicinus, and Chauncey, introduction, 1–3.
109. Blair, "Contemporary U.S. Memorial Sites as Exemplars of Rhetoric's Materiality," 17.
110. O'Connor, oral history interview with the author.
111. Blair, Jeppeson, and Pucci, "Public Memorializing in Post Modernity," 269.

CHAPTER 3
Remembering Matthew Shepard

1. Kaiser, *The Gay Metropolis, 1940–1996,* 330, 327–47.
2. Currently, a memorial bench at the University of Wyoming in Laramie constitutes the only material marker of Shepard's life and murder.
3. Moisés Kaufman, "A New Monument to Matthew Shepard," *San Francisco Chronicle,* last modified July 12, 2007, http://www.sfgate.com/opinion/open forum/article/A-new-monument-to-Matthew-Shepard-2581901.php.
4. Shepard, *The Meaning of Matthew,* chapter 11.
5. McGee, "Text, Context, and the Fragmentation of Contemporary Culture," 279.
6. Ott and Aoki, "The Politics of Negotiating Public Tragedy," 486. In 2009 Regent Media, the most recent owner of the *Advocate,* significantly cut the print publication of the magazine and moved much of its content online.
7. Morris, "My Old Kentucky Homo," 95.
8. This characterization does not, of course, reflect all possible understandings of materiality, particularly the dimension of materiality not anchored in the physical; it does, however, reflect what those who study monumentality often (though not always) mean by the term. For instance, see Selzer and Crowley, *Rhetorical Bodies.*
9. Arendt, *The Human Condition,* 173.
10. See Thomas, preface, ix.
11. Giedeon, Léger, and Sert, "Nine Points on Monumentality," 48.
12. Aristotle, *Poetics,* 10, 49–50.

13. Arendt, *The Human Condition*, 19.

14. As quoted in Rehding, *Music and Monumentality*, 21.

15. Rehding, *Music and Monumentality*, 14.

16. Huyssen, *Present Pasts*, 46–48; Hess, "In Digital Remembrance," 812–30.

17. Nora, "Between Memory and History," 8.

18. Schwartz, *Abraham Lincoln and the Forge of National Memory*, 23–25.

19. Morris, "Sunder the Children," 402.

20. Blair, Dickinson, and Ott, introduction, 16.

21. Massumi, *Parables for the Virtual*, 15.

22. Blair, Dickinson, and Ott, introduction, 16–17.

23. Petersen, *Murder, the Media, and the Politics of Public Feelings*, 5.

24. Blair, Dickinson, and Ott, introduction, 17.

25. Habermas, *The Structural Transformation of the Public Sphere*, 25.

26. Nancy Fraser, "Rethinking the Public Sphere," 109, 123, 116; among others.

27. Warner, *Publics and Counterpublics*, 114.

28. Asen, "Seeking the 'Counter' in Counterpublics," 444–45.

29. Pezzullo, "Resisting 'National Breast Cancer Awareness Month,'" 349, 361.

30. Warner, *Publics and Counterpublics*, 65–124, 75.

31. Warner, *Publics and Counterpublics*, 97.

32. Ott and Aoki, "The Politics of Negotiating Public Tragedy," 489.

33. For Carl von Clausewitz, persuasion and violence constitute different ends of the political spectrum. See Giddens, "Political Theory and the Problem of Violence," 245. For violence as occasion for rhetorical invention, see Browne, "Encountering Angelina Grimké," 56.

34. For instance, Congresswoman Virginia Foxx remarked that Shepard's memory was a "hoax." See 111 Cong. Rec. H4, 929 (2009) (statement of Congresswoman Virginia Foxx). In more recent years others have blamed a dispute over drugs as the reason for the Shepard's death. See Patrick Letellier, "20/20 Hindsight," *Advocate*, February 1, 2005, 35, and Jimenez, *Book of Matt*.

35. Ott and Aoki, "The Politics of Negotiating Public Tragedy," 499, 497.

36. Lynch, "Memory and Matthew Shepard," 228.

37. Balter-Reitz and Stewart, "Looking for Matthew Shepard," 123.

38. Browne, "Encountering Angelina Grimké," 55–56.

39. Warner, introduction to *Fear of a Queer Planet*, xxvii.

40. Browne, "Encountering Angelina Grimké," 56.

41. Harold and DeLuca, "Behold the Corpse," 272.

42. "The Good Shepard," *Advocate*, November 10, 1998, 13.

43. Chris Bull, "All Eyes Were Watching," *Advocate*, November 24, 1998, 33, 35; Jon Barrett, "Lost Brother," *Advocate*, November 24, 1998, 27, 29.

44. Walter Boulden, "Remarks of Matthew's Friends at D.C. Vigil," last modified October 14, 1998, http://www.wiredstrategies.com/shepard3.html. This speech is from an online collection known as the Matthew Shepard Resource Archive.

45. Barrett, "Lost Brother," 27.

46. Paul et al., "Suicide Attempts among Gay and Bisexual Men," 1343.

47. John Gallagher, "Matt's HIV Status," *Advocate*, March 16, 1999, 33–35.

48. Barrett, "Lost Brother," 28.

49. Boulden, "Remarks of Matthew's Friends."

50. Federal Bureau of Investigation, "Hate Crimes Statistics," http://www.fbi.gov/about-us/cjis/ucr/hate-crime/1998 (accessed February 12, 2015).

51. Lawrence, *Punishing Hate*, 23.
52. Bull, "All Eyes Were Watching," 35; "The Good Shepard," 13; *Local Law Enforcement Hate Crimes Prevention Act*, H.R. 1343, 107th Cong. (April 3, 2001); *Local Law Enforcement Enhancement Act of 2001*, S. 625, 107th Cong. (March 27, 2001); The *Congressional Record* contains numerous accounts of remarks on both of these bills throughout the 107th Congress and subsequent Congresses. President Clinton made several notable connections between Shepard and Byrd in public statements, a weekly radio address, and an official proclamation. All of these remarks are available at the William J. Clinton Presidential Library and Museum, The Archives, http://www.clintonlibrary.gov/research .html (object name "Matthew Shepard and James Byrd") (accessed February 12, 2015).
53. On reminiscing and queer time, see Foucault, "Sexual Choice, Sexual Act," 297.
54. Bull, "All Eyes Were Watching," 35; Brendan Lemon, "The State of Hate," *Advocate*, April 13, 1999, 24–28.
55. John Aravosis, "First-Hand Report from the D.C. Vigil, October 14," last modified October 15, 1998, http://www.wiredstrategies.com/shepard3.html (accessed February 12, 2015).
56. Bull, "All Eyes Were Watching," 37.
57. Bull, "All Eyes Were Watching," 37.
58. Benoit Denizet-Lewis, "It Could Have Been Me," *Advocate*, October 12, 1999, 50.
59. "An Urban Uproar over a Rural Tragedy," *Advocate*, November 24, 1998, 29.
60. ACT UP/New York, "Matthew Shepard Political Funeral," last modified October 20, 1998, http://www.actupny.org/reports/Shepard.html (accessed February 12, 2015).
61. Habermas, *The Structural Transformation of the Public Sphere*, 79; However, in some situations the state and the public are increasingly aligned, if not one in the same. See Asen and Brouwer, introduction, 2.
62. Phil Curtis, "Letter from Laramie," *Advocate*, last modified October 26, 1999, http://www.advocate.com/html/specials/shepard/laramie01.asp (site discontinued). This article appeared as a special report in the online edition, not the printed edition of the same date.
63. Comstock, "Dismantling the Homosexual Panic Defense," 81–82.
64. Curtis, "Letter from Laramie."
65. Bull, "All Eyes Were Watching," 37; See also James Brooke, "Gay Man Dies from Attacks, Fanning Outrage and Debate," *New York Times*, October 13, 1998, A30.
66. Schwartz, *Abraham Lincoln and the Forge of National Memory*, 34, 30, 31–32.
67. Smith, *Fools, Martyrs, Traitors*.
68. Jensen, Burkholder, and Hammerback, "Martyrs for a Just Cause," 335–37.
69. Smith, *Fools, Martyrs, Traitors*, 373, quoted in Jensen, Burkholder, and Hammerback, "Martyrs for a Just Cause," 337.
70. Jensen, Burkholder, and Hammerback, "Martyrs for a Just Cause," 340–41.
71. Jensen, Burkholder, and Hammerback, "Martyrs for a Just Cause," 340.
72. James Brooke, "Friends and Strangers Mourn Gay Student in Wyoming," *New York Times*, October 17, 1998, A11.
73. Ott and Aoki, "The Politics of Negotiating Public Tragedy," 490.
74. Jensen, Burkholder, and Hammerback, "Martyrs for a Just Cause," 340.

75. "The Good Shepard," 13.
76. Barrett, "Lost Brother," 28; Todd Savage, "His Story Lives On," *Advocate*, October 12, 1999, 48.
77. Bull, "All Eyes Were Watching," 37.
78. Dennis Shepard, "My Son Matt," *Advocate*, April 30, 2000, 30.
79. The Matthew Shepard Foundation, "Matthew's Life," last modified 2006, http://www.matthewshepard.org/site/PageServer?pagename=mat_Matthews_ Life (site discontinued).
80. Matthew Shepard Foundation, "Matthew's Story," last modified 2015, http:// www.matthewshepard.org/our-story/matthews-story (accessed February 12, 2015); "The Good Shepard," 13.
81. "The Good Shepard," 13.
82. Boulden, "Remarks of Matthew's Friends."
83. "The Good Shepard," 13.
84. Bull, "All Eyes Were Watching," 37.
85. Denizet-Lewis, "It Could Have Been Me," 50–52.
86. Barrett, "Lost Brother," 26.
87. The HRC, Matthew Shepard Foundation, and GLAAD all released statements highlighting Shepard's virtues.
88. Browne, "Encountering Angelina Grimké," 56–57.
89. Charland, "Constitutive Rhetoric," 133–50.
90. Jensen, Burkholder, and Hammerback, "Martyrs for a Just Cause," 336.
91. Jamieson and Campbell, "Rhetorical Hybrids," 148–49, 151.
92. Jensen, Burkholder, and Hammerback, "Martyrs for a Just Cause," 340.
93. Jon Barrett, "Defining Moments of the Decade," *Advocate*, January 18, 2000, 19.
94. Jeremy Kinser, "Stonewall 30: Can It Be Three Decades; Fast-Forward—and Back," *Advocate*, June 22, 1999, 34.
95. Michael Joseph Gross, "Matthew Shepard: Five Years Later—Pain and Prominence," *Advocate*, September 30, 2003, 27.
96. Adam B. Vary, "Is Gay Over?," *Advocate*, June 20, 2006, 102.
97. Chauncey, *Gay New York*, 286.
98. Bravmann, *Queer Fictions of the Past*, 4–6.
99. Barrett, "Defining Moments of the Decade," 19.
100. M. M. Buechner, "TIME Man of Year Poll Roils Internet," *TIME*, last modified December 21, 1998, http://www.time.com/time/nation/article/0,8599,17197,00 .html.
101. Gross, "Matthew Shepard: Five Years Later," 26.
102. Halberstam, *In a Queer Time and Place*, 44.
103. Bravmann, *Queer Fictions of the Past*, 31, 5.
104. While class was absent from many queer counterpublic critiques, it was clearly an issue. Had Shepard not been from a financially secure middle-class family he would not have been an easy victim for identification; nor would his memory have been able to thrive thanks to the legal, cultural, and economic resources that his family and supporters brought to the task.
105. Yusef Najafi, "Hope Emerges from Horror: Judy Shepard and Local Activists Reflect on the Decade since Matthew Shepard's Murder," *Metroweekly: Washington D.C.'s GLBT Newsmagazine*, last modified October 23, 2008, http://www .metroweekly.com/2008/10/hope-emerges-from-horror/.

106. Urvashi Vaid, "Post-Principle Blues," *Advocate*, December 8, 1998, 96.

107. Jasmyne Cannick, "Hate Crimes in Black and White," *Advocate*, November 6, 2007, 22.

108. Judy Wieder, "The Real Rosie," *Advocate*, December 24, 2002, http://www.advocate.com/politics/commentary/2002/12/24/real-rosie?page=0,1.

109. Juang, "Transgendering the Politics of Recognition," 243, 253.

110. Stotzer, "Violence against Transgender People," 170–79.

111. Schwartz, Ulit, and Morgan, "Straight Talk about Hate Crimes Bills," 174–76. The Matthew Shepard and James Byrd, Jr., Hate Crimes Prevention Act that became law in 2009 included explicit protections for transgender persons.

112. "Polar," comment on "Judy Shepard: Back Up HRC on Press 'Misinformation' About Leaving Transgender Behind!," *Transadvocate*, comment posted June 15, 2008, http://www.transadvcate.com/judy-shepard-back-up-hrc-on-press-misinformation-about-leaving-transgender-behind.htm (site discontinued).

113. Mark Walcott, "Past Tense," *Advocate*, October 28, 2003, 4.

114. Cannick, "Hate Crimes in Black and White," 22.

115. Bull, "All Eyes Were Watching," 37.

116. "Polar," comment on "Judy Shepard."

117. Boulden, "Remarks of Matthew's Friends."

118. Schwartz, *Abraham Lincoln and the Forge of National Memory*, 156–57.

119. Jamieson, *Eloquence in an Electronic Age*, 115.

120. Sennett, *The Fall of Public Man*, 26, 104.

121. Burke, *Rhetoric of Motives*, 55.

122. Bull, "All Eyes Were Watching," 37.

123. Barrett, "Lost Brother," 28.

124. Barrett, "Lost Brother," 28.

125. Boulden, "Remarks of Matthew's Friends."

126. Neal Broverman, "Short Answers: Romaine Patterson," *Advocate*, October 25, 2005, 22.

127. Barrett, "Lost Brother," 28.

128. Shepard, "My Son Matt," 30.

129. Shepard, "My Son Matt," 30.

130. Judy Wieder and John Gallagher, "The Shepard Family Heals," *Advocate*, October 12, 1999, 40.

131. John Gallagher, "Hiking against Hate," *Advocate*, March 16, 1999, 35.

132. Barrett, "Lost Brother," 28.

133. Barrett, "Lost Brother," 28; Bill Ghent, "Matthew Shepard Inc.?," *Advocate*, January 19, 1999, 54.

134. Bull, "All Eyes Were Watching," 37.

135. Lemon, "The State of Hate," 24.

136. Kaiser, *Gay Metropolis*, 340, 329.

137. Michael Cooper, "Killing Shakes Complacency of the Gay Rights Movement," *New York Times*, last modified October 21, 1998, http://www.nytimes.com/ads/marketing/laramie/19981021_laramie6.html.

138. Balter-Reitz and Stewart, "Looking for Matthew Shepard," 123.

139. Cooper, "Killing Shakes Complacency."

140. Barrett, "Defining Moments of the Decade," 19.

141. Jennifer Mrozowski, "More Schools Get Gay-Straight Alliances," *Cincinnati*

Enquirer, last modified August 12, 2001, http://www.enquirer.com/editions/2001/08/12/loc_more_schools_get.html.

142. Cooper, "Killing Shakes Complacency."
143. Barrett, "Defining Moments of the Decade," 19.
144. Denizet-Lewis, "It Could Have Been Me," 50, 53, 51–53.
145. Denizet-Lewis, "It Could Have Been Me," 51.
146. Cooper, "Killing Shakes Complacency."
147. Cooper, "Killing Shakes Complacency."
148. Cooper, "Killing Shakes Complacency."
149. Barrett, "Lost Brother," 28.
150. Boulden, "Remarks of Matthew's Friends."
151. Perry Bacon, Jr., "Obama Signs Bill Expanding Hate Protection to Gays," *Washington Post*, last modified October 29, 2009, http://www.washingtonpost.com/wp-dyn/content/article/2009/10/28/AR2009102804909.html.
152. House Subcommittee on Criminal Justice of the Committee on the Judiciary, *Hearing on AntiGay Violence*, 99th Cong., 2nd sess., 1986, 1–31.

CHAPTER 4
Imagining GLBT Americans

1. Quinn and Meiners, *Flaunt It!*, 3.
2. Morris, "Sunder the Children," 403–5.
3. Anderson, *Imagined Communities*, 6.
4. Rehding, *Music and Monumentality*, 42.
5. For instance, prominent examples include Beasley, introduction, 3–18; Stuckey, *Defining Americans*; Canaday, *The Straight State*; Bodnar, *Remaking America*; Kammen, *The Mystic Chords of Memory*.
6. Anderson, *Imagined Communities*, 204.
7. Bruner, *Strategies of Remembrance*, 7.
8. Vivian, *Public Forgetting*, 59, 13–14.
9. Fisher, "Narration as a Human Communication Paradigm," 8–9.
10. Fisher, *Human Communication as Narration*, 109.
11. For instance, see Gil Kaufman, "California Senate Passes Bill Requiring Gay History Education," *MTV News*, last modified May 12, 2006, http://www.mtv.com/news/1531648/california-senate-passes-bill-requiring-gay-history-education; Wyatt Buchanan and Greg Lucas, "Bill Would Include Gays in Public School Texts," *San Francisco Chronicle*, last modified April 16, 2006, http://www.sfgate.com/education/article/CALIFORNIA-Bill-would-include-gays-in-public-2537268.php.
12. Morris, "Sunder the Children," 412.
13. Olson, "Traumatic Styles in Public Address," 254.
14. Lorde, "Age, Race, Class, and Sex," 123.
15. The notion "that a single courageous State may, if its citizens choose, serve as a laboratory; and try novel social and economic experiments without risk to the rest of the country" was popularized by U.S. Supreme Court justice Louis Brandeis in 1932. See New State Ice Co. vs. Liebman, 285 U.S. 262 (1932) at 311.
16. Nora, "Between Memory and History," 8.
17. Squires, *Aligning and Balancing the Standards-Based Curriculum*, 13–14.

18. "Do You Know What Textbooks Your Children Are Really Reading?" *Fox News*, last modified September 17, 2010, http://www.foxnews.com/story/0,2933,545900,00 .html.

19. Olson, "On the Language and Authority of Textbooks," 238.

20. Clawson and Kegler, "The 'Race Coding' of Poverty in American Government College Textbooks," 181.

21. Crismore, "Rhetorical Form, Selection, and the Use of Textbooks," 133.

22. Burke, *A Rhetoric of Motives*, 57–59.

23. Clawson and Kegler, "The 'Race Coding' of Poverty in American Government College Textbooks," 184–85.

24. Gullicks et al., "Diversity and Power in Public Speaking Textbooks," 250–51.

25. Reynolds, "Textbooks: Guardians of Nationalism," 37.

26. Adorno, *The Culture Industry*, 98–99.

27. Althusser, "Ideology and Ideological State Apparatuses," 104.

28. McGee, "The 'Ideograph,'" 11.

29. Anyon, "Ideology and United States History Textbooks," 382–86.

30. Coman, "Reading about the Enemy," 327–29.

31. Ramaswamy, "Maps and Mother Goddesses in Modern India," 100, 104, 108.

32. Eagleton, *Criticism and Ideology*, 89.

33. Nash, Crabtree, and Dunn, *History on Trial*, 132, 92, 135.

34. Jensen, *Dirty Words*.

35. Novkov and Gossett, "Survey of Textbooks for Teaching Introduction to U.S. Politics," 393, 394–98.

36. Macgillivray and Jennings, "A Content Analysis Exploring Lesbian, Gay, Bisexual, and Transgender Topics in Foundations of Education Textbooks," 170–88.

37. Michael Janofsky, "Gay Rights Battlefields Spread to Public Schools," *New York Times*, last modified June 9, 2005, http://www.nytimes.com/2005/06/09/ education/09clash.html?pagewanted=all&_r=0.

38. Ceci Connolly, "Some Abstinence Programs Mislead Teens, Report Says," *Washington Post*, last modified December 2, 2004, A01, http://www.washington post.com/wp-dyn/articles/A26623–2004Dec1.html; Nicholas D. Kristof, "Bush's Sex Scandal," *New York Times*, last modified February 16, 2005, http://www .nytimes.com/2005/02/16/opinion/16kristof.html.

39. "Excerpts of Textbooks in Disputed Courses," *Associated Press*, December 9, 2005 (site discontinued). See Keesee and Sidwell, *United States History for Christian Schools*.

40. Burke, *A Rhetoric of Motives*, 21–22.

41. Burke, *A Grammar of Motives*, 406–7.

42. Katz, *Love Stories*, 49.

43. Katz, *Love Stories*, 49.

44. Mosse, *Nationalism and Sexuality*, 34.

45. Chauncey, *Gay New York*, 229.

46. Ian Drury, "Gordon Brown Apologises to Gay Enigma Codebreaker Alan Turing for 'Appalling' Persecution," *Daily Mail*, last modified September 11, 2009, http://www.dailymail.co.uk/news/article-1212703/Gordon-Brown-apologises -gay-WW2-code-breaker-Alan-Turing-appalling-persecution.html.

47. Danny Shaw, "Royal Pardon for Codebreaker Alan Turing," *BBC News*, last modified December 24, 2013, http://www.bbc.com/news/technology-25495315.

48. Sinfield, *Cultural Politics*, 41.

49. Johnson, *The Lavender Scare*, 31, 36, 55–56.

50. Johnson, *The Lavender Scare*, 144.

51. Rick Anderson, "Worst Internal Scandal in NSA History Was Blamed on Cold War Defector's Sexuality: But What If They Weren't Gay?" *Seattle Weekly*, last modified July 17, 2007, http://www.seattleweekly.com/2007-7-18/news/the -worst-internal-scandal-in-nsa-history-was-blamed-on-cold-war-defectors -homosexuality.

52. Anderson, "Worst Internal Scandal in NSA History."

53. Anderson, "Worst Internal Scandal in NSA History."

54. Hillary Clinton, "Remarks at an Event Celebrating Lesbian, Gay, Bisexual and Transgender (LGBT) Month," last modified June 22, 2010, http://votesmart.org /public-statement/520879/remarks-at-an-event-celebrating-lesbian-gay-bisexual -and-transgender-lgbt-month#.UumFOxBdV8E.

55. Bellah, "Civil Religion in America."

56. Lieven, *America Right or Wrong*, 143.

57. Larry Kramer, "Reagan and AIDS," *New York Review of Books*, last modified April 12, 2007, http://www.nybooks.com/articles/archives/2007/apr/12/reagan-and -aids; Matt Foreman, "A Letter to My Best Friend, Steven Powsner, On the Death of Former President Ronald Reagan," *Empty Closet*, July 2004, A8.

58. Koop, *Koop*, 204.

59. Perez and Dionisopoulos, "Presidential Silence, C. Everett Koop, and the *Surgeon General's Report on AIDS*," 18, 30.

60. Allen White, "Reagan's AIDS Legacy," *San Francisco Chronicle*, last modified June 8, 2004. http://www.sfgate.com/opinion/openforum/article/Reagan-s-AIDS -Legacy-Silence-equals-death-2751030.php.

61. Representative Henry Waxman, "Fighting an Epidemic in the Absence of Leadership," *Washington Post*, last modified September 4, 1985, H19. Published online at http://waxman.house.gov/fighting-epidemic-absence-leadership (ac- cessed February 12, 2015).

62. C. Everett Koop, *Surgeon General's Report on Acquired Immune Deficiency Syndrome* (Washington, D.C.: U.S. Public Health Service Public Affairs Of- fice, 1986), http://www.ncbi.nlm.nih.gov/pmc/articles/PMC1477712/ (accessed February 12, 2015).

63. Perez and Dionisopoulos, "Presidential Silence, C. Everett Koop, and the *Surgeon General's Report on AIDS*," 28–29.

64. Judy Lin, "Gay Community Seeks Recognition in Textbooks," *Contra Costa Times*, May 28, 2006.

65. Jordan Rau, "State Senate Endorses Teaching of Gays' Historical Achieve- ments," *Los Angeles Times*, last modified May 12, 2006, A1, http://articles.la times.com/2006/may/12/local/me-books12.

66. Senator Sheila Kuehl, "SB 1437: 'Bias-Free Curriculum Act,'" http://www.sen .ca.gov/ (accessed February 12, 2015).

67. Prividera and Howard, "Masculinity, Whiteness, and the Warrior Hero," 30. See also Shome, "White Femininity and the Discourse of the Nation," 323–42.

68. Rau, "State Senate Endorses Teaching."

69. Joyce Howard Price, "California Panel Backs Teaching 'Sexual Diversity,'" *Washington Times*, last modified April 7, 2006, A10, http://www.washington times.com/news/2006/apr/6/20060406-112123-7246r.

70. Greg Lucas, "Senate OKs Bill on Gays in Textbooks," *San Francisco Chronicle*,

last modified May 12, 2006, B8, http://www.sfgate.com/education/article/
SACRAMENTO-Senate-OKs-bill-on-gays-in-textbooks-2518921.php.

71. Jesse McKinley, "From TV Role in 'Dobie Gillis' to Rights Fight in Legislature," *New York Times*, last modified May 14, 2006, A16; "California Assembly Scales Back Gay-Inclusive Textbook Bill," *Advocate*, last modified August
9, 2006, http://www.advocate.com/news/2006/08/09/california-assembly-scales
-back-gay-inclusive-textbook-bill; "California Might Honor Gays in Textbooks,"
NBC News, last modified May 12, 2006, http://www.nbcnews.com/id/12754481/#
.VgGYyN9VhBd; Bill O'Reilly, "Should California Schools Put Positive Spin
on Gays?" *The O'Reilly Factor,*May 9, 2006, http://www.alacrastore.com/store
content/Voxant-TV-Transcripts/THE-O-REILLY-FACTOR-Should-California
-Schools-Put-Positive-Spin-on-Gays-2006fx050805cc256.

72. Quote by Senator Kuehl in Juliet Williams, "Senate Committee Agrees to Add
Sexual Orientation to Curriculum," *Lodi News-Sentinel*, May 4, 2006, 7.

73. Jonathan Snowden, "Press Release: SB 1437 (Kuehl): Bias-Free Curriculum
Act, Question and Answers," last modified April 18, 2006, http://dist23.casen.gov
office.com/ (site discontinued).

74. Williams, "Senate Committee Agrees."

75. "California Bill Would Require Textbooks Mention Gay's Contributions," *Diverse Education*, last modified May 2, 2006, http://diverseeducation.com/article
/5806/.

76. It is important to note here that while *American* signifies a person of U.S.
citizenship in contemporary parlance, originally *American* designated a person
from any of the nations of North and South America. This discourse is regularly forgotten as first Europeans and then the United States sought to take
exclusive ownership of the term, an only slightly veiled form of cultural imperialism.

77. It is interesting that the national character of these GLBT contributors is
more prominent than their contributions to the state of California, an element
equally required by the legislation. While Kuehl's legislation and public statements do require GLBT contributions to the nation be highlighted, they also
include required support in the area of the state. However, it is the excessive
focus upon the nation, national figures, and national consequences in the debate that contributes to the national underpinnings of the memories.

78. For instance, see Bruner, *Strategies of Remembrance*, 83.

79. Jonathan Zimmerman, "Straight History: The Danger of Trying to Put a 'Positive' Face on the Past," *San Francisco Chronicle*, last modified May 7, 2006,
http://www.sfgate.com/opinion/openforum/article/Straight-history-The-danger
-of-trying-to-put-a-2535582.php.

80. Bodnar, *Remaking America*, 72.

81. Lawrence, "Bill Would Require Textbooks."

82. Epstein, "Gay Politics, Ethnic Identity," 12.

83. Of course, drawing these kind of parallels can have unintended consequences.
As Elizabeth V. Spelman argues, comparison across groups can make it harder
to recognize significant intra-group differences, can problematize intersecting
identities, and can become a kind of imperialism of suffering—what she calls
"making your suffering mine." See Spelman, *Fruits of Sorrow*, 94, 113.

84. Greg Lucas, "Bill Expanding Gay Rights in Public School Curriculum Watered
Down," *San Francisco Chronicle,* last modified August 8, 2006, http://www

.sfgate.com/education/article/SACRAMENTO-Bill-expanding-gay-rights
-in-public-2491474.php.

85. Rau, "State Senate Endorses Teaching."

86. Buchanan and Lucas, "Bill Would Include Gays."

87. Kaufman, "California Senate Passes Bill."

88. Lawrence, "Bill Would Require Textbooks."

89. Rau, "State Senate Endorses Teaaching."

90. Faderman and Timmons, *Gay L.A.*, 334.

91. Wood, *Gendered Lives*, 247.

92. Zimmerman, *Whose America?*, 128.

93. Bodnar, *Remaking America*, 228.

94. Zimmerman, "Straight History."

95. Zimmerman, "Straight History."

96. Bravmann, *Queer Fictions of the Past*, 94–96.

97. Duggan, *The Twilight of Equality?*, 51–53.

98. William Henderson, "Cultural History," *Advocate*, June 20, 2006, 28.

99. Brian Rooney, "California Mulls Gay History in Textbooks," *ABC News*, last modified May 12, 2006, http://abcnews.go.com/WNT/story?id=1956254&page=1.

100. Rau, "State Senate Endorses Teaching."

101. Lucas, "Senate OKs Bill on Gays," B8.

102. Debra J. Saunders, "One for the Textbooks," *San Francisco Chronicle*, last modified May 21, 2006, E7, http://www.sfgate.com/opinion/saunders/article/One-for-the-textbooks-2534836.php.

103. Zimmerman, "Straight History."

104. Gustavo Serina, "Teaching Gay History," *San Francisco Chronicle*, last modified May 28, 2006, E6, http://www.sfgate.com/opinion/letterstoeditor/article/LETTERS-TO-THE-EDITOR-2496019.php.

105. Foucault, *History of Sexuality*, 17–18.

106. Mosse, *Nationalism and Sexuality*, 33–34.

107. Foucault, *History of Sexuality*, 136, 139.

108. McKinley, "From TV Role in 'Dobie Gillis,'" A16.

109. Snowden, "Press Release."

110. Moore, *Beyond Shame*, 13.

111. Morris, "My Old Kentucky Homo," 95.

112. Castiglia, "Sex Panics," 158.

113. Castiglia, "Sex Panics," 158.

114. Moore, *Beyond Shame*; Castiglia and Reed, *If Memory Serves*; *Gay Sex in the 70s*.

115. As quoted in Lucas, "Senate OKs Bill," B8.

116. Morris, "My Old Kentucky Homo," 103.

117. McKinley, "From TV Role in 'Dobie Gillis,'" A16.

118. Concerned Women of America, "'Gay' Activists Use California School Kids to Push Their Agenda," *Family Voice*, November/December 2006.

119. Gary Bauer, "The Aftershocks of Gay Marriage," *Human Events*, last modified May 30, 2008, http://www.humanevents.com/2008/05/30/the-aftershocks-of-gay-marriage.

120. "California to Include Gays in School Texts," *UPI Newswire*, last modified May 12, 2006, http://www.upi.com/Top_News/2006/05/12/California-to-include-gays-in-school-texts/UPI-91841147467478.

121. Senator Sheila Kuehl, "SB777: 'Student Civil Rights Act,'" http://www.sen.ca
     .gov (accessed February 12, 2015).
122. Mark Leno, "Sen. Leno Hails Governor's Approval of Landmark LGBT In-
     clusive Education Bill," last modified July 14, 2011, http://sd11.senate.ca.gov/
     news/2011–7–14-sen-leno-hails-governor-s-approval-landmark-lgbt-inclusive
     -education-bill.
123. "California Governor Signs Bill Requiring Schools Teach Gay History," *CNN*,
     last modified July 15, 2011, http://www.cnn.com/2011/US/07/14/california.lgbt
     .education/index.html.

CHAPTER 5
Preserving a Queer (After) Life

1. Watney, *Policing Desire*, 7–8.
2. Some efforts have been made to remedy these inequities, though practices vary
   nationwide. See Michael D. Shear, "Obama Extends Hospital Visitation Rights
   to Same-Sex Partners of Gays," *Washington Post*, last modified April 16, 2010,
   http://www.washingtonpost.com/wp-dyn/content/article/2010/04/15/AR2010041
   505502.html.
3. Cohen, "Contested Membership," 56.
4. For example, in 1992 a father sued to have his gay son's gravestone removed
   from the cemetery because it included the words *gay* and *AIDS*. See Amy Lou-
   ise Kazmin, "Judge Won't Change Gay Man's Gravestone," *Los Angeles Times*,
   last modified September 26, 1992, http://articles.latimes.com/1992–9–26/local
   /me-1001_1_alexander-lawrence. Similarly, despite the emphatic efforts described above, a feminist editor of Stein's work has leveled assaulted claims
   that Stein and Toklas were lovers as besmirching the credibility of both. Newton, "Sick to Death of Ambiguities . . . ," 10.
5. Huyssen, *Present Pasts*, 46–48.
6. Phillips, introduction, 3.
7. Bodnar, *Remaking America*, 14–18.
8. Olson, Finnegan, and Hope, "Visual Rhetoric in Communication," 1.
9. Clark, *Rhetorical Landscapes in America*, 35.
10. Clark, *Rhetorical Landscapes in America*, 9.
11. Clark, *Rhetorical Landscapes in America*, 10.
12. Morris, "Death on Display," 204–5.
13. Geertz, *The Interpretation of Cultures*, 89.
14. Morris, "Death on Display," 206–7, 213–15.
15. A text helpful in the completion of this chapter was Meyer, *Cemeteries & Grave-
    markers*.
16. Hijiya, "American Gravestones and Attitudes toward Death," 342.
17. Hijiya, "American Gravestones and Attitudes toward Death," 345.
18. Morris, "Death on Display," 205.
19. Morris, "Death on Display," 209.
20. Hijiya, "American Gravestones and Attitudes toward Death," 355.
21. Morris, "Death on Display," 210–11.
22. Morris, "Death on Display," 212.
23. Morris, "Death on Display," 214.
24. Thompson, "On the Development of Counter-Racist Quare Public Address
    Studies," 135. See also Wittig, *The Straight Mind and Other Essays*, 28.

25. Warner, introduction, xxvii.
26. Berlant and Warner, "Sex in Public," 548.
27. Foucault, *History of Sexuality,* 135–59.
28. Department of Veterans Affairs, Va. Form 40–1330 (August 2009), http://www .va.gov/vaforms/va/pdf/VA40–1330.pdf (site discontinued). A new version of the form that supersedes the previous version appears to be less hostile and shows a more ambiguous stance toward these issues. See Department of Veterans Affairs, Va. Form 40–1330 (Feb 2014), http://www.va.gov/vaforms/va/pdf/ VA40–1330.pdf (accessed February 12, 2015). See also Department of Veterans Affairs, "Federal Benefits for Veterans, Dependents and Survivors," (2010), 64–65, http://www.va.gov/opa/publications/benefits_book/federal_benefits.pdf (site discontinued). See also the 2014 version of this document, which has been updated at http://www.va.gov/opa/publications/benefits_book.asp (accessed February 12, 2015).
29. Garance Burke, "A Call for Eternal Equality: Seeking Acceptance, Gay Veterans Group Pushes for Memorial at SE Cemetery," *Washington Post,* September 14, 2003, C01.
30. Neal Broverman, "AFA, Aghast Gay Soldiers Could be Buried at Arlington, Rallies Troops," *Advocate,* last modified February 13, 2013, http://www.advocate .com/politics/military/2013/02/13/afa-aghast-gay-soldiers-could-be-buried -arlington-rallies-troops.
31. Bill McAuliffe, "House Passes 'Final Wishes' Bill," *Minneapolis–St. Paul Star Tribune,* last modified May 11, 2010, http://www.startribune.com/politics /state/93504484.html; "Editorial: 'Final Wishes' Veto is Cold, Calculating," *Minneapolis–St. Paul Star Tribune,* last modified May 24, 2010, http://www .startribune.com/opinion/editorials/94778999.html.
32. Dawn Ennis, "Laws Proposed to Protect Trans Youth as Leelah Alcorn's Death Rallies Thousands," *Advocate,* last modified December 31, 2014, http://www .advocate.com/politics/transgender/2014/12/31/leelah-alcorn-rallies-thousands -laws-proposed-protect-trans-youth.
33. Ray Henry, "R.I. Enacts Gay Partner's Funeral-Planning Rights," *Boston Globe,* last modified January 6, 2010, http://www.boston.com/news/local/rhode_island/ articles/2010/01/06/ri_enacts_gay_partners_funeral_planning_right.
34. For instance, see Mark Joseph Stern, "Church Cancels Gay Man's Funeral, Claims Service Would Be 'Blasphemous,'" *Slate,* last modified August 8, 2014, http://www.slate.com/blogs/outward/2014/08/08/church_cancels_gay_married_ man_s_funeral_because_it_s_blasphemous.html; Burwell v. Hobby Lobby. 13– 354 U.S. 2014.
35. Berlant and Warner, "Sex in Public," 548.
36. Morris, "Death on Display," 208.
37. Butler, *Gender* Trouble, xv.
38. Butler, *Bodies That Matter,* x, 22.
39. Berlant and Freeman, "Queer Nationality," 160.
40. Berlant and Warner, "Sex in Public," 548.
41. Linden-Ward, "Strange but Genteel Pleasure Grounds," 295.
42. Linden-Ward, "Strange but Genteel Pleasure Grounds," 305.
43. Morris, "Death on Display," 213.
44. Phelan, *Unmarked,* 5.
45. Warner, introduction, xx.

46. Mulvey, "Visual Pleasure and Narrative Cinema," 11.

47. Davis, "Homoerotic Art Collection from 1750 to 1920," 247–77.

48. Francis, Kellaher, and Neophytou, *The Secret Cemetery*, 172–74; Linden, *Silent City on a Hill*, 175, 275.

49. Zelizer, *Pricing the Priceless Child*, 26.

50. Mytum, *Mortuary Monuments and Burial Grounds of the Historic Period*, 63, 129.

51. Morris, "Death on Display," 213.

52. Edelman, "The Future Is Kid Stuff," 19.

53. Morris, "Death on Display," 213.

54. Woodlawn Cemetery, "History of the Landscape Lawn Plan," 2006, http://www .thewoodlawncemetery.org/landscape.html (site discontinued).

55. Warner, "Introduction: Fear of a Queer Planet," 7.

56. Edelman, "The Future Is Kid Stuff," 18.

57. Deleuze and Guattari, *A Thousand Plateaus*, 11–12.

58. Burke, "A Call for Eternal Equality," C01.

59. McGee, "Text, Context, and the Fragmentation of Contemporary Culture," 279.

60. Library of Congress, "Good Gray Poet," last modified August 16, 2010, http:// www.loc.gov/exhibits/treasures/whitman-goodgraypoet.html.

61. Hippler, *Matlovich*, 146.

62. Hippler, *Matlovich*, 133–34 (italics original).

63. Hippler, *Matlovich*, 134.

64. Hippler, *Matlovich*, 146, 133.

65. Congressional Cemetery's gay and lesbian graves vary in clarity about their occupant's sexuality. Assumptions about those interred there are based on a list updated by Michael Bedwell, various news reports on the cemetery, and the author's own interpretation. See Michael Bedwell, "The Story of His Stone," *Leonard Matlovich.com*, last modified 2009, http://www.leonardmatlovich.com/ storyofhisstone.html.

66. Gittings and Lahusen's memorial bench is now in place; Kameny's interment has been held up on account of conflicts with his estate. See Lou Chibbaro, Jr., "An End to Kameny Burial Stalemate?" *Washington Blade*, July 24, 2013, http://www.washingtonblade.com/2013/07/24/an-end-to-frank-kameny-burial -stalemate.

67. Wary of unintentionally invoking Certeau's notion of "strategy," I explicitly use the term *rhetorical strategy* in this chapter to signal the word's more conventional meaning.

68. Morris, "Death on Display," 205.

69. Blair, "Contemporary U.S. Memorial Sites as Exemplars of Rhetoric's Materiality," 46.

70. Mark S. King, "A Funny (and Very Gay) Tour of Congressional Cemetery," YouTube video, from blog and video blog collection *My Fabulous Disease*, 6:50, http://youtu.be/TdMWcfqlXhA (accessed February 12, 2015).

71. Daniel Holcombe, "Around the Gatehouse," *Heritage Gazette* (Summer 2013): 4, http://congressionalcemetery.org/pdf/Newsletter_2013_Summer.pdf (accessed February 12, 2015); Yusef Najafi, "Honor Role: Gay Veterans Gather to Honor Those Who Served," *MetroWeekly*, last modified November 8, 2006, http://www .metroweekly.com/2006/11/honor-role.

72. Blair, "Contemporary U.S. Memorial Sites as Exemplars of Rhetoric's Materiality," 47.
73. Morris, "Death on Display," 206–7.
74. This imprisonment was not necessarily in the concentration camps. Plant, *The Pink Triangle*, 181.
75. Other icons include a bald eagle, an animated cartoon character, and a Freemason symbol.
76. Bray, *The Friend*, 296.
77. Bray, *The Friend*, 8.
78. Wallace, "Alan Bray, The Friend," 846.
79. Boswell, *Same-Sex Unions in Premodern Europe*, 193, 271, and Wallace, "Alan Bray, The Friend," 846–48.
80. Bray thoughtfully recounts the difficulty in historicizing this practice in *The Friend*, 1–10.
81. Matlovich appears to have had choice over his plots and was well aware that he would spend eternity near Hoover: "When I bought the plot, I left room for two, because I still hope to have a lover someday. . . . As it is now, though, I'll have to be content with the company of J. Edgar Hoover and his boyfriend, Clyde Tolson. They aren't buried together, but J. Edgar is buried just down the row." Hippler, *Matlovich*, 134.
82. Morris, "Pink Herring & the Fourth Persona," 228–44.
83. King, "A Funny (and Very Gay) Tour of Congressional Cemetery."
84. Hank Hyena, "J. Edgar Hoover: Gay Marriage Role Model?" *Salon,* last modified January 5, 2000, http://www.salon.com/2000/01/05/hoover.
85. Blair, "Contemporary U.S. Memorial Sites as Exemplars of Rhetoric's Materiality," 38.
86. McGarry and Wasserman, *Becoming Visible*, xv.
87. Duggan, "'Becoming Visible,'" 189.
88. McGarry and Wasserman, *Becoming Visible*, 36.
89. Jo Hoenninger, "Honoring the Life of Leonard Matlovich," *Outserve/SLDN,* last modified November 26, 2008, http://www.sldn.org/blog/archives/honoring-the-life-of-leonard-matlovich.
90. However, since Matlovich's memorial and its San Francisco reproduction are both materially and geographically distinct, the meanings garnered from the reproduction can be quite different. See Blair, "Contemporary U.S. Memorial Sites as Exemplars of Rhetoric's Materiality," 38–39, 40.
91. The Adams memorial is known by various names but was officially entitled The Mystery of the Hereafter and The Peace of God that Passeth Understanding by the artist. The more popular nineteenth-century title Grief was despised by Saint-Gaudens. The Adams Memorial is the more colloquial contemporary usage.
92. Jan Garden Castro, "Making the Personal Monumental: A Conversation with Patricia Cronin," *Sculpture* 22, no. 1 (January–February 2003), http://www.sculpture.org/documents/scmag03/janfeb03/cronin/cronin.shtml (accessed February 12, 2015).
93. Castro, "Making the Personal Monumental"; Cassandra Langer, "The Second Life of Harriet Hosmer," *Gay & Lesbian Review Worldwide,* last modified January 1, 2010, http://www.glreview.org/article/article-180; "Galleries—The Bronx," *New Yorker,* last modified December 2, 2002, http://archives.newyorker

.com/?i=2002-12-02#folio=CVi; Anthony DePalma, "Sleeping Together: A Daring (and Icy) Duet," *New York Times*, February 23, 2003, http://www.nytimes
.com/2003/02/23/nyregion/urban-studies-sleeping-together-a-daring-and-icy
-duet.html (accessed February 12, 2015); Jerry Saltz, "Forever Yours," *Village
Voice*, last modified October 28, 2003, http://www.villagevoice.com/2003–10–28/
news/forever-yours; Douglas Britt, "Exhibit on 'Queer Identity' Requires Unusual Preparations," *Houston Chronicle*, last modified June 18, 2010, http://
blog.chron.com/peep/2010/06/exhibit-on-queer-identity-requires-unusual
-preparations.
94. Morris, "Death on Display," 214.
95. Blair, "Contemporary U.S. Memorial Sites as Exemplars of Rhetoric's Materiality," 39.
96. The notion of repetition as difference appears in Deleuze's *Difference and Repetition*, 30, but is dispersed through Deleuze and Guattari's work. See *A Thousand Plateaus*, x. The phrase is used most clearly by Jeffrey T. Nealon to describe how minorities can deterritorialize aspects of culture. See *Alterity Politics*, 119.
97. Certeau, *The Practice of Everyday Life*, xix.
98. Morris and Sloop, "'What Lips These Lips Have Kissed,'" 2.
99. Morris and Sloop, "'What Lips These Lips Have Kissed,'" 9.
100. Morris and Sloop, "'What Lips These Lips Have Kissed,'" 3.
101. Francis, Kellaher, and Neophytou, *The Secret Cemetery*, 3.
102. Freud, *Beyond the Pleasure Principle*, 55.
103. Edelman, "The Future Is Kid Stuff," 26–28.
104. Edelman, "The Future Is Kid Stuff," 12.
105. Castro, "Making the Personal Monumental."
106. Halperin, *Saint Foucault*, 62.
107. Castro, "Making the Personal Monumental."
108. Silverman, *Art Nouveau in Fin-de-Siècle France*, 1, 30.
109. Burke, *Language as Symbolic Action*, 45.
110. Saltz, "Forever Yours."
111. DePalma, "Sleeping Together."
112. Saltz, "Forever Yours."
113. Pablo Maurer, "At Congressional Cemetery, a Solemn Tribute to Gay Servicemembers," *DCist*, last modified August 29, 2012, http://dcist.com/2012/08/
congressional_cemetery_piece.php; "New Veterans Memorial Will Honor
LGBT Community," *WTOP*, last modified September 6, 2014, http://wtop.com/
news/2014/09/new-veterans-memorial-will-honor-lgbt-community.
114. Maurer, "At Congressional Cemetery, a Solemn Tribute."
115. American Veterans for Equal Rights, "Special Projects," January 1, 2008, http://
aver.us/category/projects (accessed February 12, 2015).
116. While it is ironic that a monument that was intended to mark same-sex desire
eternally was removed in 2010, the removal was productive on two accounts.
First, reminded of earlier concerns that marble would not weather the elements well, Cronin replaced the original *Memorial to a Marriage* with a more
substantial bronze duplicate that could live up to its eternal aspirations. Second, this replacement allowed the original piece to go on tour, further circulating the rhetorical work of the project. See Tanyanika Samuelsa, "Bronze
Version of *Memorial to Marriage* Sculpture of Artist and Her Wife Returning

to Woodlawn," *New York Daily News*, last modified September 15, 2011, http://www.nydailynews.com/new-york/bronx/bronze-version-memorial-marriage-sculpture-artist-wife-returning-woodlawn-article-1.955324. Third, a replica of the original was recently purchased for permanent display by Scotland's Glasgow Gallery of Modern Art.

117. Deitch Projects, "Patricia Cronin: Memorial to a Marriage," press release, http://www.deitch.com/files/projects/memorial%20to%20a%20marriage.pdf (accessed January 5, 2015).

118. Foucault, *Power/Knowledge*, 93, 125–33.

CHAPTER 6

In (Queer Public) Memory's Wake

1. Notably, this claim is wildly problematic. See Bravmann, *Queer Fictions of the Past*, 68–96.

2. The National Park Service theme study uses the initialism LGBT as opposed to GLBT.

3. "Your Story Is America's Story: Heritage Initiatives," National Park Service, last modified January 1, 2015, http://www.nps.gov/history/heritageinitiatives.

4. April Slayton, "Secretary Jewell Announces New National Park Service Theme Study to Interpret, Commemorate Sites Related to Lesbian, Gay, Bisexual, Transgender History," Press Release, Department of the Interior, May 30, 2014, http://www.doi.gov/news/pressreleases/secretary-jewell-announces-new-national-park-service-theme-study-to-interpret-commemorate-sites-related-to-lesbian-gay-bisexual-transgender-history.cfm.

5. Slayton, "Secretary Jewell Announces New National Park Service Theme Study."

6. "About Us," National Park Service, last modified January 1, 2015, http://www.nps.gov/aboutus/index.htm.

7. Tim Gill, "National Park Service Announces LGBT Theme Study at Stonewall," YouTube video, 2:18, from a press conference recorded by the U.S. Department of the Interior on May 30, 2014, posted by the Department of the Interior, June 6, 2014, http://youtu.be/SQKlMOo5sjM.

8. Thistlethwaite, "Building 'A Home of Our Own,'" 154.

9. Jon Jarvis, "Telling All of America's Story: The National Park Service Announces LGBT Theme Study," White House, May 30, 2014, http://www.whitehouse.gov/blog/2014/05/30/telling-all-america-s-story-national-park-service-announces-lgbt-theme-study.

10. "About Us," National Park Service; *The National Parks: America's Best Idea*.

11. Morris, "My Old Kentucky Homo," 95.

12. On subjugated knowledges, see Foucault, *Power/Knowledge*, 81. On questioning rigor, see Muñoz, *Cruising Utopia*, 65. On homonormativity, see Duggan, *The Twilight of Equality?*, 50.

13. Morris, "My Old Kentucky Homo," 95.

14. Huyssen, *Present Pasts*, 30.

15. Recent projects in the last decade include memorials in Dayton (United States), Manchester (England), Toronto (Canada), Berlin (Germany), Vienna (Austria), Rome (Italy), Dublin (Ireland), Sydney (Australia), Trieste (Italy), Saint-Malo (France), Montevideo (Uruguay), Barcelona (Spain), Sitges (Spain), and Tel Aviv (Israel), among others.

16. For instance, see Dan Savage's "It Gets Better Project," http://www.itgetsbetter.org (accessed February 12, 2015).

17. Cristina Corbin, "Pennsylvania Official under Fire for Civilian Surveillance Project, Rendell Apologizes," *Fox News,* last modified September 17, 2010, http://www.foxnews.com/politics/2010/09/17/pennsylvania-security-chief-civilian-surveillance-project.

18. On queer historiography, see Halperin, *How to Do the History of Homosexuality,* 6. On homonormativity, see Duggan, *The Twilight of Equality?,* 43–66. On gay shame, see Halperin and Valerie, *Gay Shame.*

19. Bravmann, *Queer Fictions of the Past,* x.

20. Nora, "Between Memory and History," 8.

21. Young, *The Texture of Memory,* 28.

22. Mumford, "Death of the Monument," 433–40.

23. Savage, *Monument Wars,* 310–13.

24. Huyssen, *Present Pasts,* 46.

25. Joanne Huist Smith, "Dayton May Honor Famous Lesbian Author with Memorial," *Dayton Daily News,* last modified August 19, 2009, http://www.daytondailynews.com/news/news/local/dayton-may-honor-famous-lesbian-author-with-memori/nM3r5.

26. Marchae Grair, "Historic Ohio LGBT Marker Destroyed," *Advocate,* last modified July 13, 2010, http://www.advocate.com/News/Daily_News/2010/07/13/Ohio_LGBT_Historic_Marker_Destroyed.

BIBLIOGRAPHY

"1883, April, Drs. J. C. Shaw and G. N. Ferris: 'Perverted Sexual Instinct.'" In *Gay/Lesbian Almanac*, edited by Jonathan Ned Katz, 188–91. 1983. Reprint, New York: Harper & Row, 1994.

"1883, March, Dr. William Hammond. Two Types of 'Pederasts.'" In *Gay/Lesbian Almanac*, edited by Jonathan Ned Katz, 185–87. 1983. Reprint, New York: Harper & Row, 1994.

"1883, May 27, *Detroit Post and Tribune:* Sarah Edmonds Seelye, 'The Story of a Remarkable Life.'" In *Gay/Lesbian Almanac*, edited by Jonathan Ned Katz, 191–94. 1983. Reprint, New York: Harper & Row, 1994.

"1895, September, Dr. James Weir, Jr.: 'The Effect of Female Suffrage on Posterity.'" In *Gay/Lesbian Almanac*, edited by Jonathan Ned Katz, 285–87. 1983. Reprint, New York: Harper & Row, 1994.

Adorno, Theodor W. *The Culture Industry: Selected Essays on Mass Culture*. Edited by J. M. Bernstein. 1991. Reprint, New York: Routledge, 2005.

Althusser, Louis. "Ideology and Ideological State Apparatuses." In *Mapping Ideology*, edited by Slavoj Žižek, 100–40. New York: Verso, 1994.

Anderson, Benedict. *Imagined Communities: Reflections on the Origin and Spread of Nationalism*. 1983. Reprint, New York: Verso, 1991.

Anyon, Jean. "Ideology and United States History Textbooks." *Harvard Educational Review* 49, no. 3 (1979): 361–86.

Arendt, Hannah. *The Human Condition*. Chicago: University of Chicago Press, 1958.

Aristotle. *On Rhetoric: A Theory of Civic Discourse*. Edited and translated by George A. Kennedy. New York: Oxford University Press, 1991.

———. *Poetics*. New York: Cosimo, 2008.

Asen, Robert. "Seeking the 'Counter' in Counterpublics." *Communication Theory* 10 (2000): 424–46. doi:10.1111/j.1468–2885.2000.tb00201.x (accessed February 12, 2015).

———, and Daniel C. Brouwer. Introduction to *Counterpublics and the State*, edited by Robert Asen and Daniel C. Brouwer, 1–32. Albany: State University of New York Press, 2001.

Assmann, Jan. "Collective Memory and Cultural Identity." *New German Critique* 65 (Spring–Summer 1995): 125–33. http://www.jstor.org/stable/488538 (accessed February 12, 2015).

Babuscio, Jack. "The Cinema of Camp (*aka* Camp and the Gay Sensibility)." In *Camp: Queer Aesthetics and the Performing Subject*, edited by Fabio Cleto, 117–135. Ann Arbor: University of Michigan Press, 1999.

Bailey, Robert W. *Gay Politics, Urban Politics: Identity and Economics in the Urban Setting*. New York: Columbia University Press, 1999.

Balter-Reitz, Susan J., and Karen A. Stewart. "Looking for Matthew Shepard: A Study in Visual Argument Field." In *Visual Communication: Perception, Rhetoric and Technology*, edited by Diane S. Hope, 111–26. Cresskill, N.J.: Hampton Press, 2006.

Beasley, Vanessa B, ed. Introduction to *Who Belongs in America? Presidents, Rhetoric, and Immigration*. College Station: Texas A&M University Press, 2006.

Beauvoir, Simone de. *The Second Sex*. New York: Vintage, 1989.

Bell, David, and Jon Binnie. *The Sexual Citizen: Queer Politics and Beyond*. Malden, Mass.: Wiley-Blackwell, 2000.

Bellah, Robert N. "Civil Religion in America." *Dædalus: Journal of the American Academy of Arts and Sciences* 96, no. 1 (1967): 1–21. http://www.robertbellah.com/articles_5.htm (accessed February 12, 2015).

Bennett, Jeffrey A. *Banning Queer Blood: Rhetorics of Citizenship, Contagion, and Resistance*. Tuscaloosa: University of Alabama Press, 2009.

Berlant, Lauren, and Elizabeth Freeman. "Queer Nationality." *boundary 2* 19, no. 1 (1992): 149–80. http://www.jstor.org/stable/303454 (accessed February 12, 2015).

————, and Michael Warner. "Sex in Public." *Critical Inquiry* 24, no. 2 (1998): 547–66. http://www.jstor.org/stable/1344178 (accessed February 12, 2015).

Bérubé, Allan. *Coming Out Under Fire: The History of Gay Men and Women in World War Two*. New York: Free Press, 1990.

Bessette, Jean. "An Archive of Anecdotes: Raising Lesbian Consciousness after the Daughters of Bilitis." *Rhetoric Society Quarterly* 43, no. 1 (2013): 22–45. doi:10.1080/02773945.2012.740131 (accessed February 12, 2015).

Biesecker, Barbara. "Remembering World War II: The Rhetoric and Politics of National Commemoration at the Turn of the 21st Century." *Quarterly Journal of Speech* 88, no. 4 (2002): 393–409. doi:10.1080/00335630209384386 (accessed February 12, 2015).

Blair, Carole. "Contemporary U.S. Memorial Sites as Exemplars of Rhetoric's Materiality." In *Rhetorical Bodies*, edited by Jack Selzer and Sharon Crowley, 16–57. Madison: University of Wisconsin Press, 1999.

————, Greg Dickinson, and Brian L. Ott. "Introduction: Rhetoric/Memory/Place." In *Places of Public Memory: The Rhetoric of Museums and Memorials*, edited by Greg Dickinson, Carole Blair, and Brian L. Ott, 1–54. Tuscaloosa: University of Alabama Press, 2010.

————, Marsha S. Jeppeson, and Enrico Pucci, Jr. "Public Memorializing in Postmodernity: The Vietnam Veterans Memorial as Prototype." *Quarterly Journal of Speech* 77, no. 3 (1991): 263–88. doi:10.1080/00335639109383960 (accessed February 12, 2015).

————, and Neil Michel. "Commemorating in the Theme Park Zone: Reading the Astronauts Memorial." In *At the Intersection: Cultural Studies and Rhetorical Studies*, edited by Thomas Rosteck, 29–83. New York: Guilford, 1999.

————. "Reproducing Civil Rights Tactics: The Rhetorical Performances of the Civil Rights Memorial." *RSQ: Rhetoric Society Quarterly* 30, no. 2 (2000): 31–55. http://www.jstor.org/stable/3886159 (accessed February 12, 2015).

Bodnar, John. *Remaking America: Public Memory, Commemoration, and Patriotism in the Twentieth Century.* Princeton: Princeton University Press, 1992.

Booth, Mark. *Camp.* New York: Quartet, 1983.

Boswell, John. *Same-Sex Unions in Premodern Europe.* New York: Vintage, 1994.

Bravmann, Scott. *Queer Fictions of the Past: History, Culture, and Difference.* New York: Cambridge University Press, 1997.

Bray, Alan. *The Friend.* Chicago: University of Chicago Press, 2003.

Bright, Deborah, and Erica Rand. "Queer Plymouth." *GLQ: A Journal of Lesbian and Gay Studies* 12, no. 2 (2006): 259–77. doi:10.1215/10642684–12–2–259 (accessed February 12, 2015).

Brookey, Robert Alan. "A Community Like *Philadelphia.*" *Western Journal of Communication* 60, no. 1 (1996): 40–56. doi:10.1080/10570319609374532 (accessed February 12, 2015).

———. "Speak Up! I Can't Queer You!" In *Queering Public Address: Sexualities in American Historical Discourse,* edited by Charles E. Morris III, 195–219. Columbia: University of South Carolina Press, 2007.

Brouwer, Dan. "The Precarious Visibility Politics of Self-Stigmatization: The Case of HIV/AIDS Tattoos." *Text and Performance Quarterly* 18, no. 2 (1998): 114–36. doi:10.1080/10462939809366216 (accessed February 12, 2015).

Browne, Stephen H. "Encountering Angelina Grimké: Violence, Identity, and the Creation of Radical Community." *Quarterly Journal of Speech* 82, no. 1 (1996): 55–73. doi:10.1080/00335639609384140 (accessed February 12, 2015).

Bruner, M. Lane. *Strategies of Remembrance: The Rhetorical Dimensions of National Identity Construction.* Columbia: University of South Carolina Press, 2002.

Buckland, Fiona. *Impossible Dance: Club Culture and Queer World-Making.* Middletown, Conn.: Wesleyan University Press, 2002.

Burke, Kenneth. *A Grammar of Motives.* 1945. Reprint, Berkeley: University of California Press, 1969.

———. *A Rhetoric of Motives.* 1950. Reprint, Berkeley: University of California Press, 1969.

———. *Language as Symbolic Action: Essays on Life, Literature, and Method.* Berkeley: University of California Press, 1966.

———. *The Philosophy of Literary Form.* Berkeley: University of California Press, 1973.

Burwell v. Hobby Lobby. 13–354 U.S. 2014.

Butler, Judith. *Bodies That Matter: On the Discursive Limits of "Sex."* New York: Routledge, 1993.

———. *Gender Trouble: Feminism and the Subversion of Identity.* 1990. Reprint, New York: Routledge, 1999.

Canaday, Margot. *The Straight State: Sexuality and Citizenship in Twentieth-Century America.* Princeton: Princeton University Press, 2009.

Casey, Edward S. "Public Memory in Place and Time." In *Framing Public Memory,* edited by Kendall R. Phillips, 17–44. Tuscaloosa: University of Alabama Press, 2004.

Castiglia, Christopher. "Sex Panics, Sex Publics, Sex Memories." *boundary 2* 27, no. 2 (2000): 149–75. doi:10.1215/01903659–27–2–149 (accessed February 12, 2015).

———, and Christopher Reed. *If Memory Serves: Gay Men, AIDS, and the Promise of the Queer Past.* Minneapolis: University of Minnesota Press, 2012.

Ceccarelli, Leah. "Polysemy: Multiple Meanings in Rhetorical Criticism." *Quarterly Journal of Speech* 84, no. 4 (1998): 395–415. doi:10.1080/00335639809384229 (accessed February 12, 2015).

Certeau, Michel de. *The Practice of Everyday Life.* Translated by Steven Rendall. Berkeley: University of California Press, 1984.

Charland, Maurice. "Constitutive Rhetoric: The Case of the *Peuple Québécois.*" *Quarterly Journal of Speech* 73, no. 2 (1987): 133–50.

Chauncey, George. *Gay New York: Gender, Urban Culture, and the Making of the Gay Male World, 1890–1940.* New York: Basic Books, 1994.

Chesebro, James W., ed. *Gayspeak: Gay Male and Lesbian Communication.* New York: Pilgrim Press, 1981.

Chisholm, Dianne. "The City of Collective Memory." *GLQ: A Journal of Lesbian and Gay Studies* 7, no. 2 (2001): 195–243. doi:10.1215/10642684-7-2-195 (accessed February 12, 2015).

Christiansen, Adrienne E., and Jeremy J. Hanson. "Comedy as Cure for Tragedy: ACT UP and the Rhetoric of AIDS." *Quarterly Journal of Speech* 82, no. 2 (1996): 157–70. doi:10.1080/00335639609384148 (accessed February 12, 2015).

Clark, Gregory. *Rhetorical Landscapes in America: Variations on a Theme from Kenneth Burke.* Columbia: University of South Carolina Press, 2004.

Clawson, Rosalee A., and Elizabeth R. Kegler. "The 'Race Coding' of Poverty in American Government College Textbooks." *Howard Journal of Communications* 11, no. 3 (2000): 179–88. doi:10.1080/10646170050086312 (accessed February 12, 2015).

Cleto, Fabio. Introduction to *Camp: Queer Aesthetics and the Performing Subject,* edited by Fabio Cleto, 1–42. Ann Arbor: University of Michigan Press, 1999.

Cohen, Cathy J. "Contested Membership: Black Gay Identities and the Politics of AIDS." In *Queer Studies: An Interdisciplinary Reader,* edited by Robert J. Corber and Stephen Valocchi, 46–60. Malden, Mass.: Blackwell, 2003.

Coman, Paul. "Reading about the Enemy: School Textbook Representation of Germany's Role in the War with Britain during the Period from April 1940 to May 1941." *British Journal of Sociology of Education* 17, no. 3 (1996): 327–40. doi:10.1080/0142569960170306 (accessed February 12, 2015).

Comstock, Gary David. "Dismantling the Homosexual Panic Defense." *Law & Sexuality: A Review of Lesbian, Gay, Bisexual and Transgender Legal Issues* 2 (1992): 81–102.

———. *Violence against Lesbians and Gay Men.* New York: Columbia University Press, 1991.

Crismore, Avon. "Rhetorical Form, Selection, and the Use of Textbooks." In *Language, Authority and Criticism,* edited by Suzanne de Castell, Allan Luke, and Carmen Luke, 133–52. Philadelphia: Falmer Press, 1989.

Cvetkovich, Ann. *An Archive of Feelings: Trauma, Sexuality, and Lesbian Public Cultures.* Durham: Duke University Press, 2003.

———. "Sexual Trauma/Queer Memory: Incest, Lesbianism, and Therapeutic Culture." *GLQ: A Journal of Lesbian and Gay Studies* 2, no. 4 (1995), 351–77. doi:10.1215/10642684-2-4-351 (accessed February 12, 2015).

Darsey, James. "From 'Gay Is Good' to the Scourge of AIDS: The Evolution of Gay Liberation Rhetoric, 1977–1990." *Communication Studies* 42, no. 1 (1991): 43–66. doi:10.1080/10510979109368320 (accessed February 12, 2015).

Davis, Whitney. "Homoerotic Art Collection from 1750 to 1920." *Art History* 24, no. 2 (2001): 247–77. doi:10.1111/1467-8365.00263 (accessed February 12, 2015).

Deleuze, Gilles. *Difference and Repetition.* New York: Continuum, 2004.

————, and Félix Guattari. *A Thousand Plateaus.* New York: Continuum, 2004.

D'Emilio, John. *Sexual Politics, Sexual Communities: The Making of a Homosexual Minority in the United States, 1940–1970.* Chicago: University of Chicago Press, 1983.

————. *The World Turned: Essays on Gay History, Politics, and Culture.* Durham: Duke University Press, 2002.

Derrida, Jacques. "Structure, Sign, and Play in the Discourse of the Human Sciences." In *Writing and Difference,* translated by Alan Bass, 351–70. Chicago: University of Chicago Press, 1978.

Dickinson, Greg, Carole Blair, and Brian L. Ott, eds. *Places of Public Memory: The Rhetoric of Museums and Memorials.* Tuscaloosa: University of Alabama Press, 2010.

Dow, Bonnie J. "*Ellen,* Television, and the Politics of Gay and Lesbian Visibility." *Critical Studies in Media Communication* 18, no. 2 (2001): 123–40. doi:10.1080/07393180128077 (accessed February 12, 2015).

Duberman, Martin Bauml, Martha Vicinus, and George Chauncey, Jr. Introduction to *Hidden from History: Reclaiming the Gay and Lesbian Past,* edited by Martin Bauml Duberman, Martha Vicinus, and George Chauncey, Jr., 1–13. New York: NAL Books, 1989.

Duggan, Lisa. "'Becoming Visible: The Legacy of Stonewall,' New York Public Library, June 18–September 24, 1994." *Radical History Review* 62, no. 2 (1995): 189–94. doi:10.1215/01636545–1995–62–189 (accessed February 12, 2015).

————. *The Twilight of Equality?: Neoliberalism, Cultural Politics, and the Attack on Democracy.* Boston: Beacon, 2003.

Dunn, Thomas R. "Remembering 'A Great Fag': Visualizing Public Memory and the Construction of Queer Space." *Quarterly Journal of Speech* 97, no. 4 (2011): 435–60. doi:10.1080/00335630.2011.585168 (accessed February 12, 2015).

————. "Remembering Matthew Shepard: Violence, Identity, and Queer Counterpublic Memories." *Rhetoric & Public Affairs* 13, no. 4 (2010): 611–652. doi:10.1353/rap.2010.0212 (accessed February 12, 2015).

————. "The Quare in the Square: Queer Memory, Sensibilities, and Oscar Wilde." *Quarterly Journal of Speech* 100, no. 2 (2014): 213–240. doi:10.1080/00335630.2014.959987 (accessed February 12, 2015).

Eagleton, Terry. *Criticism and Ideology: A Study in Marxist Literary Theory.* 1976. Reprint, New York: Verso, 2006.

Edelman, Lee. "The Future Is Kid Stuff: Queer Theory, Disidentification, and the Death Drive." *Narrative* 6, no. 1 (1998): 18–30. http://www.jstor.org/stable/20107133 (accessed February 12, 2015).

Ellman, Richard. *Oscar Wilde.* New York: Vintage, 1988.

Enoch, Jessica, and Jack Jordynn. "Remembering Sappho: New Perspectives on Teaching (and Writing) Women's Rhetorical History." *College English* 73, no. 5 (2011): 518–37.

Epstein, Steven. "Gay Politics, Ethnic Identity: The Limits of Social Constructionism." *Socialist Review* 17, nos. 3–4 (1987): 9–54.

Erni, John Nguyet. "Flaunting Identity: Spatial Figurations and the Display of Sexuality." In *Rhetorics of Display,* edited by Lawrence J. Prelli, 311–26. Columbia: University of South Carolina Press, 2006.

Escoffier, Jeffrey, Regina Kunzel, and Molly McGarry. "The Queer Issue: New

Visions of America's Lesbian and Gay Past." *Radical History Review* 62 (Spring 1995): 1–6. doi:10.1215/01636545–1995–62–1 (accessed February 12, 2015).

Faderman, Lillian, and Stuart Timmons. *Gay L.A.: A History of Sexual Outlaws, Power Politics, and Lipstick Lesbians.* New York: Basic Books, 2006.

Finch, Mark. "Sex and Address in *Dynasty.*" *Screen* 27, no. 6 (1986): 24–43. doi:10 .1093/screen/27.6.24 (accessed February 12, 2015).

Finnegan, Cara A. "Recognizing Lincoln: Image Vernaculars in Nineteenth-Century Visual Culture." In *Visual Rhetoric: A Reader in Communication and American Culture,* edited by Lester C. Olson, Cara A. Finnegan, and Diane S. Hope, 61–78. Los Angeles: Sage, 2008.

Fisher, Walter R. *Human Communication as Narration: Toward a Philosophy of Reason, Value, and Action.* Columbia: University of South Carolina Press, 1989.

——. "Narration as a Human Communication Paradigm: The Case of Public Moral Argument." *Communication Monographs* 51, no. 1 (1984): 1–22. doi:10.1080 /03637758409390180 (accessed February 12, 2015).

Flinn, Caryl. "The Deaths of Camp." In *Camp: Queer Aesthetics and the Performing Subject,* edited by Fabio Cleto, 433–57. Ann Arbor: University of Michigan Press, 1999.

Foucault, Michel. "Film and Popular Memory." *Radical Philosophy* 11 (Summer 1975): 24–29.

——. *History of Sexuality: An Introduction, Vol. 1.* 1978. Reprint, New York: Vintage, 1990.

——. *Power/Knowledge: Selected Interviews and Other Writings, 1972–1977.* Edited by Colin Gordon, translated by Colin Gordon et al. New York: Pantheon, 1980.

——. "Sexual Choice, Sexual Act." In *Politics, Philosophy, Culture: Interviews and Other Writings, 1977–1984,* edited by Lawrence D. Kritzman, 286–303. New York: Routledge, 1988.

Francis, Doris, Leonie Kellaher, and Georgina Neophytou. *The Secret Cemetery.* New York: Berg, 2005.

Fraser, Hilary. "A Visual Field: Michael Field and the Gaze." *Victorian Literature and Culture* 34, no. 2 (2006): 553–71. http://www.jstor.org/stable/25056319 (accessed February 12, 2015).

Fraser, Nancy. "Rethinking the Public Sphere: A Contribution to the Critique of Actually Existing Democracy." In *Habermas and the Public Sphere,* edited by Craig Calhoun, 109–42. Cambridge: Massachusetts Institute of Technology, 1992.

Freccero, Carla. "Queer Times." *South Atlantic Quarterly* 106, no. 3 (2007): 485–94. doi:10.1215/00382876–2007–007 (accessed February 12, 2015).

Freeman, Elizabeth, ed. "Queer Temporalities." Special Issue, *GLQ: A Journal of Lesbian and Gay Studies* 13, nos. 2–3 (2007). doi:10.1215/10642684–2006–029 (accessed February 12, 2015).

Freud, Sigmund. *Beyond the Pleasure Principle.* Translated by C.J.M. Hubback. London: International Psycho-Analytical Press, 1922. Google E-book. https:// books.google.com/books?id=QEpqAAAAMAAJ (accessed February 12, 2015).

Gay Sex in the 70s. DVD. Directed by Joseph F. Lovett. New Almaden, Calif.: Wolfe, 2005.

Geertz, Clifford. *The Interpretation of Cultures: Selected Essays.* New York: Basic Books, 1973.

Giddens, Anthony. "Political Theory and the Problem of Violence." In *The Politics of Human Rights*, edited by the Belgrade Circle, 245–57. New York: Verso: 1999.

Giedeon, Siegfried, Fernand Léger, and José Luis Sert. "Nine Points on Monumentality." In *Architecture, You and Me: The Diary of a Development*, edited by Siegfried Giedeon, Fernand Léger, and José Luis Sert, 48–51. Cambridge: Harvard University Press, 1958.

Gilbert, Sky. *Ejaculations from the Charm Factory: A Memoir*. Toronto: ECW Press, 2000.

Gillis, John R., ed. Introduction to *Commemorations: The Politics of National Identity*. Princeton: Princeton University Press, 1994.

Gross, Larry. "What Is Wrong with This Picture? Lesbian Women and Gay Men on Television." In *Queer Words, Queer Images*, edited by R. Jeffrey Ringer, 143–56. New York: New York University Press, 1994.

Grube, John. "No More Shit: The Struggle for Democratic Gay Space in Toronto." In *Queers in Space: Communities, Public Places, and Sites of Resistance*, edited by Gordon Brent Ingram, Anne-Marie Bouthillette, and Yolanda Retter, 127–45. Seattle: Bay Press, 1997.

Gullicks, Kristen A., Judy C. Pearson, Jeffrey T. Child, and Colleen R. Schwab. "Diversity and Power in Public Speaking Textbooks." *Communication Quarterly* 53, no. 2 (2005): 247–58. doi:10.1080/01463370500089870 (accessed February 12, 2015).

Habermas, Jürgen. *The Structural Transformation of the Public Sphere*. Translated by Thomas Burger with the assistance of Frederick Lawrence. Cambridge: MIT Press, 1991.

Halberstam, Judith. *In a Queer Time and Place: Transgender Bodies, Subcultural Lives*. New York: New York University Press, 2005.

———. *The Queer Art of Failure*. Durham: Duke University Press, 2011.

Halbwachs, Maurice. *On Collective Memory*. Edited and translated by Lewis A. Coser. Chicago: University of Chicago Press, 1992.

Halperin, David M. *How to Do the History of Homosexuality*. Chicago: University of Chicago Press, 2002.

———. *Saint Foucault: Towards a Gay Hagiography*. New York: Oxford University Press, 1995.

———, and Valerie Traub, eds. *Gay Shame*. Chicago: University of Chicago Press, 2009.

Hardt, Michael, and Antonio Negri. *Empire*. Cambridge: Harvard University Press, 2000.

Harold, Christine, and Kevin Michael DeLuca. "Behold the Corpse: Violent Images and the Case of Emmett Till." *Rhetoric & Public Affairs* 8, no. 2 (2005): 263–86.

Harpham, Geoffrey Galt. *On the Grotesque: Strategies of Contradiction in Art and Literature*. Princeton: Princeton University Press, 1982.

Hass, Kristin Ann. *Carried to the Wall: American Memory and the Vietnam Veterans Memorial*. Berkeley: University of California Press, 1998.

Hawkins, Peter S. "Naming Names: The Art of Memory and the NAMES Project AIDS Quilt." *Critical Inquiry* 19, no. 4 (1993): 752–79. http://www.jstor.org/stable/1343905 (accessed February 12, 2015).

Hayes, Joseph J. "Gayspeak." *Quarterly Journal of Speech* 62, no. 3 (1976): 256–66. doi:10.1080/00335637609383340 (accessed February 12, 2015).

Hebdige, Dick. *Subculture: The Meaning of Style*. 1979. Reprint, New York: Routledge, 2006.

Hess, Aaron. "In Digital Remembrance: Vernacular Memory and the Rhetorical Construction of Web Memorials." *Media, Culture, & Society* 29, no. 5 (2007): 812–30.

Higgs, David, ed. *Queer Sites: Gay Urban Histories since 1600.* New York: Routledge, 1999.

Hijiya, James A. "American Gravestones and Attitudes toward Death: A Brief History." *Proceeding of the American Philosophical Society* 127, no. 5 (1983): 339–63. http://www.jstor.org/stable/986503 (accessed February 12, 2015).

Hippler, Mike. *Matlovich: The Good Soldier.* Boston: Alyson Publications, 1989.

Holland, Merlin. *The Real Trial of Oscar Wilde.* New York: Fourth Estate, 2003.

Howard, John. *Men Like That: A Southern Queer History.* Chicago: University of Chicago Press, 1999.

Huyssen, Andreas. *Present Pasts: Urban Palimpsests and the Politics of Memory.* Stanford: Stanford University Press, 2003.

Hyde, H. Montgomery. *The Three Trials of Oscar Wilde.* New York: University Books, 1956.

Ingram, Gordon Brent, Anne-Marie Bouthillette, and Yolanda Retter, eds. *Queers in Space: Communities, Public Places, Sites of Resistance.* Seattle: Bay Press, 1997.

Isherwood, Christopher. "The World in the Evening." In *Camp: Queer Aesthetics and the Performing Subject,* edited by Fabio Cleto, 49–52. Ann Arbor: University of Michigan Press, 1999.

Jamieson, Kathleen Hall. *Eloquence in an Electronic Age: The Transformation of Political Speechmaking.* New York: Oxford University Press, 1988.

———, and Karlyn Kohrs Campbell. "Rhetorical Hybrids: Fusions of Generic Elements." *Quarterly Journal of Speech* 68, no. 2 (1982): 146–57. doi:10.1080/00335638 209383600 (accessed February 12, 2015).

Jensen, Richard J., Thomas R. Burkholder, and John C. Hammerback. "Martyrs for a Just Cause: The Eulogies of Cesar Chavez." *Western Journal of Communication* 67, no. 4 (2003): 335–56. doi:10.1080/10570310309374778 (accessed February 12, 2015).

Jensen, Robin E. *Dirty Words: The Rhetoric of Public Sex Education, 1870–1924.* Champaign: University of Illinois Press, 2010.

Jimenez, Stephen. *The Book of Matt: Hidden Truths about the Murder of Matthew Shepard.* Hanover, N.H.: Steerforth Press, 2013.

Johnson, David K. *The Lavender Scare.* Chicago: University of Chicago Press, 2004.

Johnson, E. Patrick. *Sweet Tea: Black Gay Men of the South.* Chapel Hill: University of North Carolina Press, 2008.

Juang, Richard M. "Transgendering the Politics of Recognition." In *Transgender Rights,* edited by Paisley Currah, Richard M. Juang, and Shannon Price Minter, 242–61. Minneapolis: University of Minnesota Press, 2006.

Kaiser, Charles. *The Gay Metropolis, 1940–1996.* New York: Houghton Mifflin, 1997.

Kammen, Michael. *The Mystic Chords of Memory: The Transformation of Tradition in American Culture.* New York: Vintage, 1993.

Katz, Jonathan Ned. *Gay American History: Lesbians and Gay Men in the U.S.A.* New York: Meridian, 1976.

———. *Gay/Lesbian Almanac: A New Documentary.* New York: Harper & Row, 1983.

———. *Love Stories: Sex Between Men Before Homosexuality.* Chicago: University of Chicago Press, 2001.

Kaufman, Moïsès, ed. *Gross Indecency: The Three Trials of Oscar Wilde*. New York: Dramatists Play Service, 1999.

Keesee, Timothy, and Mark Sidwell. *United States History for Christian Schools*. Greenville, S.C.: Bob Jones University Press, 2001.

Kennedy, Elizabeth Lapovsky, and Madeline D. Davis. *Boots of Leather, Slippers of Gold: The History of a Lesbian Community*. New York: Routledge, 1993.

Kinsey, Alfred C., Wardell B. Pomeroy, and Clyde E. Martin. *Sexual Behavior in the Human Male*. Philadelphia: W. B. Saunders, 1948.

Koop, C. Everett. *Koop: The Memoirs of America's Family Doctor*. New York: Random House, 1991.

Lawrence, Frederick M. *Punishing Hate: Bias Crimes under American Law*. Cambridge: Harvard University Press, 1999.

Lefebvre, Henri. *The Production of Space*. Translated by Donald Nicholson-Smith. Malden, Mass.: Blackwell, 2000.

Lévi-Strauss, Claude. *The Savage Mind*. Chicago: University of Chicago Press, 1966.

Lieven, Anatol. *America Right or Wrong: An Anatomy of American Nationalism*. New York: Oxford University Press, 2004.

Linden, Blanche M. G. *Silent City on a Hill: Picturesque Landscapes of Memory and Boston's Mount Auburn Cemetery*. Amherst: University of Massachusetts Press, 2007.

Linden-Ward, Blanche. "Strange but Genteel Pleasure Grounds: Tourist and Leisure Uses of Nineteenth Century Cemeteries." In *Cemeteries and Gravemarkers: Voices of American Culture*, edited by Richard E. Meyer, 293–328. 1989. Reprint, Logan: Utah State University Press, 1992.

Lorde, Audre. "Age, Race, Class, and Sex: Women Defining Difference." In *Sister Outsider: Essays and Speeches,* by Audre Lorde, 114–23. Freedom, Calif.: Crossing Press, 1984.

Love, Heather. *Feeling Backward: Loss and the Politics of Queer History*. Cambridge: Harvard University Press, 2009.

Lynch, John. "Memory and Matthew Shepard: Opposing Expressions of Public Memory in Television Movies." *Journal of Communication Inquiry* 31, no. 3 (2007): 222–38. doi:10.1177/0196859907300948 (accessed February 12, 2015).

Macgillivray, Ian K., and Todd Jennings. "A Content Analysis Exploring Lesbian, Gay, Bisexual, and Transgender Topics in Foundations of Education Textbooks." *Journal of Teacher Education* 59, no. 2 (2008): 170–88, doi:10.1177/0022487107313160 (accessed February 12, 2015).

Mann, Thomas. *Reflections of a Nonpolitical Man*. Translated by Walter D. Morris. New York: Frederic Ungar, 1987.

Massumi, Brian. *Parables for the Virtual: Movement, Affect, Sensation*. Durham: Duke University Press, 2002.

McGarry, Molly, and Fred Wasserman. *Becoming Visible: An Illustrated History of Lesbian and Gay Life in Twentieth-Century America*. New York: Penguin Studio, 1998.

McGee, Michael Calvin. "The Ideograph: A Link between Rhetoric and Ideology." *Quarterly Journal of Speech* 66, no. 1 (1980): 1–16. doi:10.1080/00335638009383499 (accessed September 19, 2015).

———. "Text, Context, and the Fragmentation of Contemporary Culture." *Western Journal of Speech Communication* 54, no. 3 (1990): 274–89. doi:10.1080/10570319009374343 (accessed February 12, 2015).

Meyers, Gretchen E. "The Experience of Monumentality in Etruscan and Early Roman Architecture." In *Monumentality in Etruscan and Early Roman Architecture: Ideology and Innovation,* edited by Michael L. Thomas and Gretchen E. Meyers, 1–20. Austin: University of Texas Press, 2012.

Meyer, Richard E., ed. *Cemeteries & Gravemarkers: Voices of American Culture.* 1989. Reprint, Logan: Utah State University Press, 1992.

Minton, Henry L. *Departing from Deviance: A History of Homosexual Rights and Emancipatory Science in America.* Chicago: University of Chicago Press, 2002.

Moran, Leslie J. "Transcripts and Truth: Writing the Trials of Oscar Wilde." In *Oscar Wilde and Modern Culture: The Making of a Legend,* edited by Joseph Bristow, 234–59. Athens: Ohio University Press, 2008.

Moore, Patrick. *Beyond Shame: Reclaiming the Abandoned History of Radical Gay Sexuality.* Boston: Beacon, 2004.

Morris, Charles E., III. "Introduction: Portrait of a Queer Rhetorical/Historical Critic." In *Queering Public Address: Sexualities in American Historical Discourse,* edited by Charles E. Morris III, 1–19. Columbia: University of South Carolina Press, 2007.

———. "My Old Kentucky Homo: Abraham Lincoln, Larry Kramer, and the Politics of Queer Memory." In *Queering Public Address: Sexualities in American Historical Discourse,* edited by Charles E. Morris III, 93–120. Columbia: University of South Carolina Press, 2007.

———. "Pink Herring & the Fourth Persona: J. Edgar Hoover's Sex Crime Panic." *Quarterly Journal of Speech* 88, no. 2 (2002): 228–44. doi:10.1080/00335630209384372 (accessed February 12, 2015).

———, ed. *Queering Public Address: Sexualities in American Historical Discourse.* Columbia: University of South Carolina Press, 2007.

———, ed. *Remembering the AIDS Quilt.* East Lansing: Michigan State University Press, 2011.

———. "Sunder the Children: Abraham Lincoln's Queer Rhetorical Pedagogy." *Quarterly Journal of Speech* 99, no. 4 (2013) 395–422. doi:10.1080/00335630.2013.836281 (accessed February 12, 2015).

———, and John M. Sloop. "'What Lips These Lips Have Kissed': Refiguring the Politics of Queer Public Kissing." *Communication and Critical/Cultural Studies* 3, no. 1 (2006):1–26. doi:10.1080/14791420500505585.

Morris, Richard. "Death on Display." In *Rhetorics of Display,* edited by Lawrence J. Prelli. 204–26. Columbia: University of South Carolina Press, 2006.

Mosse, George L. *Nationalism and Sexuality: Respectability and Abnormal Sexuality in Modern Europe.* New York: Howard Fertig, 1985.

Mulvey, Laura. "Visual Pleasure and Narrative Cinema." *Screen* 16, no. 3 (1975): 6–18. doi:10.1093/screen/16.3.6 (accessed February 12, 2015).

Mumford, Lewis. "Death of the Monument." In *The Culture of Cities,* by Lewis Mumford, 433–40. New York: Harcourt, 1938.

Muñoz, José Esteban. *Cruising Utopia: The Then and There of Queer Futurity.* New York: New York University Press, 2009.

———. "Ephemera as Evidence: Introductory Notes to Queer Acts." *Women & Performance: A Journal of Feminist Theory* 8, no. 2 (1996) 5–16. doi:10.1080/07407709608571228 (accessed February 12, 2015).

Mytum, Harold. *Mortuary Monuments and Burial Grounds of the Historic Period.* New York: Kluwer Academic, 2004.

Nash, Gary B., Charlotte Antoinette Crabtree, and Ross E. Dunn. *History on Trial: Culture Wars and the Teaching of the Past*. New York: Vintage, 2000.

The National Parks: America's Best Idea. Netflix. Directed by Ken Burns. Brighton, Mass.: PBS Distribution: 2009.

Nealon, Christopher. *Foundlings: Lesbian and Gay Historical Emotion Before Stonewall*. Durham: Duke University Press, 2001.

Nealon, Jeffrey T. *Alterity Politics: Ethics and Performative Subjectivity*. Durham: Duke University Press, 1998.

New State Ice Co. v. Liebman, 285 U.S. 262 (1932).

Newton, Esther. *Cherry Grove, Fire Island*. Boston: Beacon, 1993.

———. "The Mythic Mannish Lesbian: Radclyffe Hall and the New Woman." *Signs: The Journal of Women in Culture and Society* 9, no. 4 (1984): 557–75.

———. "Role Models." In *Camp: Queer Aesthetics and the Performing Subject*, edited by Fabio Cleto, 96–109. Ann Arbor: University of Michigan Press, 1999.

———. "Sick to Death of Ambiguities. . . ." *Women's Review of Books* 3, no. 4 (1986): 10–11. http://www.jstor.org/stable/4019778 (accessed February 12, 2015).

Nora, Pierre. "Between Memory and History: *Les Lieux de Mémoire*." *Representations* 26 (1989): 7–24. http://www.jstor.org/stable/2928520 (accessed February 12, 2015).

Norton, Rictor. *Mother Clap's Molly House: The Gay Subculture in England, 1700–1830*. London: GMP Publisher, 1992.

———. *The Myth of the Modern Homosexual: Queer History and the Search for Cultural Unity*. London: Cassell, 1998.

Novkov, Julie, and Charles Gossett. "Survey of Textbooks for Teaching Introduction to U.S. Politics: (How) Do They See Us?" *PS: Political Science and Politics* 40, no. 2 (2007): 393–98. doi:10.1017/S1049096507070667 (accessed February 12, 2015).

Olick, Jeffrey K., Vered Vinitzky-Seroussi, and Daniel Levy. Introduction to *The Collective Memory Reader*, edited by Jeffrey K. Olick, Vered Vinitzky-Seroussi, and Daniel Levy, 3–62. New York: Oxford University Press, 2011.

Olson, David R. "On the Language and Authority of Textbooks." In *Language, Authority, and Criticism: Reading on the School Textbook*, edited by Suzanne de Castell, Allan Luke, and Carmen Luke, 233–44. Philadelphia: Falmer Press, 1989.

Olson, Lester C. "Traumatic Styles in Public Address: Audre Lorde's Discourse as Exemplar." In *Queering Public Address: Sexualities in American Historical Discourse*, by Charles E. Morris III, 249–82. Columbia: University of South Carolina Press, 2007.

———, Cara A. Finnegan, and Diane S. Hope. "Visual Rhetoric in Communication: Continuing Questions and Contemporary Issues." In *Visual Rhetoric: A Reader in Communication and American Culture*, edited by Lester C. Olson, Cara A. Finnegan, and Diane S. Hope, 1–19. Los Angeles: Sage, 2008.

Ono, Kent A., and John M. Sloop. "The Critique of Vernacular Discourse." *Communication Monographs* 62, no. 1 (1995): 19–46. doi:10.1080/03637759509376346 (accessed February 12, 2015).

Osborne, James F., ed. *Approaching Monumentality in Archaeology*. Albany: State University of New York Press, 2014.

Ott, Brian L., and Eric Aoki. "The Politics of Negotiating Public Tragedy: Media Framing of the Matthew Shepard Murder." *Rhetoric & Public Affairs* 5, no. 3 (2002): 483–505. doi:10.1353/rap.2002.0060 (accessed February 12, 2015).

Padgug, Robert A. "Sexual Matters: On Conceptualizing Sexuality in History." *Radical History Review* 20 (Spring/Summer 1979): 3–23.

Paul, Jay P., et al., eds. "Suicide Attempts among Gay and Bisexual Men: Lifetime Prevalence and Antecedents." In *American Journal of Public Health* 92, no. 8 (2002): 1338–45.

Perez, Tina L., and George N. Dionisopoulos. "Presidential Silence, C. Everett Koop, and the *Surgeon General's Report on AIDS.*" *Communication Studies* 46, no. 1–2 (1995): 18–33. doi:10.1080/10510979509368436 (accessed February 12, 2015).

Petersen, Jennifer. *Murder, the Media, and the Politics of Public Feelings: Remembering Matthew Shepard and James Byrd Jr.* Bloomington: Indiana University Press, 2011.

Pezzullo, Phaedra C. "Resisting 'National Breast Cancer Awareness Month': The Rhetoric of Counterpublics and Their Cultural Performances." *Quarterly Journal of Speech* 89, no. 4 (2003): 345–65. doi:10.1080/0033563032000160981 (accessed February 12, 2015).

Phelan, Peggy. *Unmarked: The Politics of Performance.* New York: Routledge, 1996.

Phillips, Kendall R., ed. *Framing Public Memory.* Tuscaloosa: University of Alabama Press, 2004.

———. Introduction to *Framing Public Memory*, edited by Kendall Phillips, 1–14. Tuscaloosa: University of Alabama Press, 2004.

———, and G. Mitchell Reyes, eds. *Global Memoryscapes: Contesting Remembrance in a Transnational Age.* Tuscaloosa: University of Alabama Press, 2011.

Plant, Richard. *The Pink Triangle: The Nazi War against Homosexuals.* New York: Henry Holt, 1986.

Pollock, Della. "Introduction: Making History Go." In *Exceptional Spaces: Essays in Performance and History*, edited by Della Pollock, 1–48. Chapel Hill: University of North Carolina Press, 1998.

Prividera, Laura C., and John W. Howard III. "Masculinity, Whiteness, and the Warrior Hero: Perpetuating the Strategic Rhetoric of U.S. Nationalism and the Marginalization of Women." *Women and Language* 29, no. 2 (2006): 29–37.

Quinn, Therese, and Erica R. Meiners, *Flaunt It! Queers Organizing for Public Education and Justice.* New York: Peter Lang, 2009.

Ramaswamy, Sumathi. "Maps and Mother Goddesses in Modern India." *Imago Mundi* 53, no. 1 (2001): 97–114. doi:10.1080/0308569010859294o (accessed February 12, 2015).

Rehding, Alexander. *Music and Monumentality: Commemoration and Wonderment in Nineteenth-Century Germany.* New York: Oxford University Press, 2009.

Reynolds, John C. "Textbooks: Guardians of Nationalism." *Education* 102, no. 1 (1981): 37–42.

Ringer, R. Jeffery, ed. *Queer Words, Queer Images: Communication and the Construction of Homosexuality.* New York: New York University Press, 1994.

Robinson, William J. "My Views on Homosexuality." In *Gay/Lesbian Almanac*, edited by Jonathan Ned Katz, 357–58. 1983. Reprint, New York: Carroll & Graff, 1994.

———. "Nature's Sex Stepchildren." In *Gay/Lesbian Almanac*, edited by Jonathan Ned Katz, 424–25. 1983. Reprint, New York: Carroll & Graff, 1994.

Román, David. *Acts of Intervention: Performance, Gay Culture, and AIDS.* Bloomington: Indiana University Press, 1998.

————. "'It's My Party and I'll Die if I Want To!': Gay Men, AIDS, and the Circulation of Camp in U.S. Theatre." *Theatre Journal* 44, no. 3 (1992): 305–27. http://www.jstor.org/stable/3208551 (accessed February 12, 2015).

Rosario, Vernon A. *Homosexuality and Science: A Guide to the Debates.* Santa Barbara: ABC-CLIO, 2002.

Rosenfeld, Gavriel D. "A Looming Crash or a Soft Landing? Forecasting the Future of the Memory 'Industry.'" *Journal of Modern History* 81, no.1 (2009): 122–58. doi:http://www.jstor.org/stable/10.1086/593157 (accessed February 12, 2015).

Ross, Andrew. "Uses of Camp." In *Camp: Queer Aesthetics and the Performing Subject,* edited by Fabio Cleto, 308–29. Ann Arbor: University of Michigan Press, 1999.

Savage, Kirk. *Monument Wars: Washington, D.C., the National Mall, and the Transformation of the Memorial Landscape.* Berkeley: University of California Press, 2009.

————. "The Politics of Memory: Black Emancipation and the Civil War Monument." In *Commemorations: The Politics of National Identity,* edited by John R. Gillis, 127–49. Princeton: Princeton University Press, 1994.

————. *Standing Soldiers, Kneeling Slaves: Race, War, and Monument in Nineteenth-Century America.* Princeton: Princeton University Press, 1997.

Schwartz, Barry. *Abraham Lincoln and the Forge of National Memory.* Chicago: University of Chicago Press, 2000.

Schwartz, Lara, Ithti Toy Ulit, and Deborah Morgan. "Straight Talk About Hate Crimes Bills: Anti-Gay, Anti-Transgender Bias Stalls Federal Hate Crimes Legislation." *Georgetown Journal of Gender and the Law* 7, no. 2 (2006): 171–85.

Selzer, Jack, and Sharon Crowley, eds. *Rhetorical Bodies.* Madison: University of Wisconsin Press, 1999.

Sender, Katherine. *Business, Not Politics: The Making of the Gay Market.* New York: Columbia University Press, 2004.

————. "Sex Sells: Sex, Class, and Taste in Commercial Gay and Lesbian Media." *GLQ: A Journal of Lesbian and Gay Studies* 9, no. 3 (2003): 331–65. doi:10.1215/10642684-9-3-331 (accessed February 12, 2015).

Sennett, Richard. *The Fall of Public Man.* New York: W.W. Norton, 1992.

Shepard, Judy. *The Meaning of Matthew: My Son's Murder in Laramie, and a World Transformed.* New York: Hudson Street, 2009. Google E-book.

Shome, Raka. "White Femininity and the Discourse of the Nation: Re/membering Princess Diana." *Feminist Media Studies* 1, no. 3 (2001): 323–42. doi:10.1080/14680770120088927 (accessed February 12, 2015).

Shugart, Helene A. "Reinventing Privilege: The New (Gay) Man in Contemporary Popular Media." *Critical Studies in Media Communication* 20, no. 1 (2003): 67–91. doi:10.1080/0739318032000067056 (accessed February 12, 2015).

————, and Catherine Egley Waggoner. *Making Camp: Rhetorics of Transgression in U.S. Popular Culture.* Tuscaloosa: University of Alabama Press, 2008.

Silverman, Debora L. *Art Nouveau in Fin-de-Siècle France: Politics, Psychology, and Style.* Berkeley: University of California Press, 1989.

Sinfield, Alan. *Cultural Politics—Queer Reading.* 1994. Reprint, New York: Routledge, 2005.

Smith, Lacey Baldwin. *Fools, Martyrs, Traitors: The Story of Martyrdom in the Western World.* Evanston, Ill.: Northwestern University Press, 1999.

Smith, Miriam. *Lesbian and Gay Rights in Canada: Social Movements and Equality-Seeking, 1971–1995*. Toronto: University of Toronto Press, 1999.

Smith, Ralph R., and Russel R. Windes, *Progay/Antigay: The Rhetorical War over Sexuality*. Thousand Oaks, Calif.: Sage, 2000.

Sontag, Susan. "Notes on 'Camp.'" In *Camp: Queer Aesthetics and the Performing Subject*, edited by Fabio Cleto, 53–65. Ann Arbor: University of Michigan Press, 1999.

Soukup, Charles. "*I Love the 80s*: The Pleasures of a Postmodern History." *Southern Communication Journal* 75, no. 1 (2010): 76–93. doi:10.1080/10417940902741514 (accessed February 12, 2015).

Spelman, Elizabeth V. *Fruits of Sorrow: Framing Our Attention to Suffering*. Boston: Beacon, 1997.

Squires, David A. *Aligning and Balancing the Standards-Based Curriculum*. Thousand Oaks, Calif.: Sage, 2005.

Stotzer, Rebecca L. "Violence against Transgender People: A Review of United States Data." *Aggression and Violent Behavior* 14, no. 3 (2009): 170–79.

Stuckey, Mary E. *Defining Americans: The Presidency and National Identity*. Lawrence: University Press of Kansas, 2004.

Sturken, Marita. *Tangled Memories: The Vietnam War, the AIDS Epidemic, and the Politics of Remembering*. Berkeley: University of California Press, 1997.

Thistlethwaite, Polly J. "Building 'A Home of Our Own': Construction of the Lesbian Herstory Archives." In *Daring to Find Our Names: The Search for Lesbigay Library History*, edited by James V. Carmichael, Jr., 153–74. Westport, Conn.: Greenwood Press, 1998.

Thomas, Michael L. Preface to *Monumentality in Etruscan and Early Roman Architecture*, edited by Michael L. Thomas and Gretchen E. Meyers, ix–x. Austin: University of Texas Press, 2012.

Thompson, Julie M. "On the Development of Counter-Racist Quare Public Address Studies." In *Queering Public Address: Sexualities in American Historical Discourse*, edited by Charles E. Morris III, 121–46. Columbia: University of South Carolina Press, 2007.

Tilmans, Karin, Frank van Vree, and Jay Winter, eds. *Performing the Past: Memory, History, and Identity in Modern Europe*. Amsterdam: Amsterdam University Press, 2010.

Trigger, Bruce G. "Monumental Architecture: A Thermodynamic Explanation of Symbolic Behaviour." *World Archaeology* 22, no. 2 (1990): 119–32. http://www.jstor.org/stable/124871 (accessed February 12, 2015).

Vicinus, Martha. "Distance and Desire: English Boarding School Friendships." *Signs: Journal of Women in Culture and Society* 9, no. 4 (1984): 600–22.

Vivian, Bradford. *Public Forgetting: The Rhetoric and Politics of Beginning Again*. University Park: Pennsylvania State University Press, 2010.

Wallace, David. "Alan Bray, The Friend." *Speculum* 80, no. 3 (2005): 845–48.

Warner, Marina. *Monuments and Maidens: The Allegory of the Female Form*. Berkeley: University of California Press, 2000.

Warner, Michael. "Introduction: Fear of a Queer Planet." *Social Text* 29, no. 29 (1991): 3–17. http://www.jstor.org/stable/466295 (accessed February 12, 2015).

———. Introduction to *Fear of a Queer Planet: Queer Politics and Social Theory*, edited by Michael Warner, vii–xxxi. Minneapolis: University of Minnesota Press, 1993.

————. *Publics and Counterpublics*. New York: Zone Books, 2002.

Watney, Simon. *Policing Desire: Pornography, AIDS, and the Media*. Minneapolis: University of Minnesota Press, 1987.

Wittig, Monique. *The Straight Mind and Other Essays*. Boston: Beacon, 1992.

Wood, Alexander. Papers and Letterbooks. Special Collections, Toronto Reference Library, Toronto.

Wood, Julia T. *Gendered Lives: Communication, Gender, and Culture*. Boston: Wadsworth, 2009.

Yep, Gust A., Karen Lovaas, and John P. Elia, eds. *Queer Theory and Communication: From Disciplining Queers to Queering the Discipline(s)*. Binghamton, N.Y.: Harrington Park Press, 2003.

Young, James E. "Memory and Counter-Memory: The End of the Monument in Germany." *Harvard Design Magazine* 9 (Fall 1999): 1–10.

————. *The Texture of Memory: Holocaust Memorials and Meaning*. New Haven: Yale University Press, 1993.

Zarefsky, David. "Four Senses of Rhetorical History." In *Doing Rhetorical History: Concepts and Cases*, edited by Kathleen J. Turner, 19–32. Tuscaloosa: University of Alabama Press, 1998.

Zelizer, Barbie. "The Voice of the Visual in Memory." In *Framing Public Memory*, edited by Kendall Phillips, 157–86. Tuscaloosa: University of Alabama Press, 2004.

Zelizer, Viviana A. *Pricing the Priceless Child: The Changing Social Value of Children*. 1985. Reprint, Princeton: Princeton University Press, 1994.

Zimmerman, Jonathan. *Whose America? Culture Wars in the Public Schools*. Cambridge: Harvard University Press, 2002.

INDEX

mnemonicide, 3, 51, 62, 120, 175. *See also* forgetting

Montezuma II (king), 111

monumentality: abuses of, 24, 175 (*see also* Nazi or National Socialist: and monumentality); beginnings of, 21–22; definitions of, 21; characteristics of, 21–24, 92, 95, 175; queer appeal of, 24–26, 62, 131, 175. *See also* queer monumentality

monuments and memorials: attacks on (*see under* violence, antigay and/or antitrans); definition, 22; GLBTQ examples of, 23, 29, 35, 37–39, 44, 67, 145–48, 180, 185–87; as forms of public memory, 8, 13, 21; vs. monumentality, 92

museums, 8, 11, 18, 23, 26, 27, 157, 184

National Park Service, 36, 170–73, 176–77, 179–80

nationalism: and biopolitics (*see* biopolitics); and contribution (*see* contribution, rhetoric of); definition of, 95; and GLBTQ forgetting (*see* forgetting); GLBTQ people as anti- (*see* antinational, GLBTQ people as); and memory, 95; and monumentality, 95, 111–14; and queer monumentality, 109; as strategic rhetoric, 32, 95, 109; textbooks as sites of, 32, 95–97, 99–101, 178

nationality: differences in GLBTQ community, 3, 83, 111–12, 114; queer nationality, 43–47, 140–41; U.S. privilege (*see* privilege, national)

natural, rhetoric of the: as critique of GLBTQ people, 1, 78, 103–04, 106; in the garden cemetery, 134–35, 141–44, 158–67, 168, 169; GLBTQ uses in self-defense, 19, 158–67, 168, 169; and heteronormativity, 136, 141–44

Nazis or National Socialist: and monumentality, 24, 175; and persecution of GLBT people, 29, 153, 181

Newbigging, Del, 43, 46, 47, 58

nonmaterial monumentality: definitions of, 30–31, 65; effectivity of, 91–92, 176; features of (*see* affect;

affiliation; circulation; malleability); history of, 29–30, 67–68; as improving queer public memory, 184–85; vs. materiality, 67–68

O'Connor, Dennis, 44, 46, 58

official democratic memory. *See* memory, official-democratic

pederasty, 16, 19

Platen, August von, 19

Plato, 16, 176. *See also* Antiquity, allusions to

politics: civil religion and, 106–07; early GLBT, 3, 6, 27, 112 (*see also* Stonewall Riots); factor in queer monumentality, 27, 31; forgetting of (*see under* forgetting); GLBTQ people represented in, 47, 73, 84, 101, 106–07, 127, 143; growth in GLBTQ (*see* institutions, GLBTQ); postmodern (*see* power: postmodern notions of); public memory as, 8–9; and the visual (*see* visual)

polysemy, 41, 62–63

power: Certeau's models of (*see* tactics; strategies); confession, 2, 178; definition of, 24, 176; and dominant culture, 2, 3, 6, 96, 101, 106; as factor in monumental turn, 27; as feature of monumentality, 13, 21, 22, 23–24, 29–30, 33, 39, 65, 71, 86, 115, 175, 179, 185; as remedy to anti-GLBTQ discourses, 25–26, 92, 161, 168–69, 176–77, 179, 186; functions of, 24, 29, 65, 176–77, 179; limitations of, 24, 177; postmodern notions of, 17, 33–34, 136–37, 144, 161, 168–69, 186

pride: as affect, 2, 69, 79; GLBTQ event, 46, 181; limitations of, 31–32, 33, 35, 50, 130, 175; and monumentality, 25, 30, 32, 33, 39, 41, 46, 50, 152, 156, 178. *See also* shame

privilege: cisgender, 31, 58, 66, 83, 85, 92, 96, 110; class, 54, 66, 83, 85; and complicity, 106; generally, 3–4, 33, 51, 99; heterosexual, 3, 11, 51, 59, 96, 104, 106, 110, 115–16, 127, 130–31, 136–39; male, 31–32, 33, 47–48, 54, 58, 66, 83,

rhetoric: (*continued*)
  visual, 133, 155, 161, 165 (*see also*
    visual)
rigor, 6, 14, 50–51, 184. *See also* evidence
Robinson, William J., 1–4, 16, 19.
    See also psychology or psychiatry;
    sexology
Roosevelt, Eleanor, 120, 121, 125
Rustin, Bayard, 118, 119, 121

Sacred Band of Thebes, 19. *See also*
    Antiquity, allusions to
"safe" GLBTQ representations, 32, 43,
    47–48, 175
safe spaces. *See* space, safe
Saint Matthew, rhetoric of, 30, 65,
    77–83, 85, 87, 88, 92, 178
Seelye, Sarah Edmonds, 19
sex. *See under* forgetting
sexology, 1–3, 19. *See also* psychology
    or psychiatry; Robinson, William J.
sculpture. *See* monuments and memo-
    rials
shame: and affective strategies, 69, 73,
    91; and GLBTQ experience, 2, 23, 32,
    181, 182
Shakespeare, William, 2, 16, 176
Shepard, Matthew, 30–31, 64–92,
    174–79, 181, 182
sodomy or sodomite, 16, 51, 103–04
space: gay, 40–42, 44, 48, 51, 56, 60–61,
    62, 123, 174; and heteronormativity,
    40, 94–95, 101, 136–44, 158, 161–62,
    169, 175, 181; as metaphor for power
    (*see* tactics; strategies); and monu-
    mentality, 29, 56, 63, 66, 145, 148, 151,
    158, 169, 173, 184, 187; and postmod-
    ernism, 5, 34; queer, 40, 60–61, 145,
    147, 150–51, 158, 161–62, 171, 175, 187;
    safe, 3, 15, 19, 27, 59
statues or statuary. *See* monuments
    and memorials
Stein, Gertrude, 129–32, 147, 179
Stonewall Riots: analogies to, 82,
    179–80; as commemorative events/
    site, 170; as problematic, 6, 118; as
    turning point, 123, 157, 183
strategies. *See* tactics: and strategies
Student Civil Rights Act, 126–27

style: and camp (*see* camp); and epide-
    ictic, 23, 177; and failure (*see* failure,
    queer art of); of gravescapes (*see*
    gravescapes); and monumentality, 5,
    21, 23, 47–48, 133; queer, 73, 76, 118,
    129, 181; traumatic, 97–98. *See also*
    aesthetics
subjugated knowledges, 3, 62, 175
supplemental rhetorics: and camp,
    54, 57–58; definition of, 56; and
    doing monumentality better, 33–34;
    the body as, 58–61; graffiti as (*see*
    graffiti)
sworn brothers. *See* friendship.

tactics: definition of, 14; and strategies,
    14, 21.
tactical and ephemeral memories,
    4–5: bricolage as (*see* bricolage);
    as critiques to monumentality, 41,
    56–57, 60, 61, 66, 115, 182; definition
    of, 13–15; fused with monumentality,
    32–35, 129–32, 137, 144, 145, 148, 152,
    156, 161, 166–67, 169, 174, 185 (*see
    also* queer monumentality: both/and
    approach); gay and lesbian memory
    rhetorics as, 14–21, 25, 39, 108, 111,
    131, 185–86; limitations of, 61, 67, 71,
    131, 152, 169, 177, 178, 186; ongoing
    need for, 179, 180–82; vs. monumen-
    tality, 25–26, 28, 31, 131, 167, 176–77,
    178
textbooks, 26, 32, 94–103, 108–28, 175,
    177, 178, 181
time or temporality. *See* queer: time or
    temporality
Toklas, Alice B., 129–32, 147, 179
traditionalist countermemory. *See*
    countermemory: traditionalist
traitors, GLBTQ people as. *See* Martin-
    Mitchell affair
transgender: and cisgender privilege
    (*see* privilege: cisgender); critiques
    of homonormativity, 31, 54, 66, 72,
    83–85, 92, 165–66; people marginal-
    ized, 48; differential experiences of
    violence, 84, 138. *See also* cisgender;
    gender
Turing, Alan, 104, 180

CPSIA information can be obtained at www.ICGtesting.com
Printed in the USA
BVOW04*0931161016

464546BV00010B/6/P